T0376654

HANDS ON MEDIA HISTORY

Hands on Media History explores the whole range of hands on media history techniques for the first time, offering both practical guides and general perspectives. It covers both analogue and digital media; film, television, video, gaming, photography and recorded sound.

Understanding media means understanding the technologies involved. The hands on history approach can open our minds to new perceptions of how media technologies work and how we work with them. Essays in this collection explore the difficult questions of reconstruction and historical memory, and the issues of equipment degradation and loss. *Hands on Media History* is concerned with both the professional and the amateur, the producers and the users, providing a new perspective on one of the modern era's most urgent questions: what is the relationship between people and the technologies they use every day?

Engaging and enlightening, this collection is a key reference for students and scholars of media studies, digital humanities, and for those interested in models of museum and research practice.

Nick Hall lectures in film, television and media technologies at Royal Holloway, University of London. His first book, *The Zoom: Drama at the Touch of a Lever*, was published in 2018. He has also been published in the journals *Technology & Culture* and the *Historical Journal of Film, Radio and Television*.

John Ellis is a professor at Royal Holloway, University of London. He wrote *Visible Fictions* (1982), *Seeing Things* (2000) and *Documentary: Witness and Self-Revelation* (2012). Between 1982 and 1999 he ran the independent production company Large Door, making documentaries for Channel 4 and the BBC.

HANDS ON MEDIA HISTORY

A New Methodology in the Humanities and Social Sciences

Edited by
Nick Hall and John Ellis

LONDON AND NEW YORK

First published 2020
by Routledge
2 Park Square, Milton Park, Abingdon, Oxon OX14 4RN

and by Routledge
52 Vanderbilt Avenue, New York, NY 10017

Routledge is an imprint of the Taylor & Francis Group, an informa business

© 2020 selection and editorial matter, Nick Hall and John Ellis; individual chapters, the contributors

The right of Nick Hall and John Ellis to be identified as the authors of the editorial material, and of the authors for their individual chapters, has been asserted in accordance with sections 77 and 78 of the Copyright, Designs and Patents Act 1988.

All rights reserved. No part of this book may be reprinted or reproduced or utilized in any form or by any electronic, mechanical, or other means, now known or hereafter invented, including photocopying and recording, or in any information storage or retrieval system, without permission in writing from the publishers.

Trademark notice: Product or corporate names may be trademarks or registered trademarks, and are used only for identification and explanation without intent to infringe.

British Library Cataloguing-in-Publication Data
A catalogue record for this book is available from the British Library

Library of Congress Cataloging-in-Publication Data
Names: Hall, Nick, 1985– editor. | Ellis, John, 1952– editor.
Title: Hands on media history : a new methodology in the humanities and social
    sciences / edited by Nick Hall and John Ellis.
Description: London ; New York : Routledge, 2020. | Includes bibliographical
    references and index. |
Identifiers: LCCN 2019016484 (print) | LCCN 2019980154 (ebook) |
    ISBN 9781138577480 (hardback : alk. paper) | ISBN 9781138577497 (pbk. : alk. paper) |
    ISBN 9781351247412 (ebk)
Subjects: LCSH: Mass media and technology—History—Study and teaching. |
    Mass media and technology—Historiography. | Mass media and
    technology—Philosophy. | Mass media—Technological
    innovations—History. | Human-computer interaction—Philosophy.
Classification: LCC P96.T42 H367 2020 (print) | LCC P96.T42 (ebook) |
    DDC 302.23—dc23
LC record available at https://lccn.loc.gov/2019016484
LC ebook record available at https://lccn.loc.gov/2019980154

ISBN: 978-1-138-57748-0 (hbk)
ISBN: 978-1-138-57749-7 (pbk)
ISBN: 978-1-351-24741-2 (ebk)

Typeset in Bembo
by Apex CoVantage, LLC

CONTENTS

List of figures	*viii*
Acknowledgements	*xii*
List of contributors	*xiii*

Introduction: what is hands on media history?   1
John Ellis and Nick Hall

PART I
Media histories   **9**

1 Why hands on history matters   11
John Ellis

2 Bringing the living back to life: what happens when
we reenact the recent past?   26
Nick Hall

3 A blind date with the past: transforming television
documentary practice into a research method   43
Amanda Murphy

4 (De)habituation histories: how to re-sensitize
media historians   58
Andreas Fickers and Annie van den Oever

vi Contents

5 (Un)certain ghosts: rephotography and historical images 76
Mary Agnes Krell

PART II
User communities 89

6 Photography against the Anthropocene: the anthotype
as a call for action 91
Kristof Vrancken

7 On the performance of playback for dead media devices 110
Matthew Hockenberry and Jason LaRiviere

8 The archaeology of the Walkman: audience perspectives and
the roots of mobile media intimacy 126
Maruša Pušnik

9 Extended play: hands on with 40 years of English
amusement arcades 145
Alex Wade

10 Enriching 'hands on history' through community
dissemination: a case study of the *Pebble Mill project* 160
Vanessa Jackson

PART III
Labs, archives and museums 173

11 The Media Archaeology Lab as platform for undoing
and reimagining media history 175
Lori Emerson

12 Reflections and reminiscences: tactile encounters
and participatory research with vintage media
technology in the museum 187
Christian Hviid Mortensen and Lise Kapper

13 A vision in Bakelite: exploring the aesthetic, material
and operational potential of the Bush TV22 204
Elinor Groom

Contents **vii**

14 Hands on circuits: preserving the semantic surplus
of circuit-level functionality with programmable
logic devices   222
Fabian Offert

Index   *235*

FIGURES

1.1–1.4	Television film and video editor Dawn Trotman demonstrating the use of an Acmade Pic-Sync during an ADAPT project reenactment exercise.	17
1.5	Vision engineers Bill Baldock and John Coupe at work inside North 3, an outside broadcast vehicle formerly owned by the BBC.	18
2.1	A child attempts to switch on an Apple II personal computer in *Kids React To Old Computers*.	32
2.2 and 2.3	Applying for a new Blockbuster Video membership card and rediscovering the DVD case in 'Touring The Last Surviving Blockbuster Video'.	34
2.4	Bill Chesneau, Ray Sutcliffe, John Adderley and David Whitson participate in a reenactment of 1970s television film production.	38
3.1	Ex-BBC Type 2 outside broadcast truck North 3, 'on location' outside Northop Hall hotel in Flintshire.	46
3.2	Screens set up in the 'video village' monitored output from multiple fixed cameras overlooking the ADAPT project reenactment event.	47
3.3	Vision supervisor Roger Neale and vision engineer John Coupe at the camera control desk inside ex-BBC outside broadcast truck North 3.	51
3.4	Images of a live darts match displayed on preview monitors inside ex-BBC outside broadcast truck North 3, during an ADAPT project reenactment exercise.	54
5.1	Screenshot from the project, 'Traces of Lee Miller: Echoes from St. Malo'.	77

5.2	This image is interactive on the National Parks Service Klondike Gold Rush Site (https://www.nps.gov/klgo/learn/nature/repeatphotography.htm).	80
5.3	An image from the project *Traces of Lee Miller: Echoes from St. Malo*.	85
6.1	*Transit*, slag heaps of Winterslag, Genk, 2017. (Kristof Vrancken)	92
6.2	Harvesting ingredients on a contaminated area, 2016. (Kristof Vrancken)	95
6.3	Cameraless photograph: dune pansy, Abandoned Ford grounds, 2016. (Kristof Vrancken)	96
6.4	The appearance of an Anthotype Print – Lab Test, 2018. (Kristof Vrancken)	97
6.5	*Transit*, slag heap of Zwartberg (black-mountain), Genk, 2017. (Kristof Vrancken)	99
6.6	*Transit*, slag heap of Waterschei and Parking Lot, Genk, 2017. (Kristof Vrancken)	99
6.7	*Transit*, Waterschei, Genk, 2017. (Kristof Vrancken)	99
6.8	*Transit*, Genk-South, 2017. (Kristof Vrancken)	101
6.9	The potable and light-sensitive Anthropocene elixir. (Kristof Vrancken)	102
6.10	*Transit*, abandoned Ford grounds, Genk, 2017. (Kristof Vrancken)	103
6.11	Portraits *mijnKOOL*, Genk, 2017. (Kristof Vrancken)	105
6.12	*Transit*, Winterslag, Genk, 2017. (Kristof Vrancken)	106
7.1	Performance of *Videodrome* (1982) on the Dead Media Streaming Service.	110
7.2	Custom posters for some of the home video releases screened on the service.	112
7.3	Betamax streaming server.	115
7.4	Curriculum for use with the Dead Media Streaming Service.	122
8.1 and 8.2	Examples of mobile uses of the Walkman. (Photographs by Melisa Lozica and Domen Valjavec)	133
8.3	Privatization of the Walkman experience. (Photograph by Vita Vlašič)	138
8.4 and 8.5	Examples of handling the Walkman. (Photographs by Lea Plut and Ema Kranjc)	141
10.1	Former Radio WM engineer, Rod Fawcett, with the Radio WM radio car. (Photo by permission of Rod Fawcett)	164
10.2	A BBC Radio links vehicle at Burghley Horse Trials. (Photo by permission of Steve Dellow)	165
10.3	Eagle Tower Dinky toy. (Photo by permission of Cyril Thompson)	165

x Figures

10.4	Pebble Mill Eagle Tower. (Photo by permission of Stuart Gandy)	166
10.5	Rigged Eagle Towers at Silverstone. (Photo by permission of Steve Dellow)	166
10.6	Outside broadcast communications sheet. (Photography by permission of Steve Dellow)	167
11.1	Apple Platinum IIe computer, from 1987, housed in the Media Archaeology Lab.	178
11.2	5.25" floppies of 'manuscript' versions of bpNichol's digital poem "First Screening" from 1982–1983, housed in the Media Archaeology Lab.	179
11.3	Commodore 64 computer, from 1982, housed in the Media Archaeology Lab.	180
11.4	Altair 8800b computer, from 1976, housed in the Media Archaeology Lab.	181
11.5	Vectrex game console, from 1983, housed in the Media Archaeology Lab.	181
11.6	Xerox typewriter, likely from around 1987, housed in the Media Archaeology Lab.	182
11.7	Magic Lantern, likely from around 1910, housed in the Media Archaeology Lab.	182
11.8	Canon Cat computer, from 1987, housed in the Media Archaeology Lab.	183
12.1	Detail from the open workshops at the Media Museum. Printer Hans Hansen operating a Heidelberg printing press.	188
12.2	The authors 'excavating' at two of the three workstations in the MAL. From the right VHS, Commodore 64 and cassette tapes.	192
12.3	Example of interior approach to the display of media technologies at the *Finnish Museum of Games*. (Credit: Saana Säilynoja, Tampere Museums, Vapriikki Photo Archives)	192
12.4	Detail of the MAL VHS workstation. Fresh questionnaires are available on the left and the user can leave their filled-out questionnaire in the box when they leave the workstation.	193
13.1	The Bush TV22, part of the Science Museum Group collection, inventory number 1979–624/721, Science Museum Group.	204
13.2	Screen grab from *Television's Opening Night: How the Box was Born*, showing the Bush TV22 alongside the historic reenactment studio.	206

13.3	Mullard leaflet advertising its aluminized cathode ray tubes, from the Kodak Collection held at the National Science and Media Museum, 1990–5036/TI51, Science Museum Group.	212
13.4	The Pilot ACE computer is moved from its case in the *Making the Modern World* gallery; the Bush TV22 1971–76 is visible in its case in the background, 2014, Science Museum Group.	213
13.5	Photograph of the Wall of Televisions in the *Experience TV* gallery of the National Media Museum, 2006, Science Museum Group.	214
13.6	Display, including the Bush TV22, in the *Information Age* gallery of the Science Museum, 2014, Science Museum Group.	216
13.7	Queen Elizabeth II and Prince Phillip are shown the coronation on a replica Bush TV22, 2014, Science Museum Group.	217
14.1	'Die shot' (close-up photography of an integrated circuit treated with acid to reveal its circuit layout) of the Soviet KR580VM80A microprocessor. High-resolution photos like this one serve as guidelines for the reverse-engineering of computational objects, and their re-implementation by means of programmable logic devices. The pictured processor has been successfully translated to Verilog, and re-implemented on an FPGA by a group of Russian enthusiasts.	229

ACKNOWLEDGEMENTS

In February 2016, the *Hands on History* conference brought together a group of speakers, scholars, and researchers united by a common interest in reenactment and restoration as ways to explore histories of technology. Over two days at the Geological Society in London, delegates discussed – among other topics – computer gaming, photography, broadcast television, and electronic preservation. The conference was organized as part of ADAPT, a research project funded by the European Research Council under the Horizon 2020 scheme (grant agreement number 323626). Some of the papers presented at *Hands on History* appear in this edited collection, and we are grateful to everyone who took part and made the conference such a stimulating and inspiring event.

The editors would like to thank, for their patience and generosity, the 15 authors whose work features in this collection. We are also thankful for the support of Stephanie Janes, who provided vital assistance in the organisation of the conference and in the early preparation of this volume. We are grateful to Natalie Foster and Jennifer Vennall at Routledge for commissioning the book and for supporting it throughout the production process, and to Ting Baker for her skilful and sharp-eyed copyediting.

Finally, we thank our friends and colleagues in the Department of Media Arts at Royal Holloway, University of London and – above all – our families for their constant love and support.

CONTRIBUTORS

John Ellis is Professor of Media Arts at Royal Holloway, University of London, and was the principal investigator on the ERC funded ADAPT project. Between 1982 and 1999 he ran the independent production company Large Door (www.largedoorltd.com) making documentaries about media-related issues for Channel 4 and the BBC. Beginning with a series made using one inch video and 16mm film (Channel 4's cinema series *Visions*), his final production was shot on DVcam (*Riding the Tiger*, about the handover of Hong Kong). His books include *Visible Fictions* (1982), *Seeing Things* (2000) and *Documentary: Witness and Self-Revelation* (2012). He was an editor of *Screen* magazine and is currently an editor-in-chief of *View: the Journal of European TV History and Culture*. He has taken a keen interest in the preservation and use of TV material and is chair of education charity Learning on Screen.

Lori Emerson is Associate Professor in the Department of English and the Intermedia Arts, Writing, and Performance Program at the University of Colorado at Boulder. She is also Founding Director of the Media Archaeology Lab. Emerson writes about media poetics as well as the history of computing, media archaeology, media theory, and digital humanities. She is currently working on two book projects: the first is called *Other Networks* and is a history of telecommunications networks that existed before or outside of the Internet; the second is called *THE LAB BOOK: Situated Practices in Media Studies* (forthcoming from the University of Minnesota Press), which she is co-writing with Jussi Parikka and Darren Wershler. Emerson is the author of *Reading Writing Interfaces: From the Digital to the Bookbound* (University of Minnesota Press, June 2014). She is also co-editor of three collections: *The Johns Hopkins Guide to Digital Media*, with Marie-Laure Ryan and Benjamin Robertson (2014); *Writing Surfaces: The Selected Fiction of John Riddell*, with Derek Beaulieu (Wilfred Laurier University Press, 2013); and *The Alphabet Game: a bpNichol Reader*, with Darren Wershler (Coach House Books 2007).

xiv Contributors

Andreas Fickers is the director of the Luxembourg Centre for Contemporary and Digital History (C²DH) and head of the DH-Lab. He studied history, philosophy and sociology and is currently Professor for Contemporary and Digital History at the University of Luxembourg. He took his PhD in 2002 at RTWH Aachen University and worked as Assistant Professor for television history at Utrecht University (2003–2007) and Associate Professor for comparative media history at Maastricht University (2007–2013). He's head of the FNR funded Doctoral Training Unit 'Digital History & Hermeneutics' (DTU) and coordinates the Trinational doctoral school together with Prof. Dr Dietmar Hüser (Universität des Saarlandes) and Prof. Dr Hélène Miard-Delacroix (Université Paris-Sorbonne). He's also principal investigator of the Impresso project and co-editor of *VIEW, the Journal of European Television History and Culture*. He's currently the Luxembourg national coordinator of DARIAH-EU and member of the joint research board of Humanities in the European Research Area (HERA).

Elinor Groom is the Curator of Television and Broadcast for the National Science and Media Museum in Bradford, responsible for a collection of broadcast technology that includes John Logie Baird's experimental apparatus, production equipment from the BBC and the ITV network, and roughly a thousand domestic television and radio receivers. At the museum she has been an academic liaison for a number of broadcast heritage research projects, and in 2018 she curated the major exhibition Action Replay: Great Innovations in Sports Broadcasting. She has also been a curator for the BFI National Archive's television collection, which contains approximately 800,000 programmes and is growing by the hundreds every day. She is a trained moving image archivist and gained experience at the East Anglian Film Archive in Norwich, the Image Permanence Institute and the George Eastman House in Rochester, NY. Her PhD examined the emergence of the ITV regional franchise network in the 1950s and 1960s through analysis of the Southern Television document archive, and was jointly supervised by the University of Nottingham and the BFI National Archive.

Nick Hall lectures in film, television and media history in the Department of Media Arts at Royal Holloway, University of London. He researches at the interface between media technologies and media cultures. Between 2013 and 2018, he worked on the ADAPT project, which examined the historical development of British television broadcast production technology. His first book, *The Zoom: Drama at the Touch of a Lever*, was published by Rutgers University Press in 2018. His research has also been published in the journals *Technology & Culture* and the *Historical Journal of Film, Radio and Television*.

Matthew Hockenberry is a media historian and technologist whose research examines critical developments in the epistemology of assembly. His work centres on the history of logistics, tracing the media forms and material practices of decentralized production throughout the nineteenth and twentieth centuries to examine the impact they've had on digital infrastructures and objects like the mobile phone. He is particularly concerned with how media archaeological approaches to the networks of production can reveal transitional moments of mediation within histories of paperwork, telecommunication, and computation. As a visiting scientist with the MIT Center for Civic Media and Tangible Media Group he developed Sourcemap, a collaborative platform for mapping supply chains and sharing "where things come from", and he writes regularly on the state of global supply through the lens of its most emblematic objects.

Christian Hviid Mortensen is currently a postdoc at the IT University of Copenhagen, where he researches hybrid museum experiences and the challenges of digital innovation in the cultural sector. From 2007 to 2018 Christian was a curator of media heritage at the Media Museum (Odense, Denmark). His research interest is the dynamics between media, culture, heritage and memory. Christian is also journal manager for the peer-reviewed journal *MedieKultur: Journal of Media and Communication Research*.

Annie van den Oever is Professor of Arts, Culture, Media and Film at the University of Groningen and founding editor of the international book series *The Key Debates: Mutations and Appropriations in European Film Studies*, published by Amsterdam University Press. She has been an editor of *NECSUS, the European Journal of Media Studies*, sits on the editorial board of the academic journal *IMAGE & TEXT*, and is Head of the Film Archive & Media Archaeology Lab, University of Groningen.

Vanessa Jackson is a former BBC series producer, and now course director of the BA (Hons) Media Production at Birmingham City University, teaching practical television production skills to undergraduates. She completed her practice-based PhD in television historiography, under the supervision of Professor John Ellis, at Royal Holloway, University of London in 2018. Her research interests include the history of television, as well as the uses of social media in community history projects. She has also published on the use of social media in enhancing student employability, and student engagement.

Lise Kapper holds an MA in Modern Culture and Cultural Communication an MA in Museum Studies. She is curator of exhibitions and education at the national Danish Media Museum (Odense, Denmark). Her curatorial practice is highly experimental. It works in the cross section between material agency and user engagement focusing on non-formal learning strategies. Theoretically, Lise Kapper is grounded in New Museology, Media Archaeology, and Phenomenology.

Mary Agnes Krell is a digital artist whose work spans performance, interactivity and narrative. Her work has been shown on multiple continents and she regularly collaborates with artists and thinkers from around the world. Mary has long

xvi Contributors

been interested in narrative, performance and mediated art. She is interested in the intersection of performance and digital media and has used her work with Forced Entertainment and the Lee Miller Archives as a point of departure. Her work has been funded in the UK by the AHRC, the British Academy, Arts Council England and commercial partners. Mary has also been an associate member of Forced Entertainment as a digital author. With them, she created a number of interactive works that were exhibited around the world at venues including the ZKM (in Karlsruhe, Germany), the ICA (in London) and The Art Institute of Chicago. Nightwalks, an interactive virtual reality piece created in collaboration with the company, won the Transmediale in 2000. She also performed in the inaugural tour of The Voices.

Jason LaRiviere received his PhD from the department of Media, Culture, and Communication at New York University. His writing has appeared in *boundary 2*, *e-flux*, *Parrhesia*, and *The Brooklyn Rail*. His current project considers compression as a technical process and philosophical concept.

Amanda Murphy is executive producer of Storyfutures Academy, the UK's national centre of excellence in immersive storytelling (a partnership between the National Film and Television School and Royal Holloway, University of London), and was the ADAPT project's digital producer. For ADAPT, Amanda produced and directed all the filmed reenactments that reunite technical TV personnel with the equipment they once worked with. Amanda is an established TV producer and executive producer who has won among others, Royal Television Society and European Broadcasting Union Rose d'Or awards for establishing hit series including *Big Brother* (she was senior producer of the first UK series in 2000) and *Supernanny* (she was the founding producer and executive producer for Channel 4 and on *Supernanny USA* for ABC in the United States). Amanda has produced a wealth of documentaries and primetime series and has served on Royal Television Society award panels. She most recently won an AHRC Research in Film award for *Missed Call* (directed by Victoria Mapplebeck) and continues as a visiting mentor and workshop tutor at the National Film and Television School.

Fabian Offert's research focuses on interpretable machine learning, critical technical practice, digital preservation, and their intersection. Currently, he is a doctoral candidate in the Media Arts and Technology program at the University of California, Santa Barbara, where he also teaches. He is a fellow of the Regents of the University of California and was a visiting scholar at the University of California, Berkeley. His work is frequently featured in both critical and technical contexts, among others at NIPS, ECCV, SIGGRAPH, Deutsches Museum, and Harvard University. Before coming to California, Fabian served as Assistant Curator at ZKM Karlsruhe where he was responsible for several large-scale media art exhibitions. He received his Diploma degree from Justus Liebig University Gießen, where he was a student of composer and director Heiner Goebbels and a fellow of the German National Academic Foundation.

Maruša Pušnik is Associate Professor at the Department of Media and Communication Studies, University of Ljubljana, Slovenia. She teaches courses on history and theory of media, popular culture and everyday life. Her research interests include cultural history of media, collective memory and nationalism as communication process, and women's genres. She published *Popularizacija nacije* (Popularization of nation, Ljubljana, 2010) and co-edited *Remembering utopia: the culture of everyday life in socialist Yugoslavia* (Washington, 2010).

Kristof Vrancken studied photography at Luca School of Arts in Genk (Belgium), where he has worked as a researcher and lecturer in hybrid media since 2008. His work is characterized by a sense of 'twisted cleanliness'. Kristof focuses on the fringes and non-places of society in a poetic manner. The absence of human presence is characteristic in this approach. The presence of man, however, is evoked through the visible remnants of human activity. His findings, mixed with absurdity and dark humour, are the key to his visual work. Since September 2015 Kristof is working on an artistic PhD project The Sustainist Gaze in which he investigates the extent to which visual artists can give shape to sustainist design in an active and socially critical manner, and the effect that applying sustainist design principles has on visual language, method, material use and photographic techniques. The interdisciplinary approach results in an interesting hybrid interface in which the role of the image within design and the role of design within the image are questioned.

Alex Wade is Senior Research Fellow at Birmingham City University. With a background in Sociology, he has previously written on space and time, French social theory, Pac-Man and sexting, with his most recent book, The Pac-Man Principle: A User's Guide to Capitalism published by Zero Books in 2018. His current work examines the link between the cold war and the development of videogames in the UK and the regional variations which have given rise to the 'videogame industry' today. He is chair of the History of Games Research Committee, which looks to further interest in the histories of all games around the world.

INTRODUCTION

What is hands on media history?

John Ellis and Nick Hall

A relationship with technology is central to being human, but it is not well understood. Humans create technology and have done since the earliest times, and this is commonly taken as a sign of what distinguishes humanity from the sub-primates. Equally, though, our technologies create us, enabling the activities and experiences and forms of social organization that make us who we are. This intimate imbrication of technologies in the formation of human bodies, minds, and structures of feeling is less well appreciated. To understand fully this reciprocal relationship between humanity and its technology is becoming an ever more urgent task. The world that we experience is one where technology seems to be taking control (which is not necessarily a new perception of human life), but also a world where the affordances of our technologies are having a detrimental effect on the planet we inhabit (which is a new and urgent perception). Hands on history is a central method in the overdue rethinking of the reciprocal relationship between humanity and the technologies it creates.

The hands on approach validates physical encounters and revalues 'skills' as the basis of the generation of knowledge and thought, as Ellis argues in his contribution to this collection. Hands on history techniques involve various forms of physical exploration of technologies as means of understanding how technologies have changed, and how they have changed us. History provides a distance, a 'making strange' (Shklovsky 1991) which, in this case, makes it much easier to reflect upon how our bodies relate to technologies and how we have taken for granted views about the use of technologies. Humans habitually adapt themselves physically and mentally to their technologies. Almost all technologies have affordances which remain unexploited. It is difficult to perceive these two features of our relationship with our everyday technologies. An encounter with the technologies of the past, once equally familiar but now fallen into disuse, will more readily reveal the double sided relationship between machines and people, bodies and tools, perceptions and potentials.

It may seem strange to make this argument at a point when so much technology is disappearing into black boxes or into the virtuality of data. However, it is exactly this development that gives urgency to the task of understanding the nature of the relationship between humans and technologies. Traditionally, we have conceptualized communication, as John Durham Peters (1999) has explored so eloquently, as the attempt to externalize the mind's thoughts through a process of dissemination which is always less than ideal, but equally enables us to exist as humans. However, we are now embarking on a phase of existence where communication is involuntary, where our every physical movement 'sheds' data through our own everyday communication devices (and the routine devices of public surveillance) which can then be recuperated and processed. This involuntary communication has become meaningful through the deployment of the new range of computational technologies. The old saying "What we do speaks volumes" has now become literal fact because it can be collected, measured, compared, and processed. So it seems to us as though we are developing a new relationship with technology, the like of which we have not experienced before. The value of the hands on history approach lies in enabling researchers to see this rather more as another chapter in the long relationship between human bodies and technologies.

The hands on approach also emphasizes the issue of technological affordances. We may shed data as a fact of modern life, but the uses to which this data is put, and what the machines are that learn from it, is increasingly concentrated in a narrow range of the affordances of this new technological dispensation. As Zuboff (2019) persuasively argues, the whole of our being (including the evanescence of moods and the confidentiality of the personal) is now subject to collection, processing, deduction, and – crucially – marketization. This marketization takes the form not only of predicting future behaviour but also of channelling it through the further processing of the data which returns to us. This is a particular use of the affordances of the new data-driven technology. It is not the only use, as even Google was once keen on telling its customers. A few years ago, Google's ever optimistic public presentations promoted 'artificial intelligence' (AI) as it was then known as the universal panacea. The standard presentation example was that of the prediction of flu epidemics from the search patterns of individuals looking for 'cold and flu remedies' and similar terms. This remains a rather lonely example of the use of AI in public service rather than at the service of regulation and commercial exploitation.

Hands on history defamiliarizes our relationship with technologies. As a novel approach, it allows us to explore what we understand but do not know that we know. It allows us to reassess our culture in terms of its physical encounters with its tools and technologies, and to use this understanding for further reflection. As Ellis argues, hands on history takes a number of complementary forms, all of which are explored in this volume. Hands on history provides a framework in which we can obtain and explore a machine for its affordances, experiment with combinations of machines to discover how they work together and what they might be capable of achieving, and discover and document the communities that have developed advanced skills in combination with the machines within defined historical contexts. This framework offers further opportunities: we can document the ensembles of machinery, the technical arrays and the working practices into which they are or were inserted. We can experiment with using, or getting professionals to use, those technical arrays in the way that they were once used, and enhance our understanding of both the affordances of the machines and the affordances of their host institutions or workplaces.

Hands on history is already a flourishing practice in museum display, primarily aimed at the engagement of children and families. It promotes the physical exploration of objects liberated from their display cases. This encourages curiosity, tactile engagement, and exploration that leads, hopefully, to further learning. Academic researchers are increasingly turning to hands on history practices as well, often in response to digitization and technological changes. The term 'hands on' is often used to describe the physical engagement with archival documents, rather than their digital avatars. These approaches are based on two assumptions:

- The assumption of authenticity, that the physical objects have properties that can hardly be reproduced in other media.
- The assumption that physical interactions with objects produce forms of knowledge that cannot easily be translated into concepts.

The knowledge gained from hands on activities is a necessary, but often underrated, aspect of learning. Roger Kneebone, professor of surgical education at Imperial College London, argues that "the ability to do things with your hands, with tools, cutting things out and putting things together [. . .] is really important in order to do the right thing either with operations, or with experiments". He is concerned that "We have noticed that medical students and trainee surgeons often don't seem as comfortable with doing things with their hands [as] they used to, even perhaps five or ten years ago" (Weaver 2018). Kneebone ascribes this decline in physical skills to the increased engagement with screen-based activities.

The emphasis on tactile learning is important for understanding the past as well as for preparing to encounter the future. To work with authentic historical documents and objects is to develop an empathy with the people and practices for whom those objects were of central importance in either everyday or especially significant practices. Often, the regular users of these historic objects developed specific physical skills in using them. Kneebone has developed simulations of past medical practices, bringing together retired surgeons who carry out operations on realistic silicone models to demonstrate techniques that have since fallen into disuse. A similar approach was been adopted by the ADAPT research project examined here by Ellis, Hall and Murphy. In Kneebone's simulations, the surgeons are often assisted by current medical students (Kneebone and Woods 2012), and the whole activity is filmed "to capture the unspoken context of the contributions

4 John Ellis and Nick Hall

of assistants, scrub nurses, anaesthetists and other members of the surgical team", which are often ignored in existing written and even filmed accounts (ibid.). Hands on history concentrates on the physical interactions that are often overlooked or downgraded in intellectual practice as 'mere skills', as Ellis's chapter emphasizes. As a result, a hands on approach often reveals the work of subaltern groups and individuals: the assistants, the artisans, the technical staff.

Hands on history involves a range of practices from the informal to the highly elaborate. They are united by the perception that the material world cannot be fully understood without physical encounters, and that, further, practices in the material world are poorly documented or misunderstood. Within this movement, hands on media history is a relatively new branch. It has been conceived at a time when the taken-for-granted practices of the analogue media era are disappearing into the past, leaving behind a substantial legacy of obsolete equipment whose use quickly became obscure. The existence of these puzzling artefacts has produced a media archaeology movement. An essential corrective to the predominant historical myth of perpetual innovation and improvement in media (a tendency identified by Fickers and van den Oever in this volume) this movement examines forgotten or 'dead' media as Bruce Sterling (1995) defined it, often through a direct physical engagement with pieces of technology. The work of Siegfried Zielinski and Wolfgang Ernst has been formative for this movement. Zielinski's larger historical project of 'variantology' involves an archaeological approach to media technologies, as well as writing extensively on time-based media and media history (Zielinski and Wagnermaier 2005). Around 2013, Ernst founded a pioneering collection of working examples of obsolete media technologies at Humboldt University, the Medienarchäologischer Fundus (Media Archaeology Resource). This initiative has been the inspiration for many of the collections described in this book. In her chapter, Lori Emerson gives a vivid account of the development of a Media Archaeology Lab within the institutional context of University of Colorado at Boulder. Emerson also explores the dramatic impact that this hands on approach has had to learning and research within the university, overturning many of the traditional separations of academic thinking.

Media archaeology is concerned with what could have been, what might have been, and what fleetingly was. Emerson analyses the information architecture of the Canon CAT from precisely this perspective, highlighting its distinctive approach to documents and their retrieval which is markedly different to the standard Microsoft-derived model that we are now used to. Media archaeology is interested in technologies that were abandoned (often for no good reason), as well as in imagining new uses for technologies that eventually fell by the wayside. This exploration of the potential affordances of historic technologies is explored in several essays in Huhtamo and Parikka's influential collection *Media Archaeologies: Approaches, Applications, and Implications* (2011). As his essay in this collection demonstrates, Kristof Vrancken owes much to this approach in developing his extraordinary exploration of the early nineteenth century anthotype photographic method. He seizes on the vegetable basis of the process to give it a startlingly contemporary re-use. Often through community based projects, he uses anthotype photography as a way of understanding the problems of post-industrial society: the legacy of pollution, the overvaluation of permanence and digital perfectibility, the reliance on technologies whose internal workings are hidden from their users.

Media archaeology is also interested in the specific effects or feel of abandoned media technologies (see Huhtamo and Parikki, 2011). In their chapter, Matthew Hockenberry and Jason LaRiviere describe the Dead Media Streaming Service, which revives disused video formats to reproduce their specific 'aura' through a film streaming service. The chosen formats are directly related to the moment of the cultural impact of the films, or even, as in the case of Cronenberg's *Videodrome* to the technologies directly referenced in the film's own narrative. Pušnik's essay shows the strong attachment that citizens often had with 'their' piece of technology through her vivid analysis of the users of Walkman cassette tape players.

Media archaeology focusses on what could have been as well as what was. This emphasis is important as a way of avoiding the dominant way of thinking about media technologies, criticized by Fickers and van den Oever in this volume, which studies only what was rather than the whole range of affordances of any piece of technology. It is all too easy to take as natural or inevitable the systems that emerged from the complex negotiations between users, manufacturers and broader social interests. This social process of realizing specific technological affordances (and, by implication, downplaying others) has been charted by social constructivist historians of technology. Through its contrasting emphasis on exploring all potential affordances of technologies, the media archaeology approach can produce a distinctive hands on practice. This practice seeks to find uses for media technologies beyond those for which they were originally designed, as well as revisiting the specific 'structure of feeling' (Williams 1977) that inhabited their one-time use.

The media archaeology approach works best when applied to processes or independent pieces of equipment rather than the complex arrays that are often deployed in media production, either together or serially in an interdependent production chain. It is hard to see what unrealized affordances exist in a specialized piece of equipment like an Acmade Compeditor, commonly known as the 'picsync', designed for the specific purpose of synchronizing moving images and magnetic sound when they are being married together during film editing. Many of the chapters in this collection are centred around the attempt to deal with this technological legacy: the legacy of the realized affordances of technologies and technologies designed for specific purposes, as many media technologies were. It emphasizes the way in which those technologies were once owned by or used by people in both work media and media play and pleasure. Several of the chapters are the result of the ADAPT research project on the major ways in which television programmes were made in the analogue era. Ellis, Hall, and Murphy discuss the particular variant of the hands on history approach which this project adopted.

This collection examines a wider range of hands on history approaches which, together, represent a sustained attempt to come to terms with the legacy of 'obsolete' media equipment that now surrounds us. This involves both specialized production equipment made bespoke or in small batches, and consumer equipment that was usually produced by the millions on a production line. They have one thing in common: they were linked together by complex and interdependent relationships: from television production to television sets and home videotape; from games consoles to specifically designed software; from the Walkman to the commercial distribution of music by radio or pre-recorded cassettes.

Specialist items of equipment, designed and produced for very specific purposes, present a number of problems for subsequent generations. Not only can their purpose often be obscure, but also they present problems for reuse or recycling. The question of loss and waste, and the problems of electronic waste in particular, have been raised by writers as diverse as Gabrys (2011), Parikka (2015) and Strauven (2013) specifically in relation to media equipment, and is raised again in this collection by Emerson. The rate of equipment obsolescence in media industries is high. Equipment tends to be used intensively and then discarded. This tendency is intensified by the push for ever-newer consumer experiences and the lack of compatibility between proprietary systems and older versions, often simple things like software or styles of physical connectors, as Hockenberry discusses in relation to videotape.

The move from analogue to digital media systems has been particularly wasteful in this regard. 'Backwards compatibility' has not been a priority for manufacturers and innovators who have sought instead to gain market advantage by selling 'all-new' systems. Many consumers prefer a bricolage approach, marrying older but familiar equipment with the new. But the dominant approach to the marketing of technology has forced consumers to abandon technologies to which they have become profoundly attached, as Pušnik demonstrates in relation to the Walkman, and, in a very different context, Wade describes in relation to arcade games. Those involved in the hands on history movement are all, to some degree, involved in a stubborn resistance to such trends. The amateur collectors and maintainers of equipment; the curators of hands on museum collections; those who study media history through the prism of production studies or media archaeology; those who reconstruct historic media events or techniques; and even those who simply use old equipment as decorative items: all are engaged in a form of stubborn resistance to the onward rush of equipment obsolescence.

The approaches to hands on media history in this collection tend to focus on exploring and understanding the social implementation of media technologies. The chapters range from production to consumption, from still to moving image, from sound recordings to gaming. Together they interrogate 'history' as well as the meaning and importance of its 'hands on' variant. To work with the hands on approach to history of media inevitably brings to the fore issues of memory and repetition, since much media history is still "within living memory". Jackson's essay in this collection discusses the citizen curation of memories of a TV work culture, working up material and reminiscences volunteered through a Facebook group into a more substantial history of the BBC's now-demolished Pebble Mill studios. She asks the crucial question of who this history is for: the participants and their circle, or a wider public.

Several essays in this volume address practices of reenactment, recreation, and simulation. Nick Hall's contribution to this volume teases out the various practices involved in 'reenactment' where popular TV formats and social media encounters with 'old' technologies demonstrate the widespread appeal of the hands on exploration of the past. He discusses the ADAPT project's approach to reenactment as an active process of remembering for the participants who were reenacting or recalling their younger selves. Amanda Murphy provides a guide to this complex process of revival of old broadcast technologies in the hands of their expert users. Mary Agnes Krell provides another approach in her discussion of 'rephotography', which involves reenacting in the present the precise position and disposition of a photographer in the past in order to measure historic change and distance rather than to emulate the past. Reenactment involves both gain and loss, both remembering and forgetting, in a complex process of understanding history as a process of change whilst trying to recover as much as possible of the haptic experience of the past. The emulation of early computer games as proposed by Fabian Offert is a good example of this process. He discusses how the software emulation of hardware that is no longer operational brings old games back to life so that they can be used by their one-time expert players as well as new participants. However, this process strips away the last vestiges of the rich social environment into which many of these games were deployed: the subversive and slightly seedy world of the arcades described by Alex Wade. It is a truism that our memories are treacherous, yet that we all depend on them for our orientation in the world. The hands on approach can stimulate memories that have remained latent or hidden, leading to a productive questioning of our settled accounts of our past, confronting us with 'things we have forgotten about' and reviving a different, earlier, sense of self.

The hands on history approach to media provides a new approach to understanding one of the central questions of modern life: the relationship between people and the technologies they use. It forces us to re-evaluate simplistic accounts of technological progress, as Fickers and van den Oever demonstrate here. It show that, as Ellis discusses, the habitual division between mind and brain is an inadequate model for understanding the co-evolving relationship between technologies and humans. This relationship has long been one of mutual adaptation, requiring the development of skills which are the basis of any process of intellectual apprehension of the world in which we live. Finally, the hands on approach also shows that our current direction of technological development is a choice rather than a given, the result of social negotiations and human decisions rather than an inevitable movement.

8 John Ellis and Nick Hall

Bibliography

Gabrys, Jennifer (2011) *Digital Rubbish: A Natural History of Electronics*. Ann Arbor: University of Michigan Press.

Huhtamo, Erkki and Parikka, Jussi (2011) *Media Archaeologies: Approaches, Applications, and Implications*. California: University of California Press.

Kneebone, Roger and Woods, Abigail (2012) "Bringing surgical history to life" *British Medical Journal*, 345 https://doi.org/10.1136/bmj.e8135

Parikka, Jussi (2015) *A Geology of Media*. Minneapolis: University of Minnesota Press.

Peters, John Durham (1999) *Speaking into the Air: A History of the Idea of Communication*. Chicago, IL: University of Chicago Press.

Shklovsky, Victor (1991) *'Art as Device', in The Theory of Prose*. Bloomington, IL: Dalkey Archive Press.

Strauven, Wanda (2013). "Media Archaeology: Where Film History, Media Art and New Media (Can) Meet." In *Preserving and Exhibiting Media Art: Challenges and Perspectives* (eds). Hediger, V., Saba, C., Le Maitre, B., and Noordegraaf, J. Amsterdam: University of Amsterdam Press.

Sterling, Bruce (1995) "The Dead Media Manifesto." International Symposium on Electronic Arts, Montréal http://www.deadmedia.org/modest-proposal.html.

Weaver, M. (2018) "Medical Students 'Raised on Screens Lack Skills for Surgery'." *The Guardian*. 30 October. [online]. https://www.theguardian.com/society/2018/oct/30/medical-students-raised-on-screens-lack-skills-for-surgery.

Williams, Raymond. (1977) *Marxism and Literature*. Oxford: Oxford University Press.

Zielinski, Siegfried and Wagnermaier, Silvia M. (eds) (2005). *Variantology – On Deep Time Relations of Arts, Sciences and Technologies*. Cologne: Verlag der Buchhandlung König.

Zuboff, Shoshana (2019) *The Age of Surveillance Capitalism*. London: Profile Books.

PART I

Media histories

1
WHY HANDS ON HISTORY MATTERS

John Ellis

The hands on approach to history responds to the presence of complex technologies in all aspects of human existence since the industrial revolution, and in particular to the recent growth of 'black box' electronic devices. The 'gamble' of the hands on approach is that the physical experience of machinery brings insights that cannot be gained in any other way. It is a commonplace that most people, faced with an unfamiliar piece of technology, do not read the instruction manual. Instead, they try it out. The interaction of body, mind, and machine that results from these encounters enables learning and develops skills. So it is with the experience of an unfamiliar piece of historical technology. Written descriptions are not enough to develop a real understanding of the machine and its functioning. Physical experience is needed to inform the understanding, and to eliminate misapprehensions and misunderstandings. Once someone has handled a film projector, they can more easily understand how it worked, what its particular affordances were, and what 'aura' it could create in the cinematic experience. Similarly, just to pick up a film camera gives a vivid experience of its particular 'heft', its weight, balance, and manoeuvrability, and that physical experience gives insight into how it could (and could not) be used in practice.

To go this far is a valuable educational experience, and should be a key part of any researcher's training. Beyond it lie a further series of questions. It is clear to begin with that the experience of handling a single piece of technology as a novice will be very different from that of either an experienced user or a trained professional user. This leads some to propose a 'media archaeology' that seeks to explore the many potential affordances of the many machines that come down to us from history, rather than the affordances that were realized in the context of their historically situated use (Ernst 2012; Parikka 2012, etc.). This certainly works with mechanical devices of all kinds (Huhtamo and Parikka 2011), and it is important in encouraging researchers to enter into a new mindset: that of the skilled user of a

12 John Ellis

technology. However, its application to the 'black box' technologies that are now proliferating is less obvious, as these technologies are effectively scattered across the physical and the virtual, between the tool at hand and the software and data services that it requires to give it life.

Moreover, the affordances of technologies are always realized within historically situated institutional implementations, and technologies are often designed with these in mind. Institutional considerations will also bear down even on those seeking alternative or counterfactual uses, just as much as they do on mainstream and everyday uses. Experimental media archaeology will always take place within institutions of experimentation or 'play': universities, museums, hackathons, and so on. Histories of the institutions of television broadcasting exist for many national contexts. Equally, we also have several traditions of advanced analysis of the products of the process, the films, and programmes. But there are hardly any accounts of the space that lies between the decisions by executives to invest in and deploy particular suites of technologies, and the emergence of those films and programmes on the other. This is the underexplored realm of enactment or operationalization. Often labelled misleadingly as 'media practice', this is the complex arena where creative decisions are made in full awareness of the institutional requirements for particular kinds of aesthetic products. Media professionals know what is required of them and they deliver it; they equally know that one of the requirements of them is a degree of originality or innovation, and they will often look to the underexplored affordances of the available technology to help deliver that degree of innovation. 'Media practice' is therefore a dynamic realm which is best understood by addressing the interplay of people and machines, and machines with other machines.

It is also clear from media practice that machines, even analogue machines, are not typically used alone: they occur in larger ensembles, as part of complex processes that have various stages or involve the use of several machines at once. To film using celluloid involves a camera, lights, and sound recorders; the product of that initial process then passes through further stages of film development, editing, dubbing, and printing, and, finally, projection. Each stage involves particular skills and individuals with a high level of skill in one stage may well be unable to carry out a basic operation in another. Hands on history has to come to terms with these key aspects of the imbrication of humans with technologies. It has to enable the novice users to translate their experiences and insights into a full understanding of the human/technological ensemble which, at a particular moment in history, was capable of producing extraordinary objects and experiences. Hands on history, in other words, has to come to terms with the processes of that skilled individuals went through, just as much as it has to enable an exploratory and experiential approach to learning.

This implies a process of documentation of the work of skilled individuals. Alongside the experiential knowledge generated by handling and experimenting with old machines, the hands on approach has to develop of knowledge bank of information about the skilled use of those machines in the circumstances of their historically situated implementation. These certainly involve industrial and institutional contexts of which we have authoritative accounts as noted earlier. However, when it comes to accounts of the operation of the machines involved, we run up against a set of problems. The users of the technologies, as a rule, do not have the descriptive or analytic discourses to describe systematically what they used to do. So much is tied up in their muscle memory, in the things that they had to learn to do automatically. The approach adopted by the ERC funded ADAPT research project (2013–8) was to go beyond interviews and stage encounters between equipment and their skilled users.[1] The simplest of these encounters involved individuals explaining and demonstrating particular pieces of equipment. Even these encounters yielded far more than a conventional interview because the physical presence equipment triggered fresh memories and the opportunity to handle it once again enabled a voyage of discovery. The ADAPT project was also far more ambitious in enabling encounters between teams of former professionals and the arrays of equipment they used, together, to produce television. The chapters by Amanda Murphy, Nick Hall, and Vanessa Jackson in this collection all explore aspects of this work.

In a way, this method simply develops what most individuals do when they are faced with a piece of equipment. They do not reach for the instructions handbook, even in the increasingly rare cases where such a thing is provided. Instead, they resort to the audio-visual 'how to' material that can easily be found on YouTube and elsewhere. Audio-visual accounts are clearly the preferable complement to the physical experience of a piece of machinery as they, too, demonstrate the involvement of hand and eye, mind and body. The ADAPT project applied this insight successfully to documenting the activities of the skilled professionals who made broadcast television programmes in the analogue era, as is described by Murphy and Hall elsewhere in this collection. This process of documentation requires considerable modifications to traditional research methods. It requires that curators and researchers enter unfamiliar kinds of engagements with objects and with people. It also requires a fresh approach to the presentation of documentation (for example, as 'how they used to' videos as well as written accounts).

The hands on method renders visible and perceptible aspects of human experience that have been neglected by exclusively written, word-based analyses. The use of audio-visual documentation of hands on practices makes visible much that has escaped analysis in the past. Viewing filmed footage opens up the world to a fresh process of seeing. The viewer is enabled to see actions, attitudes and exchanges that would have been overlooked by even alert observers during the actual filming. Multiple camera points of view can capture interactions of people with people, people with machines, and machines with machines that are simply too complex or too fleeting to be apprehended in the flow of events. Recent media theory (Nichols 1991; Renov 1993; Bruzzi 2006; Ellis 2012, etc.), has emphasized that documentary filming is a specific form of intervention into the world, enabling a reconstruction of vision that is both mobile and analytic. The camera and the sound recorder can be seen as new extensions of the human, enabling new explorations of the world by the very act of preserving moments

14 John Ellis

for later inspection. Further, they enable forms of selection and rearrangement of motion in time and space that can open them up to further analysis. This is particularly the case when using a set-up of multiple cameras and sound recorders, as is now possible. From this perspective, it might seem odd that the filming of activities (rather than interviews) is not a more standard approach to social research. However, the technological arrays that would be both suitable and affordable are only just becoming available, and, as Amanda Murphy explores in this collection, the current working practices of television also require adaptation before they can be deployed in a research setting.

The gains from a hands on approach will be great. Researchers will at last be able to perceive that which is not easily articulated in words alone. The 'hands on' method combines audio-visual recording and with the direct sensory experiences of researchers. Researchers deploy a combination of audio-visual recording of skilled users with the immersion of the researcher into similar or analogous physical interactions with those machines. They would both experience for themselves and observe the experiences of others. This would enable researchers to perceive the physicality of human/machine interactions; to grasp the processes that are not verbalized by the human participants in those activities; and, importantly, to observe the activities of teams of humans working with arrays of machinery.

The hands on approach provides a solution to the problem of ethnography so eloquently posed by Geertz (1973) in describing his method of 'thick description':

> Doing ethnography is like trying to read (in the sense of 'construct a reading of') a manuscript – foreign, faded, full of ellipses, incoherencies, suspicious emendations, and tendentious commentaries, but written not in conventionalized graphs of sound but in transient examples of shaped behaviour.
>
> (Geertz 1973, 10)

Geertz further emphasizes that any kind of ethnographic description

> is interpretative; what it is interpretive of is the flow of social discourse; and the interpreting involved consists of trying to rescue the 'said' of such discourse from its perishing occasions and fix it in perusable terms.
>
> (Geertz 1973, 20)

Audio-visual recording using multiple cameras enables the fixing of Geertz's 'perishing occasions'; and then the researcher's own hands on experience guides the interpretive process. This hands on approach provides access to the experiences of the skilled users of technologies, whether they are professionals going about a defined task, or citizens interacting with the many devices that populate the everyday world. So this method can tell us about how 'being in the world' has been and is now constituted. It can reveal the nature of what has been termed 'the new hybrid', or 'hybrid agents': how human and machine work together as a single entity. As Daniel Miller (2010, cover) remarked "things make us just as much as we make things", an insight that only increases in relevance as microelectronics are deployed across everyday life.

The 'gamble' of the hands on approach is therefore an intellectual approach that has important consequences for our attitudes to knowledge and learning. The hands on approach to technologies explored here would have several stages, each of which has its own value and importance for the researcher. In summary, they are:

1. To obtain and explore a machine for its affordances. The researcher(s) see, feel and understand how it works and what it might be capable of doing when free of the institutional constraints in which it was, historically, deployed.
2. To experiment with combinations of machines to discover how they work together and what they might be capable of achieving, understanding the way that machines have a transformative and combinatory potential.
3. To discover and document the communities that have developed advanced skills in combination with the machines within defined historical contexts.
4. To document the ensembles of machinery, the technical arrays and the working practices into which they are or were inserted.
5. To experiment with using, or getting professionals to use, those technical arrays in the way that they were once used. This will discover 'from the inside' what mutual adaptations were involved of people to machines, machines to people, and people to people.
6. To understand both the affordances of the machines and the affordances of the institutions or work-places into which they are or were inserted. These two classes of affordances are mutually determining: the individuals operating within institutions explore the affordances of the technologies; the institutions mould these affordances to their aims; and the designers of technologies take account of their institutional deployment.

The importance of the hands on approach

The approach outlined above has yielded substantial insights when deployed in the ADAPT project. Two examples will demonstrate their nature. Early in the project's history, an initial experimental 'simulation' (as the project designated professional/equipment encounters, see Hall) was mounted using an extant 16mm film cutting room that survived at the London Film School. Once commonplace when most television production outside studios or major live events used film, these technological arrays have almost disappeared. In addition to the iconic editing table (Steenbeck being a key manufacturer), these rooms included large amounts of ancillary equipment: bins for the off-cuts of footage, cans for storage of film reels, rewind benches and cores to wind film round, chinagraph pencils to mark them with, and, crucially, a Pic-Sync for coordinating the strips of magnetic 16mm

16 John Ellis

footage to which the sound tape recordings had been transferred to the 16mm film footage. We were fortunate find this survival that still contained all these items in working order. The simulation also involved two generations of editors, Oliver White and Dawn Trotman.

Dawn Trotman had begun as Oliver's assistant and had quickly graduated to being an editor in her own right. She began cutting 16mm film for a variety of purposes (news, documentary, inserts into studio drama) at the BBC's regional centre in Birmingham (see Vanessa Jackson's chapter in this collection) and ended up as the senior coordinating editor for the BBC's flagship and highly popular early Sunday evening magazine series *Countryfile*, a digital editing operation that she carried out using professional equipment largely based in her home.

When Trotman was reunited with the Pic-Sync, a machine that she used daily when starting out in film editing, she reacted in a highly specific way. When Trotman met the Pic-Sync again, it had already been loaded with two film strips. As a professional, she knew not to intervene in an existing set-up, but she immediately wanted to discover whether she still could remember how to use it. So, giving a verbal account as she goes, her hands hover over the intricate machine as she mimes how her hands used to move. Her physical muscle memory enables her to recall and give an account of the stages of work that she used to go through. In a conventional interview, she would not have easily (if at all) been able to give a detailed and comprehensible account of the activity of syncing up, because that would require her to describe both machine and her operation of it in a way that separated the one from another. For her, the machine and her actions in operating it were an indivisible unit.

Again, a later simulation reunited a group of BBC vision engineers with their 1970s workspace in the outside broadcast truck or 'scanner', North 3. On sitting down in their workspace for the first time for over 30 years, they all instinctively adopt the same physical position in relation to the controls that they operate. They sit well back in their seats, with arms outstretched in front of them, fingers splayed and hovering over the controls (see Figure 1.5). They developed this distinctive stance as a means of hand/eye coordination. They were required to scan a number of monitors in front of them for potential faults in the adjustment of the three or four cameras being used. They had to react as quickly as possible by making compensatory adjustments. This stance is a learned reaction to this set of circumstances, and provides the best way of carrying out their work. Here, the technology has changed its operators, and their bodies alone contain the information that guides them to take this stance. Even if they did, by some exceptional effort, produce an adequate account of how the equipment worked and how they worked with it, we would still run up against the 'instruction manual' problem described earlier. They would simply not be aware that they had learned this way of arranging their bodies. So the researcher, as a novice user, would find it difficult or impossible to relate their own physical orientations towards the technology in the way that professionals used to. No written account of the work of its previous operators would have remarked on this.

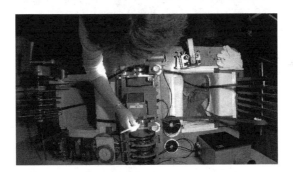

FIGURES 1.1–1.4 Television film and video editor Dawn Trotman demonstrating the use of an Acmade Pic-Sync during an ADAPT project reenactment exercise.

FIGURE 1.5 Vision engineers Bill Baldock and John Coupe at work inside North 3, an outside broadcast vehicle formerly owned by the BBC.

These examples demonstrate that the hands on approach reveals important information about the relationship between humans and the technologies that they use habitually. They show the inadequacy of much current everyday thinking about our relationships with the machines that we use and that use us. These habits of thought are framed within a problematic of mind–intentionality–agency that relegates physical objects and technologies to the status of things which do our bidding and simply aid us to achieve our intentions. When we conceptualize 'tools', we tend to regard them as objects which enable us to carry out our predetermined plans: we think, they do. We regard tools are the extension of capacities within the brain and the body. We believe that tools enable us to realize our previously planned intentions; that *Homo sapiens* has agency, and things do not. In such a perspective, skilled practice tends to be regarded as habit, an automatic engagement with the material world, which explains the often self-deprecating or even subservient attitudes of many 'technicians'.

Against this attitude can be set the idea of the 'hybrid agent' where the body and the tool become an extended unit, 'the tooled body', a new kind of perceptual and cognitive unit. Latour uses the telling example of the gunman, which, once expressed in English, provides a literal rendering of the fusion of human and tool. As Latour puts it:

> neither the isolated gun nor the isolated individual can bear the responsibility for the act of killing. The responsibility lies, on the one hand, in the way those two agents come together to construct a new hybrid agent—the gunman—and, on the other, in the socio-technical network that supports and makes possible such a meeting.
>
> (Latour 1999, 190)

This careful formulation emphasizes that the hybrid agent is socially constructed. It requires a specific culture to enable the encounter to take place by making the technology of the gun available, and by the 'support' that it provides in supplying an ethical framework justifying the deployment of the gun not simply for 'deterrence' but for practical action. Latour concludes that for this hybrid actor, "action involves a coalescence of human and non-human elements, and thus the responsibility for action must be shared among those elements" (Latour 1999, 182). The implications of this position are clear: gun culture as well as the gunman are responsible for the specific action of killing. But so deeply ingrained is the attitude that tools simply do our bidding that the person is punished and the culture or subculture escapes.

Another example can be found in the idea of the 'cameraman' or, better, 'filmer': the hybrid agent constructed in the organized encounter between a camera and its experienced operator. The veteran filmer Brian Tufano provided a clear example of this when enabled by a hands on history experiment conducted as part of the ADAPT project. Tufano's long career as a cameraman began when he was promoted to the role at the BBC in 1963, almost coinciding with the introduction of a new generation of 16mm film cameras that were far lighter than was previous possible. Tufano left the BBC in 1978 to shoot feature films, including *Trainspotting* (1996), *Billy Elliot* (2000) and *Kidulthood* (2006). At the BBC, he was a crucial member of the team making the BBC2 documentary series *Man Alive*, which pioneered a form of documentary that emphasized personal stories and real-life situations.

Tufano demonstrated the series of cameras he had worked with as an assistant, showing the problems that they posed for hand-held work. "You could hardly be subtle with something like this [Arriflex ST with external blimp], or even this [self-blimped Arriflex ST] which was considered great in its day." Tufano was part of a wide movement amongst filmers in the mid-twentieth century, a movement that sought to produce a new kind of hybrid agent: a filmer who could move within situations rather than observe them from a series of more or less fixed positions. They wanted to get the camera off the tripod, and be "mobile" as he puts it, moving into the action as it developed, in concert with the sound recordist. Although enabled to move around within events, they continued to conceive of their role as one of observation, rather than intervention. Hence Tufano's use of the words 'subtle' and 'unobtrusive'.

Tufano comments on the lightweight Éclair camera after he has held it and repeated some familiar actions. He tells how he "suddenly felt a sense of *freedom*" and emphasizes that the Éclair was balanced and felt comfortable when hand-held. He then pauses and reflects, producing rather haltingly the statement that "I thought of my body as a kind of Steadicam": the device, invented far later, which compensates for the movements of the body which, when transmitted to the camera, can produce a distractingly 'wobbly' image. It was a matter of "being as flexible as possible" and "going into the gym and building up your upper body strength and your legs". This is a clear description of a cameraman adapting his body to the equipment he was using. He goes further to outline some new perceptual methods that he had to learn as well: "if you go into a dangerous situation, you need to be as alert as possible, so its learning to use left eye as well as your right eye". When the right eye is looking down the camera viewfinder, the natural response is to close the left eye. However, the vigilant filmer needs to keep the left eye open and to monitor what is going on around. As well as these physical and perceptual modifications to himself, Tufano also made a series of modifications to the camera, installing an exposure meter and using a particular set of controls for the zoom lens that best suited his mode of operation. Finally, he adopted a newly developed battery belt to replace the battery box designed to be slung across the shoulder.

Tufano gives a clear account and demonstration of the process of mutual adaptation necessary to produce a new fused entity: the hybrid agent of the Éclair filmer. The machine offers new affordances whose realization in practice required physical and perceptual changes in the cameraperson, as well as adaptations of the machine to the operator. Tufano's vivid analysis of this process offers the same radical perspective as that of Bernard Stiegler who regards the human as a prosthetic being: "The prosthesis is not a mere extension of the human body; it is the constitution of this body qua 'human'" Stiegler (1998, 152). The camera here is not a tool of a human; it is a prosthesis that allows the extension and mutation of human perception and action into a new field. The camera takes the human capacity of vision and allies it to the process of recording. As part of a larger ensemble of technologies, it participates in a process that brings that recorded event to others who can observe in tranquillity. The new hybrid agent of camera and filmer extends that capacity for recorded seeing by giving it a mobility within the action being filmed as it develops. It provides the ability to follow and observe human actors, to shift focus and attention within a space, to reframe according to the dictates of the action or the editorial preoccupations of the filmer. This new hybrid actor is capable of a new kind of intervention in events that is qualitatively different from that of the eyewitness, and enables a further new kind of seeing in those who witness events through the recorded and edited images and sounds (see Frosh and Pinchevski 2009). The filmer effectively rethinks time, space and events for a new category of absent and distant viewer. We are still working through the implications of this new hybrid actor for society.

Latour's account of the new hybrid 'gunman' is couched in terms of a story of combining two hitherto separate entities. That is what gives it an explanatory impact. Tufano's account of his process of becoming what I have called 'an Éclair filmer' requires that we go further. It requires a more detailed examination of the encounter between person and technology to ask what we do when we think, and in particular whether we are mistaken in our understanding of the relationship between our minds and our tools.

The archaeologist and anthropologist Lambros Malafouris (2013) has developed fresh approach to this issue from his theorization of the earliest toolmaking activities of humanity. Drawing on ideas from Latour, Appadurai, and others, he proposes a 'material engagement theory', which posits that human think through things.

> Human cognitive and emotional states or processes literally comprise elements in their surrounding material environment. . . . Our ways of thinking

are not merely causally dependent upon but constituted by extracranial bodily processes and material artifacts.

(Malafouris 2013, 228)

We do not think and then use things, in other words. Rather, we think through and with the material world. Thinking emerges through the material engagement with things in the world and is formed and developed in those encounters. Malafouris gives the example of a Stone Age person engaged in the activity of hand-knapping: using a suitably shaped flint to create a keen-edged handaxe from another piece of flint.

> Instead of seeing in the shaping of the handaxe the execution of a pre-conceived 'internal' mental plan, we should see an 'act of embodying.' . . . In tool making, most of the thinking happens where the hand meets the stone. There is little deliberate planning, but there is a great deal of approximation, anticipation, and guessing about how the material will behave. . . . Sometimes the material collaborates; sometimes it resists. In time, out of this evolving tension comes precision and thus skillfulness. Knapping, then, should be seen more as an active 'exploration' than as a passive 'externalization' or 'imposition of form'.
>
> (2013, 235)

This is a dramatic example of thinking with and through the material world, and has many similarities with the accounts of filmers as they engage with the events they are filming, whether they are pre-planned or spontaneous. The remark that "there is a great deal of approximation, anticipation and guessing about how the material will behave" could well be applied to documentary filmmaking and even to many kinds of fiction as well. The "evolving tension" that arises in repeating the action to gain "precision and thus skilfulness" describes the difficult process of acquiring the skills necessary for the task.

Malafouris is dealing with what might appear to be a simple cultural process, one of creating tools from the interaction of two natural objects and one human. This may appear to be a long way from the situations encountered today. However, the knapping of flints is always already inserted into a pattern of activity, and required by defined needs: the knapped flints are used for making weapons, scraping skins, cutting meat, and carving bone. The activity takes place, in other words, within an always-already existing technological context where other tools like fire also exist and call into existence the need for sharp edged implements. Malafouris is describing an encounter with objects (in this case drawn from the natural world) which is essentially no different from our contemporary encounters with the always-already existing world of technological objects that we are able to deploy . . . if we can discover how to operate them.

So Malafouris's description of the combined physical/mental process of creating knapped flints can be applied equally to the activity of editing, the remaking of the captured sounds and images into a meaningful ensemble. Editing is famously an iterative process of trying out combinations of material to find out what works best as a meaningful whole. In film editing, this is a physical process (director Charles Crichton described in the documentary *Distilling Whisky Galore* (Grigor 1991) working as assistant to Zoltan Korda who ripped the film with his teeth). Digital editing dispenses with the directly physical encounter with strips of film, but the same iterative process is still at its heart. Colour grading, telecine and sound mixing other processes also involve the same exploratory process of material engagement. The material is in the eye and ear rather than the hand. Technicians vary elements and their combination to discover what 'works' for the particular purpose they have in mind. It is no different from flint-knapping except that the desired result is not a sharp edge that can be sits well in the hand, but an audio-visual text that is both meaningful and pleasurable for its anticipated users.

Malafouris makes a distinction between the mind and the brain. The mind, he claims, exists in the interaction of human and tools. This distinction reveals the imbrication of the human and the physical in processes which lie beyond the brain. It also requires that we regard the concept of 'agency' in a different way. The power to act is usually seen as an exclusively human capability. However Malafouris argues that "Agency and intentionality may not be innate properties of things, but they are not innate properties of humans either; they are emergent properties of material engagement" (2013, 148–149). Agency emerges from the interaction of humans and the material world. Agency and intentionality emerge from the encounter between the human and the material world into which she or he is born, a world that in our time increasingly involves everyday and intimate technologies.

> Our starting point cannot be that of conscious agency as an innate property of humans. The feeling of agency should be seen as an emergent property of action rather than as an a priori possession of the embodied biological organism. From this perspective, achieving agency is a process inseparable from becoming human.
>
> (2013, 215)

This much emerges from actor network theory. Malafouris then ventures into research in neuro-psychology, citing the famous (or infamous) research into the brain development of London taxi drivers who are required to have a comprehensive knowledge ("The Knowledge" as they call it) of the location and interrelation of London's streets. Research has shown that the acquisition of The Knowledge produces physical changes in the brains of taxi drivers, with an increase in the size of the hypothalamus. Research into musicians has revealed similar enhancements of their capabilities when compared to non-musicians.

> It appears not only that musicians have extraordinary motor and sensory skills, and better somatosensory discrimination abilities, but also that, relative

> to non-musicians, they have an increased ability to learn new tasks, and they show enhanced motor and sensory learning capabilities . . . Several studies comparing musicians with non-musicians clearly indicate important structural and functional changes in the brains of the former as a result of intense sensory and motor training associated with musical expertise.
>
> (2013, 46)

Intense physical training is required to play a musical instrument to a high standard. As Tufano showed, the requirements for the highest achievements in operating a handheld 16mm camera are equally exacting. Similar skills are required of many who work within the media industries today: a co-ordination between hand, machine, eye and ear that are not easy to acquire. As Murphy points out, there is a considerable difference between the footage that results from camera movements made by an inexperienced user, and the 'useable move' that will be provided by a skilled user. This is a distinct skill that has to be acquired by practice. Yet we still think of what is learned here as skills or crafts rather than knowledges. There is an implicit downgrading of these 'skills' in relation to other forms of learning. The material engagement approach requires that we re-evaluate our approach to the idea of 'skills' and their acquisition. What we call 'skills' are in fact adaptations of humans to their new circumstances of operation. The change from first acquaintance with a technology to becoming a skilled operator is one of (observable) physical change, and (not yet researched) biological changes as well. Malafouris' material engagement theory offers a means of understanding and theorizing an area that many media studies scholars find mysterious: the area of 'media practice'. More widely, it also enables us to understand the potential of hands on approaches to the study of the relations between technologies and their humans, or humans and their technologies.

In the past, intellectuals have conceived of their own activity of thought as something that can only take place through stratagems of avoidance of the physical: by shrugging off the preoccupations of everyday existence to servants and to women; by regarding the physical world as a necessary encumbrance, to be endured and overcome; by creating ivory towers. The intellectuals of the past, beginning with the early elites who first gained control the surpluses of agriculture, expressed their power through their emancipation from the physical, the better to be able to think and reflect. So the notion that thinking takes place through material engagement runs counter to the long history of intellectual activity and so seems rather more radical or difficult than it is in practice. It runs against a dualism of the physical and the mental which sets the two in opposition to each other. This same dualism is that which Heidegger (1977) identified and criticized in his essay on technology, a dualism that sees thought as existing separate from the physical world and hence able to instrumentalize that world. This attitude he summed up in the idea that humanity to rethink nature as a 'standing reserve', as the raw material that waits for the human intelligence to exploit it. This attitude is that of the Anthropocene: the ability to have, through the application of technologies, a

24 John Ellis

profound and pervasive impact on the nature of the world. A hands on approach to knowledge will begin to enable a move away from this mindset, to see the human as the product of a continuing process of material engagement with both nature and technologies. The perception that nature is a 'standing reserve', criticized by Heidegger, is based on the misconception that human intentionality and agency are separate and antecedent to action, rather than produced within the encounter of hybrid agents and the material world.

The self-awareness of the hands on researcher in trying to adopt the adaptations of the skilled operators is important in developing an understanding what those adaptations were. This new methodology, then, requires techniques of physical self-awareness that are different from the contemplative or analytic skills of the past. These new analytic approaches are all the more important as we become aware of the challenges and affordances of our future. We need an awareness both that we are continuously adapting through new material engagements, and that we are actors in a world whose very existence is threatened by our misapprehension of our material engagements as manipulation of a world that stands 'in reserve', ready to do our bidding.

We live in a time when understanding this relationship has become an urgent task. Our period is one in which vast populations are being taken (or are taking themselves) through a whole range of new material engagements, with whole classes of new electronic technologies which are redefining everyday existence. The affordances of these technologies bring with them a large range of new material engagements and hence series of adaptations of our bodies and our minds. We are all digital technicians now, using our opposable thumbs for new purposes, adapting our vision and physical disposition for screen work of different kinds. We are altering our internal perceptions of time as we adapt our management of time. We are substituting writing for speech, moving images for writing. Donna Haraway (1991) famously pointed out that humans have always been cyborgs, moulding and combining their bodies to whatever tool they were using. More recently, Andy Clark has claimed that humans are 'natural-born cyborgs' because of this continuous adaptation of our minds through their material engagements: "Many of our tools are not just external props and aids, but they are deep and integral parts of the problem-solving systems we now identify as human intelligence" (Clark 2004, 5–6). The range of hands on history approaches acknowledges the complex realities of this insight. Hands on approaches will develop an understanding of our place in a world through which thinking becomes possible, together with which we think.

Note

1 This chapter and the videos to which it refers were produced as part of the ADAPT project funded by the European Research Council (ERC) under the European Union's Horizon 2020 research and innovation programme (grant agreement No. 323626).

Bibliography

Bruzzi, Stella (2006) *New Documentary: A Critical Introduction*. London: Routledge.

Clark, Andy (2004) *Natural-Born Cyborgs*. Oxford: Oxford University Press.

Ellis, John (2012) *Documentary: Witness and Self-Revelation*. London: Routledge.

Ellis, J., Murphy, A. and Hall, N., 2018. ADAPT. Available from: https://doi.org/10.17637/rh.c.3925603.

Ernst, Wolfgang (2012) *Digital Memory and the Archive*. Minneapolis: University of Minnesota Press.

Frosh, P. and Pinchevski, A. (eds) (2009) *Media Witnessing: Testimony in the Age of Mass Communication*. London: Palgrave Macmillan.

Geertz, Clifford (1973) *The Interpretation of Cultures*. New York: Basic Books.

Grigor, Murray (1991) *Distilling Whisky Galore*. London: Large Door/Channel 4 Television, 8 January.

Haraway, Donna (1991) A Cyborg Manifesto: Science, Technology, and Socialist-Feminism in the Late Twentieth Century. In *Simians, Cyborgs and Women: The Reinvention of Nature*. London: Routledge.

Heidegger, Martin (1977) *The Question Concerning Technology*. New York: Taylor & Francis.

Huhtamo, Erkki and Parikka, Jussi (eds) (2011) *Media Archaeologies: Approaches, Applications, and Implications*. Berkeley, CA: University of California Press.

Latour, Bruno (1999) *Pandora's Hope: Essays on the Reality of Science Studies*. Cambridge, MA: Harvard University Press.

Malafouris, Lambros (2013) *How Things Shape the Mind: A Theory of Material Engagement*. Boston, MA: MIT Press.

Miller, Daniel (2010) *Stuff*. Cambridge: Polity Press.

Nichols, Bill (1991) *Representing Reality: Issues and Concepts in Documentary*. Bloomington: Indiana University Press.

Parikka, Jussi (2012) *What is Media Archaeology?* Cambridge: Polity Press.

Renov, Michael (1993) *Theorizing Documentary*. New York: Routledge.

Stiegler, Bernard (1998) *Technics and Time 1*. Stanford, CA: Stanford University Press.

2

BRINGING THE LIVING BACK TO LIFE

What happens when we reenact the recent past?

Nick Hall

We live in an age of reenactments of the recent past. In recent years, three types of reenactment have grown in importance. Historical reenactment television has flourished since the early 2000s, lately turning its attention to histories well within the memory of many viewers. Meanwhile, as portable digital video recording equipment and access to high-speed internet has become widespread, many thousands of people have committed their own reenactments, recreations, and rediscoveries to web platforms like YouTube. Some of these emerge from the efforts of individuals to record their own memories or preserve equipment: a new form of 'history from below'. Others are imitations of historical reenactment or enquiry, confected to draw an audience and to raise advertising revenue. Together, these forms of reenactment – produced without formal research methodology, with entertainment their primary concern, and always adopting a hands on approach to their interactions with technology – create the cultural backdrop against which scholarly and investigative reenactments now take place. The importance for contemporary scholars of public engagement leads to an inevitable blending of the two, for video recordings of investigative reenactments must jostle for space alongside the characteristic media forms of the digital era: clickbait and viral video.

Digital video platforms – with YouTube in the vanguard – provide an outlet for historical reenactments of every type. Elderly machinery has been dusted off and restarted for the cameras; children are introduced to obsolete computer technologies little older than themselves; hipsters tour 'the last' video rental store. No longer is the historical reenactment limited to geographically specific locations. The muddy field of a Civil War reenactment and the rigging of a restored tall ship are joined by the everywhere of the internet. Historical reenactments on television and in digital media blur the lines between reenactment, simulation, and performed memory, and they draw the 'past' that is available for memory work closer to the present. In turn, these popular entertainment reenactments alter the conditions under which investigative reenactments and simulations take place. It is this conjunction that I am interested in exploring: between a culture now immersed in immediate, online, user-generated reenactments of the past, and the more sober and systematic efforts of media historians. As other chapters in this volume indicate, these two approaches to the past are not in contention: they nourish and inspire one another. What they hold most importantly in common is that they are not concerned with raising dead ancestors – in other words, they do not want to bring the distant past back to life. Instead, they seek to bring the *living* back to life. Inspired and informed by practices of experimental media archaeology, they find neglected, forgotten, failed, obsolete or dead practices and technologies and resuscitate them for education or entertainment.

In this chapter, I trace the development of this new form of reenactment, which has emerged out of the conjunction of historical reenactment television and online digital video. I examine two examples of online reenactment: revisitations of holdout Blockbuster franchises in the USA, and the viral video format "Kids React. . .". I consider the ways in which the unspoken and unselfconscious methodologies behind these viral videos tessellate with approaches taken by recent historical reenactors, taking as my principal example hands on research into historical technological processes in television production. At the centre of this discussion is the problem of the reenactment of the recent past, in which individuals replay everyday behaviours that previously typified their working lives. This is a form of reenactment unlike any other that has been routinely performed. It offers unique opportunities to obtain valuable and richly detailed memories about past working practices and obsolete technologies. However, this approach challenges traditional ways of thinking about historical evidence and oral testimony. It privileges emotion and affect over historical rigour. The emotional reunion with a long-discarded technology is intrinsic to any reenactment of the recent past, but this emotional evidence can be challenging to interpret and introduce to the historical record. Alongside this methodological challenge is a practical one. Online reenactments tend to place vital historical testimony onto the precarious spaces of online video platforms. There, videos which do not immediately attract a mass audience risk sinking into the algorithmic sediment: the thick layer of digital content that is rarely watched and hard to find, because it lacks metadata or because nobody links to it. Thus, in addition to its primary methodological provocations, hands on historical reenactments also make a further case for the necessity of secure, non-corporatized digital public space into which the digital products of online hands on history may be deposited.

Reenacting the recent past on television

Television's preoccupation with the recent past can be traced to the fly-on-the-wall documentary boom of the late 1990s. *The 1900s House*, produced in 1999 for Channel 4, was one of the first television series to immerse 'ordinary people' in a confected past. The series stripped the Bowler family – mother, father, and three teenaged children – of their modern clothing and comforts and sent them, dressed as Victorians, to live in a Victorian terraced house. The series' solemn commitment to authenticity set the tone for historical reenactment television. The opening episode documented the family's three-day preparatory visit to the Museum of Domestic Culture at Shugborough Hall, while the marketing material surrounding the programme insisted that the family would "abide by a strict set of rules in an effort to live exactly as Victorians would have done" ("Programme highlights: 1999 week 38 page 46" 1999). *The 1900 House* thus established the parameters for the genre, enumerated by Michelle Liu Carriger as "a reality TV/documentary format, painstaking facsimile replicas of historical environments, and the casting of regular contemporary people as the main subjects of the programs, relying on the dynamic of reenactment for their content" (Carriger 2010, 135). The series was followed by sequels covering more recent history, including *The Edwardian Country House* (Channel 4, 2002), *The 1940s House* (Channel 4, 2001), *Coal House* (BBC Wales, 2007) and *Coal House at War* (BBC Wales, 2008).

Over the past decade, television has become bored with the distant past, and has turned its attention to reviving more recent technologies and lifestyles. "Technological time travel" documentary series *Electric Dreams* (BBC Four, 2009), ostensibly educational and produced in partnership with the Open University, remodelled a family home and watched as its inhabitants struggled with resurrected and restored domestic technologies from the 1970s, 1980s, and 1990s. The parents recalled each of the technologies with fondness or exasperation, while their four children experienced them afresh. More recently, and without any veneer of educational purpose, Channel 4 aired *That's So Last Century* (2015), a compilation of celebrities showing their children the technologies of their past. That same year *Back In Time For Dinner* (BBC, 2015) transported a family to each decade from the 1950s to the 1990s, but – having run out of historical road – the sequel series *Further Back In Time For Dinner* (BBC, 2017) turned the historical tide to cover the first half of the century, in its first episode returning viewers to an historical milieu first glimpsed 17 years earlier in *The 1900s House*.

Throughout television's circular tour around the fads and fashions of the twentieth and early twenty-first centuries, certain constants remained. While historical foci shifted, television's experimental methodology remained fairly fixed. A "typical" family – always a husband and wife, always more than two children (a mixture of boys and girls, teenagers and younger) – was recruited, their house transformed, their clothes replaced. In each of these series, children act as surrogates for the broader television audience. Their innocent commentary on the differences between 'then' and 'now' incites explanatory narration which might otherwise seem too overtly didactic for entertainment television. Above all, historical reenactment television was hands on, challenging its participants to make bread in coal ovens, and wash clothes with dolly and mangle, feeling the awkwardness and unfamiliarity of their labour at the very tips of their fingers. No matter how remote or recent the reenactment, the family was always put to hardship, so that the novelty enjoyed as they first encountered their new surroundings was certain to wear off before the end of the first episode. Historical reenactment television never went without an early emotional breakdown: witness Joyce Bowler, driven to tears of rage by an accumulation of frustrating Victorian kitchen technologies in the second half-hour of *The 1900 House*, or Rochelle Robshaw's profound annoyance at her husband's disappointment in her dish of 1950s liver in *Back In Time For Dinner*. These episodic crises fit into a larger narrative pattern: as Vanessa Agnew puts it,

> we find that each of the *House* series traces a similar arc—estrangement from familiar surroundings, depravation [*sic*] in the historical setting, the precipitation of a crisis, followed by resolution (or expulsion from the group), and finally reintegration into the present.
>
> (Agnew 2007, 303–304)

It was these emotional facets of historical reenactment television, among other factors, which prompted Agnew to worry about the genre's tendency to privilege affect over rigorous historical analysis (Agnew 2007). Recent developments in the genre have shown her anxiety to be well founded. Television's ruthless pursuit of the marketable format has seen historical reenactment further boiled down to its most dramatic and energizing affective moments, then repeated – with minor variations – ad nauseam across the world. Family relationships and childish reactions come to the fore, just as they do in other reality genres. *Gordon Ramsay's Kitchen Nightmares* and *Supernanny* – superbly entertaining examples of reality TV – are more than close cousins of the crudest forms of historical reenactment; they are siblings, jostling for space in the same crowded television schedules and replay apps. In the light of shows like *That's So Last Century*, the solemn dedication of *The 1900 House* to historical fidelity (however partial, however problematic) seems almost as antiquated as its subject matter.

Reenactment, clickbait, and 'procrastitainment'

So much for historical reenactment television; moving image media has moved on, and taken reenactment with it. Now we have a new historical reenactment format to contend with: a broad, decentralized, disorganized movement of amateur historians and video producers who populate YouTube with boutique reenactments and "procrastitainment" videos. To understand this new genre, the definition of reenactment must be broadened almost beyond recognition. Online, hardly anybody feels the need to dress up in period clothing in order to sample the primitive user interface of Photoshop 1.0. Nobody receives training in the language and social mores of the 1970s before 'retro unboxing' a Polaroid camera. Such videos are casually, almost thoughtlessly, made: there are no 'consultants' credited to vouch for the reenactment's authenticity. Nevertheless, these videos represent a decisive, almost obsessive, effort to thoroughly document the technologies of the recent past. With hundreds of millions of views between them, their influence should not be underestimated. The viral success of the web series *Kids React*

30 Nick Hall

undoubtedly inspired television's *That's So Last Century*. What historical reenactment television started in the late 1990s, the web continued in the mid-2010s, albeit in almost unrecognizable form.

Online historical reenactment videos reflect a particular attraction to the recent past. This attraction has a number of sources. Online video is often cheaply produced, with relatively little planning. Although YouTube is an increasingly professionalized space, serendipitously or casually captured footage remains its mainstay. It is far more likely that a YouTube creator finds an old phone in a desk drawer, or purchases a cheap obsolete model from eBay, than arranges to access the same equipment within a museum. As a result, mass-produced quotidian technologies are lavished with attention by YouTube's reenactors, while less widespread equipment is more neglected. Aside from this production constraint, the audience for such videos is relatively young, especially when compared to a typical television audience. Nostalgia, for YouTube's core audience, means technologies that developed, flourished, and fell into disuse within the last few decades: DVD players, the original Sony PlayStation, and the first-generation iPhone are all candidates for the instant nostalgia treatment of the online video historical reenactment. Fortunately, it does not matter that the target audience is so narrow, and their nostalgia so alienating for a general audience. These would be significant problems for a television documentary: indeed, after the broadcast of the first episode of *That's So Last Century*, one newspaper review complained that the show's nostalgia had missed its target.

> Amusing as it was to see Vic Reeves's daughter call a cassette tape a record, and Dom Joly's son try and take a selfie with an archaic Nikon, most of us do remember when chemists dobbed customers in for their naughty snaps and people re-recorded TV shows over old episodes of *Top of the Pops* on VHS.
>
> (Wyatt 2015)

In the ultra-narrowcast space of YouTube, such criticisms carry no weight and are rarely made. Audiences can select their own precise historical interests, and those who wish to indulge their own nostalgia can select precisely the era and exactly the technology that they wish to revisit. YouTube's bottomless archive of dead technologies allows for fine distinctions: former owners of the Nokia 3310 can indulge themselves with videos of that phone, but there are countless entirely different video records of the (almost identical) Nokia 3330 as well. Videos that are annoying, patronizing, or mistargeted can simply be stopped and an alternative selected. The viewer must select the historical account that suits them, rather than (as on broadcast television) the producer needing to cater to the audience. The best – those that most capture the spirit of nostalgia for each generation and technology – might, algorithms permitting, rise to the top of trending lists. Here, online reenactment is a first draft of history, and the aspiration is not to historical rigour but to attracting views and viral circulation.

The majority of online reenactment is generated by individual users, who create highly personal videos which impart their own memories, experiences, and contexts of use upon the reenactment accounts that they produce. "I remember this," is the characteristic refrain of producers and narrators as they stumble upon a game, ringtone, or design quirk which triggers a particular nostalgic response. Like historical reenactment television, the emphasis is on hands on interactions with old technologies: equipment is handled and manipulated, buttons pressed and functions tested. Often, the camera tightly frames the hands of the user as they perform these actions. Reenactments of the use of old technologies – "retro unboxings", "living with the iPhone 2G for a week", "how to go online on a 1970s era computer" – represent a form of historical narrative that is largely controlled by the individual user of the technology, rather than by academic historians or by technology companies (Ross 2014; The 8-Bit Guy 2014). They may be seen, in this way, as a peculiar form of 'history from below'. Though this history has no explicit ideological project, and is largely shared with the world from within the corporate context of commercial platforms like YouTube, it nevertheless emancipates stories of technological innovation and use from their corporate frame and places them firmly in the hands of end-users. This is only possible because the technologies under scrutiny are recently obsolete, and have fallen into disuse well before the death of their original users.

The apparent democracy of YouTube's platform is, of course, illusory and unstable. The platform has followed a familiar path: at first a chaotic and disorganized space, as its user base has grown its sorting, suggestion, and trending algorithms have become more sophisticated. Tight integration with Google's advertising sales platform has led to the emergence of professional content creators – traditional media firms alongside the new phenomenon of creative media entrepreneurs known as YouTubers – who compete for the small income attracted by individual views. Inevitably, this professionalization and commercialization has led to the development of a range of loose genres. Regular visitors to YouTube will easily recognize the vlog, the unboxing video, the tutorial, the review, and the computer game playthrough. Within these genres, we also find formats akin to those found in broadcast television, of which *Kids React* is a primary example.

In its hyperactive emotional interactions with 'old technology' and other historical artefacts, the web series *Kids React* takes to its furthest extent Agnew's criticism of historical reenactment television's "historical representation that both takes affect as its object and attempts to elicit affect" (quoted in Carriger 2010, 136). The series is all performance and affect and scarcely any historical substance. *Kids React* is a sprawling format, conceived in 2010 by Benny and Rafi Fine, who trade as Fine Brothers Entertainment. The format is simple and repetitious: children are shown things – television programmes, viral videos, politicians making speeches, and so forth – and their reactions are filmed. There are various thematic sub-series within the broad format, including *Kids React! Technology*, in which old technology is placed in the hands of children and teenagers and their reactions

FIGURE 2.1 A child attempts to switch on an Apple II personal computer in *Kids React To Old Computers*.

recorded. In this series, the most-watched video is *Kids React To Old Computers* (FBE 2014). Produced as a promotional tie-in with the American cable series *Halt And Catch Fire*, *Kids React To Old Computers* features rapidly edited, intercut footage of children and teenagers of different ages 'reacting to', then operating and asking questions about an Apple II computer. An unseen adult answers their questions and prompts them to carry out tasks: they switch the computer on, load a floppy disk, and use the command line interface to perform a simple mathematical operation.

Though glossily and expensively produced, the kids of *Kids React* almost pass for genuine. However, as the technology writer Drew Gardner has pointed out, there is nothing 'real' about the reactions in *Kids React*:

> The Fine Brothers found all the children in Kids React from notices the brothers placed on LACasting.com. The show would be more accurately titled Child Actors React. The children are the subjects of the show, but they are also actors playing video bloggers, cast in that role by an agency. There is a viral element at work here, but the viruses have been manufactured in a laboratory.
>
> (Gardner 2014)

As Gardner remarks, the series represents a long tradition of "capitalizing on the affective labour of children", which reaches back to the radio origins of *Kids Say The Darnedest Things* and extends into contemporary clip shows like *America's Funniest Home Videos* and *You've Been Framed*. The focus of *Kids React* is always on cuteness and precocity, on creating viral, shareable moments that can be enjoyed in a moment of spare or squandered time; hence, *procrastitainment*. The *Kids React To . . . Old Technology* series stands out from other strands in the *React* format, because rather than having child actors react to other viral videos, they are invited to react to tangible historical technological artefacts: the Sony Walkman cassette player, VHS VCR, rotary phones, Game Boy, typewriters, "90s internet", and so on. Just as in so many historical reenactment television series, here children once again stand in for an audience that is working through the passing of technologies from present to past.

Indeed, the repeated attempt to capture history at the very moment of its passing from past to present is what is most striking about historical reenactment videos on YouTube. A disconnected series of amateur videos documenting the decline of the Blockbuster video rental store chain is a case in point. In the late 2010s, under pressure from online streaming services, the video rental chain Blockbuster began to collapse. The company's demise was gradual. Stores closed in waves during a series of bankruptcies and restructuring plans. By 2013 only a few hundred stores remained in the United States and by 2017, seven years after Blockbuster filed for bankruptcy, all but a handful of the firm's 9,000 stores had closed. Blockbuster's slow withering created a zombie brand. When Blockbuster stores were a fixture of malls and shopping streets across the developed world, they could be overlooked as a too-familiar feature of the retail landscape. Now, the bright blue-and-yellow signage on the surviving outlets could not be ignored. No longer ubiquitous and mundane, hold-out Blockbuster franchises located in unremarkable shopping malls were a rarity and spoke of decline. Only a few years earlier, to step into a Blockbuster outlet had been to glimpse the cutting-edge of home entertainment technology. Now, with the brand in freefall and rent-by-mail services on the rise, the doors to a Blockbuster were a portal to a very recent past.

The same technological advance that ultimately killed Blockbuster – the ability to stream high definition video across the internet – created a new opportunity to record the company's demise. Armed with digital camcorders or smartphones, YouTube content creators visited Blockbuster outlets ironically, attending the stores not to borrow a DVD but to document the absurd nostalgia of the zombie video rental store. K. Ryan Jones's *Touring the Last Surviving Blockbuster Video* is one of the earliest examples, uploaded to YouTube in March 2013 (Ryan Jones 2013). If *Kids React* follows the producing principles of Hollywood television, then videos documenting the decline of Blockbuster embody the spirit of Dogme 95. Ryan's video starts with a *Blair Witch Project* style title: "On a normal Thursday, at the beginning of a normal trip between Dallas, TX, and Wichita, KS, something extraordinary and heretofore thought lost was unearthed". This gives way to a short video seemingly shot on a smartphone: "We have made an amazing discovery, like a rare animal, an endangered species, some might even say extinct: a Blockbuster Video". Jones then leads the camera operator around the video store, delivering a satirical commentary on the store which is perfectly 'preserved' "just as we remembered it". The camera orbits Jones as he holds his head in his hands and smiles in delight, aping the behaviour of the arriving family in *1900 House* and the reactions of reenactment participants reunited with old but familiar equipment. But the video is not entirely a comedy performance: Jones briefly interviews two apparently genuine customers of the shop who make a seemingly unscripted

34 Nick Hall

FIGURES 2.2 AND 2.3 Applying for a new Blockbuster Video membership card and rediscovering the DVD case in 'Touring The Last Surviving Blockbuster Video'.

contribution to the video. Jones' mockery of Blockbuster is contrasted with the sincerity of the customers, middle-aged Midwestern women who declare "we love doing that" (going to a video rental store). At the end of the video Jones opens a new Blockbuster account and receives a membership card, which he will likely never use; for him, the transaction is satirical, but for the employee it is a matter of daily working life in a video franchise which – he must know – is likely soon to close with the loss of his job.

Jones's tour of the 'last surviving Blockbuster' is not the only video of its kind to be found on YouTube. Three years later Blockbuster Video was the subject of a video in Chris Stuckmann's "Retro Rewind" series. With the characteristic hyperbole of viral video Stuckmann explains

> my wife and I actually drove out of state to Indiana to one of the few remaining Blockbusters that are still in existence. We thought they were all gone

Bringing the living back to life **35**

but there are still a handful of people who have been able to hold on to their franchises, and we walked around an actual Blockbuster and, oh my gosh, it was *insane*.

(Stuckmann 2016)

As Blockbuster outlets became rarer, media organizations including the BBC, Vice, and Bloomberg News made their own media-historical pilgrimages. In July 2018, CBS Morning News dispatched a reporter to one of the last existing Blockbuster stores in the United States, in Bend, Oregon. The journalist, Jamie Yuccas, performed similar rituals to those of Jones and Stuckmann, admiring the alphabetically arranged shelves of DVDs, highlighting the antiquated point-of-sale computer equipment at the store's desk, and interviewing young adults for whom the retail experience was akin to a museum visit.

These examples of 'reenactment' on YouTube and in mainstream news media are highly specific and rather extreme. *Kids React* represents the most commercial, most formatted, and arguably least historiographically viable form of online video reenactment. Comic videos of moribund Blockbuster stores represent another form of reenactment that professional historians might struggle to identify as historical work. They share more with improvised comedy than with the practice of historical documentation. Yet it should be no surprise that the forms of historical record found on YouTube are unrecognizable to us, because YouTube – and the concept of an online video platform in general – is almost brand new. Moreover, YouTube, with its millions of hours of video content and almost global availability, is a symptom of a new technological reality: it has never been so easy to document the present in video and share and preserve the results. Taking advantage of this ease, most online videos document the present accidentally, without much thought for posterity. The examples here point towards a more specifically historical, but not much more self-conscious, use. Here, digital video records and dramatizes the present *in the process of becoming the past*. Taking advantage of the developing forms of a brand new media, they present a form of reenactment that is naturally unrecognizable from what has gone before. Yet there can be little doubt that the videographer or journalist who opens a new Blockbuster video account for no reason other than to demonstrate the process, and display the charmingly obsolete paper membership card, is staging a form of reenactment. Likewise the children, struggling to understand what a 5¼-inch floppy disk is and how it might be loaded into an Apple II personal computer are reenacting the past every bit as much as the Civil War reenactor in full battle dress. And this activity is not confined to the viral giants of the procrastitainment genre. As *Kids React* and its ilk goes viral at the surface, thousands of hours of video footage of old technologies are uploaded to YouTube. Much of this material slips without trace into the platform's unseen depths, where obscure titles and incomplete metadata condemn video material to just a handful of hundred views per year. Despite this obscurity these videos are accumulating to form a vast library of everyday experiences with, and memories of, newly obsolete media technologies. Future generations may be bequeathed an

36 Nick Hall

unparalleled source of evidence of their twenty-first century ancestors' interactions with technology, if the video material we uploaded can be properly catalogued and preserved.

Bringing the living back to life

Wherever new media trends and new technological opportunities appear, academic research projects follow. And so it is with historical reenactments of the recent past, of various forms. As other chapters in this collection demonstrate, media archaeology labs, filled with ancient and obsolete computer and audiovisual equipment, have flourished within universities and museums across the world. In the United Kingdom, diverse academic projects have embraced new opportunities offered by digital video. Roger Kneebone and Abigail Wilson have recreated historical surgical practices through simulation, recording the reenacted procedures "in high definition using multiple static and roving videocams with sound" (Kneebone and Woods 2012, 33). Media historian Andrew Ireland researched the history of British television drama production by remaking a contemporary episode of *Doctor Who* using the practices and technologies of 1960s studio television production (Ireland 2012). Beyond the academy, in 2006 members of the Test Card Circle – a British organization for television history enthusiasts – marked the 70th anniversary of regular television transmissions by mounting a live outside broadcast using a 1960s television truck once operated by Southern Television. The output of the broadcast, *TV70*, was recorded and distributed on DVD but eventually withdrawn due to copyright restrictions. As the costs of creating digital video fall, and video content creation skills become more widespread, projects like these are becoming more common.

ADAPT, a research project that investigated the history of British television production technologies by way of a series of video recorded historical reenactments, provided an opportunity not only to research the history of British television, but also to closely observe the working dynamics of reenactments which feature living participants.[1] Elsewhere in this volume, Amanda Murphy describes the practical considerations involved in mounting the simulations carried out for this project. Here, I shall confine myself to noting some of the features of recent-past historical reenactments which differentiate them from more traditional reenactments, and which tie them more closely to the informal and amateur reenactments described above. In particular, it can be noted that reenactments carried out with living participants intensify the collapse of temporal boundaries. This was further intensified, in the case of the ADAPT reenactments, by the absence of costumes for participants and by the porous boundaries between the reenactment space and the world surrounding it. In short, having participants wear their own clothes, and not fencing them in to a 'reenactment space', tends to make the past seem closer and more familiar. Beyond these practical concerns, we can note a marked difference in the type of memory work being conducted. In a traditional reenactment, 'modern' participants learn historical skills which are new to them. In ADAPT's reenactments, as in any carried out with survivor-participants, old skills are not learned afresh but revived and remembered.

Historical reenactments of any sort collapse temporal boundaries. Carrying out reenactments with living participants brings this collapse to the fore. The boundary between past and present, porous in any reenactment, melts away almost entirely when the recent past is simulated. ADAPT carried out historical reenactment experiments with people who had, in the past, worked in technical production roles in British television. When recruited, many participants were found either in retirement or in second careers. When participants were still working in the industrial role which was to be reenacted they were often working with a radically changed set of technologies. (Were the technologies not radically changed, there would be little point in carrying out a reenactment.) To give a number of illustrative examples: when ADAPT reunited outside broadcast producers and engineers who had joined the BBC in the 1960s and 1970s, all had retired from the Corporation and none was still working in their former role. Simulations of other technologies recruited individuals who were not yet retired but were working in radically different settings or with technologies that had evolved beyond recognition. A television editor who had learned her craft with 16mm film at a Steenbeck table, for example, was now working with digital non-linear editing software. At the very least, participants came to reenactments prepared to revive past versions of themselves. Others – those whose had not retired or left broadcasting – volunteered to perform a day's work, simply swapping contemporary tools and equipment for those they had used in the past. The television editor took a day away from her Avid editing console to return to cutting 16mm film at a Steenbeck. As a result, to participants in reenactments of the recent past, the 'gap' between the present and the reenacted past often seemed remarkably small. After the shock of a reunion with old equipment and former colleagues, the next emotion expressed was often of surprise at how close the past seemed to be: though it has been so long, participants commented, *it seems like yesterday*.

There are many reasons why the past seems so recent to such participants. Some have nothing to do with the conditions set by the investigators, and everything to do with the workings of human memory. Many reenactments have asked participants to recall the work they did in their formative years, during the "reminiscence bump" thought to enhance memories of a person's teenage years and twenties. These memories, more detailed and vivid than those made during the years of middle age, will naturally seem surprisingly close to the present day. Furthermore, participants in reenactments such as these are usually recruited weeks or months in advance and tended to be 'auditioned' by the investigators via a telephone call or series of emails. During the period between the project's initial contact with the participant and their arrival in the reenactment space, all participants – whether consciously or subconsciously – reflected upon the history of their working life. In most cases, this process was entirely conscious. In fact, it was solicited to some degree by the project team. Participants recalled old anecdotes and made efforts to remember old equipment. Often, they presented themselves in the reenactment space with a cache of personal archive documents, bringing payslips, photographs, and contracts as written counterparts to their memory. The overt outcome of this process is one of generous memory-sharing – "I thought you might like to see . . ." – but this everyday phrase masks a complex underlying process of memory retrieval. The participants, arriving with folder of photographs in hand, had spent some time in their memory boxes (physical and mental), and had in the process drawn themselves closer to their own past. Under these conditions it is little wonder that by the time the reenactment takes place, the reenacted past 'seems like yesterday'.

Other, more physical, conditions of reenactment may have the tendency to make the past seem closer and more familiar. One of these is the absence of costume. Costumes carry great importance in traditional historical reenactments. A reenactment of the distant past requires its audience to suspend their disbelief in much the same way as a theatre performance or film screening. Suspension of disbelief may be aided by detail and authenticity: the more comprehensively realistic the reenactor's costume, tools, and patterns of speech, then the more likely it is that the audience can immerse themselves temporarily in the reenacted world. In some reenactments – especially those in which the reenactment takes place both for the pleasure of the reenactors and for the entertainment or education of the audience – this immersion must also help the performers to enjoy their own activity. However, in this context, detail and apparent authenticity can also work against the suspension of disbelief. It creates a stronger contrast between the reenacted event and the modern world in which it takes place. However accurate the stitching on the Tudor reenactor's coat, however strong the smell of gunpowder after the musket fight, the audience must eventually return their attention to smartphones, car parks, their own modern dress: to all of the trappings of their modern environment. In the reenactment of the distant past, then, detail and authenticity works both for and against believability: creating a deeper immersion within the

FIGURE 2.4 Bill Chesneau, Ray Sutcliffe, John Adderley and David Whitson participate in a reenactment of 1970s television film production.

reenactment event, but a stronger contrast between *then* and *now*. In an investigative reenactment of the recent past, involving living survivors, the reverse is true. Participants take part in the event wearing their own clothes: modern dress, not a costume. This is partly because the recent past creates an assumption that costuming may not be necessary. There seems to be little difference between the casual shirt, shoes, and trousers worn by a location camera operator in the 1970s and the same outfit worn by the same person 40 years later. (An historian of clothing, of course, might point to advances in synthetic and breathable fabrics. For true fidelity even to the recent past, reenactment organizers may conclude that even such a recent reenactment demands a costume constructed only from materials available in the 1970s or 1980s.)

The lack of a costume is just one of the ways in which the boundary between the reenactment and modern world – often a prominent delineation in a more traditional reenactment – is blurred and sometimes completely erased. Participants in ADAPT simulations were not fenced into a reenactment space. Neither were any of their contemporary accessories – such as mobile phones – confiscated or voluntarily surrendered during the reenactment process. Across a number of different simulations, this lack of a boundary created various challenges to historical fidelity. The project's simulation of 16mm location film shooting was interrupted and modified on a number of occasions when equipment stopped working and needed to be fixed using tools or accessories kept in vans parked outside the reenactment space. Participants traversed an invisible boundary between past and present, bringing tools and knowledge of the present into the space of the past. They were not discouraged from doing so and there was no suggestion that, by doing so, they compromised the integrity of the experiment. On another occasion, during one of the most important moments of a simulation of outside broadcast television production, one of the participants took a call on his mobile phone.

The final characteristic of ADAPT's historical reenactments, which it shares with informal online reenactments of the sort described above, may also be the most important. Participants do not self-consciously adopt 'characters'; instead, they 'play' themselves. Consequently they do not acquire or learn about skills, but revive and remember skills they once learned and, perhaps, still practise. This makes for a dramatic comparison with the traditional historical reenactor, who must learn how to hold and safely operate a Civil War musket, or – in the example described by Agnew and Cook – learn how to climb the masts and negotiate the rigging of a tall ship. There are plenty of online videos depicting the learning of new skills, but what unites most historical reenactments of recent technologies is the display of reawakened skills, and the performance of the connection between the intellectual statement "I remember" or "It seems like yesterday" and the physical experience of recalling where to put one's hands in order to operate a piece of machinery. This transaction is at the crux of what historical reenactment of recently used technologies must achieve, and it is for this reason that participants are neither dressed up in costumes nor fenced into an historical world nor asked to play a character they are not. These theatrical flourishes, though tempting because

40 Nick Hall

they are so effectively modelled by historical reenactment television formats, must be avoided because they would hinder the very transaction that we are trying to get to: the reawakening of lost, forgotten, or dormant skill.

Conclusions

Historical reenactment television in its later phase; viral tech-nostalgia on YouTube; academic reenactments of the recent past: all profoundly different, but all born of a single historical moment. These are the cultural products of cheap, ubiquitous video camera equipment and widespread high speed internet access. Improbably, Facebook and YouTube have become laboratories for media archaeologists, enthusiasts, curators, and researchers. On these platforms, where historical research is performed without fanfare, funding, or institutional support, reenactments are pushed directly to the attention of the 'crowd' – that epithet for the vast undifferentiated mass audience thought to inhabit the world wide web. The crowd, though, is discriminating and specialist, and its members add their own expert memories and reminiscences, often detailing not only what they know and remember but also how they felt.[2]

In the historical spaces of the web, feelings matter. Affect has become a currency of online video, and so it is perfectly natural that emotional responses to old technologies should permeate online video reenactments. With affect as its fuel, the drive to capture and preserve nostalgia for recently deceased technologies is leaving a valuable digital exhaust: an unrivalled, semi-democratic, grassroots documentation of contemporary technologies. Never have everyday technologies, in full working order and in all their variations of design and permutations of usage, been so comprehensively and diversely documented by contemporary users. Future historians will not regret the personal and emotional investment put into these videos. Instead, such evidence of affect will be a vital component of their understanding of not only how technologies work but what they meant to the people who used them.

The practice of video-recording reenactments of the use of technologies and placing the resulting footage online may be relatively new, but as this chapter has demonstrated, it emerges from a series of well-established sources. Its roots are in the fields of historical reenactment and oral history, while the method of presentation and preservation owes much to technologies and visual styles developed by the 'legacy' media of scheduled television. The online platforms where these videos reside are not as revolutionary as they once seemed; what at first appeared to be disruptive new technology startups have become firmly entrenched in traditional corporate media structures. Online reenactment videos can, as I have tentatively argued here, be a form of history from below. But uploading the results to YouTube or shared on Facebook is simply to entrust the fruits of this labour to multibillion dollar tech giants. Online video sharing and social media have brought to the surface, and to some degree democratized, a shared impulse to record and reenact history before it fades from living memory. However, to secure the evidence of these reenactments for the future, a further revolution is needed. Online video reenactments should be another impetus to develop the long-proposed notion of the digital public space: a posited "arrangement of shared technologies, standards and processes that will be collaboratively developed and commonly applied" (Ageh 2013, 6) in order to provide a non-corporatized, publicly owned space in which – among other purposes – cultural heritage might be preserved for the long term.

Notes

1 ADAPT was a research project that investigated the history of television production technologies by reunited retired television production professionals with obsolete equipment. The project filmed a series of historical reenactment exercises. The project received funding from the European Research Council (ERC) under the European Union's Horizon 2020 research and innovation programme (grant agreement no. 323626). The results can be viewed at http://www.adaptTVhistory.org.uk and the full collection of digital videos filmed during the project is located at https://doi.org/10.17637/rh.c.3925603.
2 The online debate around ADAPT has been relatively muted because the project did not exist in a social media space like Facebook nor offer a comment facility on its own website. A stronger example of this sort of ongoing debate may be found in initiatives such as Jackson's *Pebble Mill Project*, discussed by Jackson elsewhere in this volume.

Bibliography

Ageh, T. (2013) Why the Digital Public Space Matters, in Hemment, Drew et al. (eds.) *Digital Public Spaces*. Manchester: FutureEverything, 6–7.

Agnew, V. (2007) History's Affective Turn: Historical Reenactment and Its Work in the Present. *Rethinking History*. [Online] 11(3): 299–312.

Carriger, M. L. (2010) Historionics: Neither Here nor There with Historical Reality TV. *Journal of Dramatic Theory and Criticism*, 24(2): 135–149.

FBE (2014) *Kids React To Old Computers*. [online]. Available from: https://www.youtube.com/watch?v=PF7EpEnglgk.

Gardner, D. (2014) *Looking at YouTube: KIDS REACT and Procrastitainment* [online]. Available from: http://www.indiewire.com/2014/07/looking-at-youtube-kids-react-and-procrastitainment-133373/.

Ireland, A. (2012) *'Conditions of Time and Space': A Re-enactment Experiment with the British TV Series Doctor Who*. Ph.D thesis. Bournemouth: Bournemouth University. [online]. Available from: http://eprints.bournemouth.ac.uk/20444/.

Kneebone, R. & Woods, A. (2012) Bringing Surgical History to Life. *British Medical Journal*, 345(7888): 32–33.

"Programme highlights: 1999 week 38 page 46". *Channel 4 Press Packs*. London: BUFVC. Available at: http://bufvc.ac.uk/tvandradio/c4pp

Ross, A. (2014) *How to Go Online on a 1970s Era Computer (the Apple 2). Email, Chat, News Groups and even Twitter!* [online]. Available from: https://www.youtube.com/watch?v=aNnJPNejdJ4.

Ryan Jones, K. (2013) *Touring the Last Surviving Blockbuster Video*. [online]. Available from: https://www.youtube.com/watch?v=ORp-RRSwtmU.

Stuckmann, Chris (2016) *Blockbuster Video – Retro Rewind*. [online]. Available from: https://www.youtube.com/watch?v=8VUyJYpPwks.

The 8-Bit Guy (2014) *Living with the iPhone 2G for a Week. Is it Obsolete?* [online]. Available from: https://www.youtube.com/watch?v=g5PYhs_DnFI.

TV70. Available from: http://405-line.tv/tv70/.

Wyatt, D. (2015) That's So Last Century, Channel 4 – TV review: You'd have to be under 16 not to recognise these gadgets. *The Independent*. 8 December. [online]. Available from: https://www.independent.co.uk/arts-entertainment/tv/reviews/thats-so-last-century-channel-4-tv-review-youd-have-to-be-under-16-not-to-recognise-these-gadgets-a6765626.html.

Yuccas, Jamie. (2018) *Visiting America's last Blockbuster store.* [online]. Available from: https://www.youtube.com/watch?v=QAdRzpcdCbs

3

A BLIND DATE WITH THE PAST

Transforming television documentary practice into a research method

Amanda Murphy

Hands on history can involve many different kinds of hands, those of one-time professionals or skilled users, and those who are encountering an old technology for the first time. A physical encounter with an obsolete technology can transform our understanding of the machine and its potential. But once those technologies had skilled users, who developed complex group working practices around their equipment. The ADAPT project set out to film and analyse the skilled users of historic television equipment as they re-encountered and used it again for the first time in many years.[1] This chapter reflects on how this experimental media archaeology project was conducted. It discusses the methods we used and the lessons we learned, and in particular how I was able to adapt my skills as a television producer to the requirements of an academic research project.

The initial proposal for ADAPT envisaged the filming of a series of reconstructions of the process of working with particular technological arrays, in which veteran industry professionals were to be reunited with the technologies they used at particular points in their careers and filmed while they worked with them, discussing the strengths and weaknesses of the machines and the prevailing ways of working with them. My role on the project was to act as the producer of these 'reconstructions', 'reenactments' or 'simulations'. The project's uncertainty about how to define this approach indicates how novel it was, and how much it was my responsibility to develop the method. The professionals were not asked to reenact the making of a particular programme, nor to reconstruct a specific historical moment. Nor were they asked to simulate their old working practices. Instead, they were asked to do for real in the present what they once did in the past. Their difficulty in recalling how a particular equipment function once worked would be invaluable research data, as were their own reflections on how they used to work, and their reflexive reenactment of working habits and workplace banter. The participants were offered a blind date with their past, enabled and recorded by the research team.

44 Amanda Murphy

My role as the project's producer involved adapting contemporary television production practice to the requirements of this unpredictable hands on research. I came to the project after a substantial career in mainstream event-based factual television. I was a senior producer on the first series of *Big Brother* in 2000 for Channel 4. I then produced both the UK and US versions of *Supernanny*. Both depended on the unpredictable behaviours of large casts of human beings. Both necessitated the recruitment and management of huge teams, overseeing the construction of ambitious sets or houses. So did ADAPT. But the mission of these broadcast shows was always to deliver new and compelling content aimed at drawing large audiences. Academic research has different priorities, and its available resources will always be meagre in comparison with the television industry. This chapter reflects on the method we developed in ADAPT, which involved revising standard television working methods to capture skilled hands on work processes for research purposes.

The hands on approach was crucial as it offers far more than a traditional interview with veterans about their past work. Approaching the project as if it were a television production was useful in breaking down each element required into a sequence or scene. It was clear we needed real reactions at the point at which the veterans were 'reunited' with old kit; it was clear we needed to understand how the equipment worked; and it was clear we needed to see full crews or teams in action in order to see machines and their operators working together. As in television, these sequences would deliver a rich mix of emotional responses and insightful factual information. The sequences we sought to film fell naturally into four categories:

1. Reunion
2. Demonstration
3. Equipment-in-use, or a team performance of some part of the television production process
4. Group discussion and reflection.

Approaching all the filming in the same way throughout the life of the project meant that all filmed events had a consistency and that the resulting videos feel like a connected collection.

However, unlike *Big Brother* or any kind of television or digital production, there was no broadcaster and no commissioning platform, and therefore no specific identified audience. There was no intention of 'narrowing down' the project's output by, for example, editing it into one main piece of work for a defined audience. Research has different priorities. Everything is potentially useful evidence. In short, we were not producing a 60-minute documentary for BBC Two. Instead, the ADAPT material was to be made available for free to a wide range of viewers, from academics and students to film and television fanatics, collectors, technical experts and the wider public. For some, the whole event would be essential viewing; others would simply want a particular aspect or a general overview. So our editing and presentation had to be radically different from that of linear broadcast TV. The solution was to produce 'long', 'medium' and 'short' packages for each particular filmed sequence. These equated to full-length real-time edits, a documentary length cut and bitesize social media friendly 'tasters'. For academics and educators, these cuts might constitute 'research data', 'seminar screening', and 'lecture clip'. While the pace and tone was similar throughout, this method of presentation at least meant the viewer could decide how much and for how long they wanted to spend looking at it. It also allowed the research team to present extracts at conferences and to contribute material to the *History of the BBC* website.

Initial challenges

The amount of research needing to be done by the producer in television's pre-production phase can easily be underestimated. While academics generally regard research as an ongoing and often never-ending process, the television producer requires all of her research to be completed in advance. An initial scoping study is required to decide on what particular areas of television production can be covered and why, whom to approach and cast, what technology to seek out, and how to begin to mount an event that can deliver useful filmed content.

As I began the research towards the ADAPT reenactments, the greatest challenge was in locating technology dating back to the 1960s and 1970s. Much of it is obsolete, and display models in museums were of no use as they have very rarely been maintained in working order. Yet the project's aim to recreate how television used to be made required technology in some kind of working order. To obtain working examples, we relied heavily on enthusiasts and collectors, and on finding a network of engineers with the time and expertise needed to bring the machinery back to life. Mounting events in venues that could offer the right conditions for veteran crews to be reunited with and again use the kit of their past, presented further challenges. Considerations included type and size of venue given the sizeable kit and army of people filming would potentially involve, ensuring sufficient light and power, ease of access for hefty equipment, and for some level of comfort to accommodate older participants.

The second challenge was to locate and cast retired television technicians and crew. This relied on mostly informal networks and was a long process, one that is usually undertaken in television by a casting team. To ensure an authentic representation of television production crews of the past, we needed to unite the right combination of men and women with the tools of the trade they once used. So, what do you find first: the working equipment, or the capable veteran? Clearly, we needed both: ideally full teams and full arrays of kit, as television was made by vast crews using interconnected machinery. It was a complicated jigsaw puzzle especially given the very limited original technology available. Our veteran participants also needed to be willing to 'act' as their former selves in the roles they once worked. They had to be physically fit enough to do a day's work and to be able to form part of a crew alongside others. They needed to be clear and ideally dynamic speakers so as to engage the eventual viewers. They had to have at least some memory of their old working practices, along with an ability to explain arcane technical terms and workplace jargon. Balancing these expectations was delicate.

The most extensive casting operation lay behind the most ambitious of the ADAPT filmed events: the reenactment of a live sports outside broadcast with a 1969 ex-BBC Type 2 truck known as North 3. This was filmed in May 2016 over four days at a Welsh hotel. A 19-strong veteran team recorded a 1970s-style darts match using original first-generation colour television cameras and sound equipment. Detailed research was required to understand the full array of kit used in outside broadcasts in this period including variations both regionally and between broadcast companies. We were fortunate in finding a rare partially working Type 2 truck and a willing participant in its owner Steve Harris.[2] Steve and I either spoke or emailed daily over the following six months. Between us we created a network of mostly retired and highly capable engineers to help Steve continue his restoration work on the truck, wrestling the vast amount of 50-year old machinery back to life. Once this process was set in motion, I began to search for and cast 19 veteran crew needed to cover all key roles.

The casting process required an understanding of the hierarchies and delicate nature of teamwork. One of my attempts to cast a supervisor into a more junior role – effectively demoting him for the purposes of our reconstruction – led to a near revolt before any camera had rolled. I also had to dispatch some of the newly found skilled crew to assist Steve Harris further in the hugely ambitious mission of getting his old outside broadcast unit into a working state. Once reunited with the old equipment, they were no longer valuable on camera as participants in the reenactment, because one of our requirements was that participants should re-encounter the equipment for the first time at the beginning of the reconstruction, so that their

FIGURE 3.1 Ex-BBC Type 2 outside broadcast truck North 3, 'on location' outside Northop Hall hotel in Flintshire.

initial reactions could be captured on camera. So this vital technical restoration process depleted my potential cast and meant I had to find more participants.

Location research was also vital for this particular shoot. The location needed to be able to accommodate what might be a sizeable entourage (a full research project crew filming another crew) and be fit for purpose. We had access to the television studio at Royal Holloway's campus near London and had used this for other reenactment exercises. But here the equipment dictated the location. Steve Harris' base is more than 200 miles north of London in the town of Hawarden in Flintshire. The diesel engine of the Type 2 outside broadcast truck – originally installed in 1969 – was incapable of a 200-mile journey, and we needed access to Steve's extensive range of spare parts. So finding a location nearby was crucial. A local hotel whose success lay in weekend weddings was persuaded to allow the project to move in during the quieter mid-week period. They agreed to their function room being transformed into a sports venue, installed a substantial extra power circuit so we didn't blow the fuses, and made space on their driveway for the huge OB truck. When filming was underway, windows were propped open to accommodate hefty cabling. A café area was inhabited by the project's film crew, alongside a makeshift 'video village' from where I directed the fixed rig. The hotel provided bed and board for cast and crew, and traditional evening meals of beef bourguignon and sponge pudding added to the 1970s atmosphere. Given the ages of the crew and the demands of the long film days, providing such comforts was essential.

In television, there is typically a skilled production management team to help with logistical planning, event scheduling, health and safety, travel, hospitality and legal compliance. ADAPT's initial budget underestimated this work, just as it did the subsequent editing of the material. We have learned that filmed reconstructions need to map out such roles at the planning/bid stage. Logistical issues can be many and varied: we needed to work out who might be called in to a remote location

FIGURE 3.2 Screens set up in the 'video village' monitored output from multiple fixed cameras overlooking the ADAPT project reenactment event.

48 Amanda Murphy

to safety test very old electrical equipment, and we had to determine what size van would fit a 1" videotape machine.

Furthermore, our experiences when planning this reenactment highlighted the importance of keeping notes throughout the production process. In television production, troubleshooting practical issues tends to take priority over the documentation of the research processes involved. Television research notes (which can include informal interviews, casting, technical and logistical information) are typically more casual as they serve mostly as *aide memoires* for how and what to capture during filming. As these are of little use after a broadcast, they can lack the accuracy essential to academic use. The use of an audio recorder for all conversations and interviews ahead of the filming is essential, alongside the use of standardized documents when making research notes, fact checking and amending all documents to ensure accuracy throughout. These techniques can help to ensure that, in the frantic work of producing a television event, useful research notes are created which will benefit the final outputs of the project.

Finding old equipment and retired crews

Casting for the reconstruction of technological processes involves finding both people and technologies. For all of the project's reenactments, it was critical to match up the right people with the right working machinery, as it was paramount to the project to provide the requisite array of interdependent working kit. There were many variants and different technical specifications depending on where and on what specific piece of kit the veteran crews worked, as well as real limits as to what equipment could be found or made to work. The sensible thing would have been to involve participants in the process of locating and engineering their old kit to be sure it was indeed the correct item. However, this process would have compromised one of the key aims of the project, which was to capture the very first moment when a veteran crew member is reunited with the equipment of their past.

In order to get around this casting problem, it became apparent that we needed to involve people who had specific knowledge of the technology of the day and could guide us behind the scenes. These came in the form of enthusiastic collectors and engineers. They would not take part in the reconstructions, but would assist us in the planning. It took considerable time to find collectors interested in the period of television equipment that we were seeking. These turned out to be amateur curators: individuals who had taken it upon themselves to keep the past alive or save obsolete artefacts from being junked by maintaining, re-using or displaying them. None we encountered were attached to any large organization or museum. All were found by word of mouth through a network of 'old boys'. Once found, they proved not just extraordinarily helpful but utterly invaluable to the project. Their knowledge extended beyond the technology, to the era in which the much-loved machine best shone. More critically, they had the engineering skills to revive the old technology. Finding and re-connecting networks of engineers and collectors was a long and time-consuming job. Some knew each other from the past, and even so had to rummage through old address books in order to remake old connections. This was an unforeseen element of the project. It paid dividends, because the collectors, restorers and enthusiasts with whom we worked made possible the fitting together of a seemingly impossible jigsaw. This jigsaw consisted of old kit that could then work with other old kit via revived old connectors and old adaptors, old vision desks, and old sound desks reunited with rack-mounted circuits and miles of cabling. It took several months to reassemble such an array of complex machinery, and prepare it to be transported and filmed in full use.

While this work went on, we forged ahead with finding a crew of retired outside broadcast crew to work on our reconstruction. Retired professionals often have their own networks, especially when they worked within large organizations. In the UK television industry, numerous reunion groups (including TelOBians and VT Old boys) responded positively to the idea of the ADAPT mission and opened their doors to us. They helped spread the word and enabled us to start to cast interested and capable veterans to film. We also placed adverts in *Prospero*, the magazine for BBC pensioners, calling for participants. This widened the reach and brought in many recommendations of pioneers to consider, of colleagues some thought suitable and led to a number of volunteers coming forward. This approach led to reconstructions that tended to emphasize the role of the BBC.

Seeking out and drawing on the experiences of other research or filmed projects – like the Pebble Mill project and the British Entertainment History Project – helped spread the word in useful quarters too.[3] These informal networks helped build strong, cohesive teams of participants. One former camera operator called another former camera operator, retired engineers called other retired engineers, and support grew in this way. However, when trying to research video tape editing and the changes brought about by non-linear and Avid, finding participants was more difficult as the all-encompassing 'tape editing' focus covered a much greater period of time than any other reenactment event. Editors, whose work is more solitary in nature, were not typically part of reunion groups and networks so were much harder to find.

In television production, the initial process of finding contacts and potential participants is followed by a process of casting. Casting involves initial conversations and meeting people to assess their willingness and suitability as individuals, but also as part of a group of people who will work together on the reconstruction and will offer complementary skills and accounts. Casting is required to construct a cohesive group rather than an assemblage of individuals who have nothing (or too much) in common. A comprehensive and updated database of all contacts is necessary during the casting phase. For ADAPT keeping data records was crucial especially as there was rarely a paper trail to the mostly older generation we were dealing with and who seemed to prefer a telephone chat to email or social media.

One problem with participants through informal social networks was that we received entirely male crew recommendations in the early days. We were aware

50 Amanda Murphy

that most television crews of the past had at least one female member – often the PA (producer's assistant) – but these proved elusive. They were not to be found at any of the reunion events we attended, and nor did they respond to our call for help in *Prospero*. So, it took a much longer trawl and numerous calls to key producers of the era to reach these more hidden but important members of past television technical teams. While staying true to the era and genre represented, it is important for research projects to consider gender and diversity of participants. For ADAPT, having one of the filmed events set in the 1980s and 1990s was key. In recreating how video tape editing was done in the 1980s and the changes through the 1990s when digital editing came in with Avid and Lightworks, there was a great opportunity to include pioneering women in editing and graphics roles such as Renee Edwards (one of the UK's first Avid editors) and Nyree Kavanagh, who taught herself Quantel Paintbox, a graphics hardware package that revolutionized television post-production.

Casting

The participants in our filmed 'simulations', reenactments or reconstructions were asked to do something unusual: to participate in a blind date with their past, and to 'play' their former selves. The project had initially used the term 'simulation' to distinguish this activity from that of historic reconstructions. It soon became clear that television veterans were confused by the term. They seemed to think we were asking them to pretend to use old equipment, rather than actually operate. I started to use the terms 'recreate' and 'reenact'. Both seemed to more accurately describe what we were doing behind the scenes in setting up the conditions of an 'event' for the veterans to respond to. These definitions also seemed to help potential participants understand that what we were expecting of them was some kind of recreating of their past. We were asking people still living to remember and recreate an element of their former lives. Getting them to act as their former selves was an unusual request, and one that does not seem to have been made before in this way. Conceptual artist Jeremy Deller, in his 2001 recreation *The Battle of Orgreave*, used 800 historical reenactors and 200 former miners to achieve his recreation of the infamous battles between police and miners during the Miners' Strikes of 1984. It was a filmed event, the aim of which was to explore the complexities of that bitter struggle. Deller did not ask any of his participants to comment in any way on what they are doing or recalling or feeling during the filming or reenactment. Some, like art critic Alex Farquharson, suggested that what he had produced was more a 'flashback' than a 'reenactment', suggesting a general uneasiness of definition around this kind of work.[4]

The ambition of ADAPT was to capture, through hands on reenactments, how television was made as far back in time as possible. It soon became evident that the 1960s was about as far back as we could with this methodology. Technicians and professionals from this period were now in their seventies and eighties. Working with older retired participants brought with it a series of specific challenges.

A blind date with the past 51

We needed to ensure that they were mentally and physically capable of long and taxing film days. They had to be able to remember (at least in part) working methods and practices of 40 or more years ago. And they needed to be able to operate an array of complex and cumbersome equipment they had likely not seen for many decades. They were also expected to act in the role they held back in the 1960s and 1970s, even if that was a much more junior position than they had achieved by the time they retired.

To help ensure the safety and wellbeing of our participants, we recruited students to act as 'shadows' to the veteran crew. There were real health and safety concerns around older participants feeling able or determined to pick up and lift heavy machinery. Much of the equipment was exceptionally cumbersome and weighty, particularly old outside broadcast machinery. Students wore dark colours so as to be discreet and intervened whenever possible to take over this task. Students also watched out for participants' welfare, looking for signs of fatigue or hunger. When necessary they suggested a break, or ensured that a chair was nearby. Most of our participants were very fit for their ages given their physical careers, but many also overestimated their capabilities. They were hard to stop once they took on what they frequently referred to as 'dedication to the output'. During their careers, this meant ensuring that programmes went to air on time; they transferred this commitment to our project. As a result of their participation, students were able to learn from the pioneers themselves about how analogue television was made, while telling tales of smartphone filming and digital platforms in return. It seemed that both benefitted equally from their time together.

Working with a diverse team of retired professionals brought a number of challenges that we did not anticipate. Asking the veterans to 'act' as their former selves also meant that at times some took on a 'presenter' mode, addressing the camera while explaining their skill even though they were never asked to do that. Some of them interrupted each other mid-sentence, in an attempt to provide clearer

FIGURE 3.3 Vision supervisor Roger Neale and vision engineer John Coupe at the camera control desk inside ex-BBC outside broadcast truck North 3.

52 Amanda Murphy

descriptions. And those acting in more junior assistant roles found it hard to resist taking over the tasks of those in roles more senior. Not all of our participants were fully cooperative with our interest in using obsolete, and often technically imperfect, technology. During our reenactment with 16mm film technology, one participant struggled to remember how a particular microphone worked and went to great lengths to point out how much he didn't like it and didn't want to use it given that he owned 'better', more recent, microphone, which he had brought along with him. He went so far as to switch out the old for his own piece of newer technology. No amount of explaining the purpose of the project could assuage his concern with providing the best quality sound he could.

Throughout our reenactments, there was no such thing as success or failure, either for the veteran crews or for the project. So, while the mission felt enormous, it was useful to remind ourselves that whatever happened when we brought veteran men and their old machines together, it was all of interest to the project. Old habits or processes forgotten were as interesting as all those remembered. Collective memory, while an important element, may not be reliable as factual truth. Frequently told anecdotes can have a way of elevating the more banal or humorous aspects of an event at the expense of what really took place. However, the premise of the project was always clear, and the structure created space for surprising outcomes.

Filming

ADAPT used the most modern digital technology to film the equipment and practices of the past. We used small, lightweight portable and fixed cameras to overcome our key challenges: how to capture entire teams working simultaneously; how to be unobtrusive but ensure the capturing of the entire experience; and how to comprehensively understand what they were doing given the highly technical nature of their work. As an academic research project, we wanted to involve students in our work as much as possible. In the first year or so, students were recruited to both film and edit, but this was not sustainable in the longer term. It was not appropriate to ask students, still training and developing their skills, to take on the critical responsibilities of filming, data-wrangling, and editing our larger reenactment exercises.

For our more complex activities, we employed the services of professional camera operators and sound recordists. Working alongside our trainee students, these crew members contributed a wide range of valuable ideas on how to best capture content. Their more extensive experience made it easier for us to obtain the exact types of shots we needed to capture the 'hands on' aspects of the reenactments. Breaking with documentary conventions, which tend to emphasize close-ups and talking heads, we needed loose mid-size and wide shots. These guaranteed that bodily movements, hands, and machine could be seen in context. In order to follow the spontaneous actions of the crew, we decided to use handheld cameras. The professional camera operators we worked with were also experts in the art of moving with the camera, creating what television professionals often refer to as 'useable moves', whereby the movement of the body is used to create flow from a close up to a wide shot. This gentle body motion, stepping back and forth to change shot size rather than zooming in or out with the camera, allows all footage to be useable in the edit. However, it is a physically demanding 'dance' that can take professionals or even seasoned crew time to perfect.

Where the number of participants was low, and reenactments took place in small spaces, four cameras were sufficient to cover the action. Students operated cameras and sound for both of these events with the university supplying all sound and Sony broadcast-standard cameras. To ensure that nothing was missed, handheld cameras were supplemented with two locked-off wide angle overhead cameras. Miniature GoPros were initially used as fixed cameras, but their lack of timecode caused challenges in the editing process, and full-sized Sony cameras on tripods were used for later exercises. The advantage of the wide angled overhead cameras is that the entire 'experience' of the participants could be fully captured as these cameras were set to record continuously. They provided a real-time record of all activity, a useful perspective of where veterans and machinery interacted, and proved invaluable in the edit supplementing where the camerawork struggled or a vital action had been overlooked. This enables detailed academic analysis, for example, on how long it took a veteran crew to set up and light a documentary interview, and what all crew members were doing with what machine at the same time. Single camera coverage selects an aspect of this process for the viewer, where a wide overhead camera allows viewers to choose for themselves what they are interested in.

The reenactment of a 1970s-style live outside broadcast involving a crew of up to 20 presented far greater challenges. Outside broadcast crews of the analogue era comprised a team of anywhere from 20 to 60 or more technicians. It became clear it was not going to be possible to replicate it or achieve it with fewer than 20 veteran crew members. Key challenges then were around the sheer numbers of veteran crew to cover as they work to simultaneously achieve the broadcast of a live show. The confined space within which they achieve this also created difficulties. The vintage outside broadcast truck, which acts as the heart of the broadcast operation, is narrow and can typically house up to ten veteran crew. They work in the three tight longitudinal sections amidst racks of monitors and machinery, a spaghetti of cables and live feeds. There was simply no space for any of our project film crew to fit, and so we adopted the working practices of one of the most recent innovations in factual television: fixed rig production, the technique used to film contemporary fly-on-the-wall documentaries like *24 Hours in A&E*, *Hospital*, and the *Educating . . .* series.

Fixed rig shooting is the chosen method for all sorts of television series where the content of the show or the space dictates that cameras be installed and left unmanned as they record. They are small and discreet so can be fixed in a number of places offering a rich mix of angles and coverage, and they allow participants to go about their business undisturbed. A more naturalistic result can be achieved

FIGURE 3.4 Images of a live darts match displayed on preview monitors inside ex-BBC outside broadcast truck North 3, during an ADAPT project reenactment exercise.

as the subjects can feel free from a watchful eye and perhaps therefore, free from concern of being judged for any memory failure. All of these benefits come at a high price: this is an expensive way of filming, which requires a professional team to install the equipment and record from it, though costs can be reduced by opting for small fixed (non-zoom) cameras such as the Marshall CV502-MB model used for our outside broadcast reenactment.

A television production company – Lion Eyes – was contracted to install, maintain, and capture video feeds from our fixed rig camera. Led by Martin Riley, who acted as technical director, the Lion Eyes team rigged cameras in two large spaces. Cameras were installed in the outside broadcast vehicle, and in a large function room in the hotel used as a location to stage a live sports event for their filming. Our veteran crew needed to move freely between both spaces. Cameras were required to capture the crew as they rigged and installed cameras, lights, sound, set, and all the connected technology in the truck. A total of 14 fixed rig cameras, 20 radio microphones and four ambient microphones captured comprehensive audio and video of all crew in all spaces at all times as they worked simultaneously with their complex array of kit to rig, rehearse, and record an outside broadcast of the period. Such extensive coverage afforded the project the potential of watching and hearing each and every crew member at any given moment and to understand the communication and production processes involved throughout.

Editing

ADAPT's filmed reenactments generated huge amounts of data. The decision to keep all the evidence of the process contrasts with television production practice, which is to discard material that is not used for the final broadcast. Fixed rig productions, whose filming technology we used to document the reconstruction of an outside broadcast, typically record the outputs of just a fraction of all the cameras that they use. They use a process of live selection of camera outputs, radically reducing the amount of data that they store for the later editing process. The research decision to record all 14 cameras at all times (using no live selection), generated 11 terabytes of footage – enough data to fill over 2,000 DVD-Rs. This had a significant impact on the edit in terms of amount of data, storage, and content management. RAID storage drives big enough to store this sizeable archive had to be found and purchased, as this proved beyond the university infrastructure at the time. Managing such a large volume of footage resulting from multiple camera sources was a complex and lengthy task. Logging the material was a major challenge in itself, and the footage had to be organized and edited before researchers could conveniently use it.

As with all productions, there was an array of challenges to face once editing began. Some were unique to the project, and many emerged from the fact that interruptions from the production crew were kept to a minimum, and the reenactment was allowed to flow naturally. In the edit, we needed to decipher multiple simultaneous audio tracks. We needed to deal with jargon and confusing technical terminology – the same piece of equipment often going by various different names. We need to consider how to condense a full day and a half of veteran crew rigging into a viewable form, while reflecting the multiplicity of different professional roles.

In total, our footage provided fresh and revealing material that is experiential and offers far more than the more typical interview with retired professionals. We see them re-live their past work, remembering and reflecting while doing so. They indulge once again in the professional culture that formed a huge part of their working careers, falling easily back into old habits and hierarchies – complete with bad jokes. This produced some vivid research data. These blind dates with the past demonstrate everyday working practices and habits that could not have been accessed in any other way. These professionals' reflections on the hands on recalled experience of their own pasts provides further data about changing (and unchanging) attitudes over lifetimes.

We edited our video material throughout the project, initially creating a temporary website and free YouTube channel while we were deliberating on the best short and long term repositories for the asset. We used YouTube and Vimeo to share filmed footage and guided interested parties from our website to our YouTube channel which housed a selection of clips. As the project evolved and grew in ambition and complexity the amount of archive material at stake increased. As the project concluded, we launched a comprehensive website and transferred all of our video material to Figshare, a long-term digital repository.[5]

Conclusion

ADAPT was a highly ambitious project. It aimed to unite two very different groups – a group of academic researchers and a group of retired television

56 Amanda Murphy

professionals – around a common purpose. Our shared goal was the preservation of television history. We wanted to show, in depth and detail, how television used to be made. We sought to highlight the hands on expertise and hard work that went into making television in the days before digital video cameras and non-linear editing.

As this chapter has shown, uniting these two groups around a series of filmed reenactments also required the adaptation of one professional skill – documentary television production – into the context of academic research. As the project's digital producer, it fell to me to make this challenging translation. The benefit of many years of experience in coordinating and producing major documentary television series enabled me to unite a disparate group of veteran participants, collectors, and enthusiasts. But, when filming, I had to resist some of my professional instincts. It was tempting, for example, to 'over produce' the participants, by asking them to demonstrate technology in a certain way, or to recount on camera the stories they had told me during the casting process. But the project required that I leave them uninterrupted, so that they felt the freedom to experiment with the old kit, to explore how it works, and to engage and re-connect with each other. My priority, in short, was to allow their memories to be triggered through the hands on experience rather than from a lot of short sharp pokes from a producer.

Refashioning my documentary production skills to suit the constraints and demands of ADAPT was a complex process, but one that has helped the project to deliver an important result. Ultimately, the process of filming reenactments for ADAPT has created a new kind of research output. Our filmed encounters between operators and machines are not oral history interviews: they lack the structure and formality that tends to mark out such activities. Nor have we produced generically conventional documentaries. Instead, we have applied some of the techniques of fixed rig television filming in a new way. By assembling old equipment and retired crews, we have set up the conditions under which extensive observation of 'hands on history' experiments can take place. The resulting footage, made widely available in long form, can now be adapted and built upon by anyone who chooses to download it. Selections from our filmed reenactments have been featured on the BBC's *History of the BBC* minisite and have been watched and share thousands of times on YouTube.[6] They have also been displayed at the National Science and Media Museum in Bradford as part of the Arts and Humanities Research Council's Being Human festival.

Aside from these publications and outputs, the project created one further important benefit. It has created new networks and invigorated existing ones. Uniquely, by uniting participants and researchers around reenactment exercises, we have been able to reconnect engineers and technical crews who had lost touch with each other. Information and technology is being shared between them as never before, to the benefit both of the individuals involved – and to the history of television. The dividends of this new methodology need not be limited to media history: our techniques are readily transferrable to almost any other aspect of technology or culture where a hands on approach might be beneficial.

Notes

1 ADAPT was a European Research Council funded project that investigated the history of British broadcasting technology. It ran from 2013 to 2018 and was based at Royal Holloway, University of London. The project received funding under the European Union's Horizon 2020 research and innovation programme, grant agreement no. 323626.
2 For more information about Steve Harris's restoration and preservation work see http://www.vintageradio.co.uk/htm/tvprojects2.htm
3 See http://www.pebblemill.org and https://historyproject.org.uk
4 See Farquharson, A. (2001) Jeremy Deller: The Battle of Orgreave. *Frieze* (61). [online]. Available from: https://web.archive.org/web/20120429192405/https://frieze.com/issue/review/jeremy_deller.
5 The project's website can be accessed at www.adaptTVhistory.org.uk, and the Figshare repository at royalholloway.figshare.com/ADAPT.
6 See https://www.bbc.co.uk/historyofthebbc/research/programming/bbccolour

4

(DE)HABITUATION HISTORIES

How to re-sensitize media historians

Andreas Fickers and Annie van den Oever

As Tom Gunning argues:

> Every new technology has a utopian dimension that imagines a future radically transformed by the implications of the device or practice. The sinking of technology into a reified second nature indicates the relative failure of this transformation, its fitting back into the established grooves of power and exploitation. Herein lays the importance of the cultural archaeology of technology, the grasping again of the newness of old technologies.
>
> (Gunning 2003, 56)

Newness is a transient phenomenon, a single phase in a longer history. David Park, Nicholas Jankowski and Steve Jones convincingly argue that the canon of media history focuses on the early periods of the histories of media, rather than the middle or late periods in their 'Introduction' to *The Long History of New Media: Technology, Historiography, and Contextualizing Newness* (2011). There is an obvious focus on media history's 'constitutive moments'. In a sense, media history "comes to us as a kind of prepackaged new media history" (Park et al. 2011). It is indeed worth stepping back from this for a moment, as they suggest, to "inquire about the role that newness plays in media, and in our histories of the media". There is a series of questions that comes to the fore: the epistemological questions about the *over* focus of media scholars on newness; the theoretical assumptions that guide them in this direction; and the critical, historiographical question "where are the histories of 'middle' and 'late' periods for media?" (Park et al. 2011).

This last question marks a serious problem in the field of media history: there is a notable gap in media historiographical research. The question then is: *why* are the middle and last phases missing? Is this due to a well-known, second problem in historiographical research: the tendency to create a *linear* if not *teleological* version of media history? As Andreas Fickers and Anne-Katrin Weber (2015) argued, on the one hand, "the diachronic perspective incorporates the inherent danger of producing linear or even teleological narratives, thereby neglecting the implicit openness of all historical development"; on the other hand, the "synchronic studies are confronted with the danger of overemphasizing the newness of specific historical events and in messing up the potentiality of history with its actual manifestations".

A third and significant problem in the field of media history is that media novelty is both *over* studied as well as *under*theorized: conceptual constancy is lacking. The question then is: how to conceptualize the new (and renewal; and the "once new", as Tom Gunning labelled it in 2003). This question is even more pressing at this very point in time. Conceptual constancy is needed to elongate and synthesize the study of (new) media history. As Benjamin Peters stresses, "a conceptual constancy in the idea of novelty" is badly needed in a world of "torrential technological change" which causes "the near-instant obsolescence of studying new media": what is new on one day is obsolete the next (Peters 2009, 25).

In an attempt to reassess the 'new' in the term 'new media', Park and a range of contributors have sought to *historicize* and *contextualize* rather than theorize media newness. Their study reflects on a range of older (standard) studies on newness in media history by Lisa Gitelman, Carolyn Marvin, and others; they inspired a number of studies that have deepened the argument that the new and the novelty phase of media are *overvalued* in media studies and that an overfocus on newness is part of a rhetoric of the new in line with the marketing strategies of the industry institutionally framing new devices as something revolutionary if not utopian. The 'rhetoric of newness' has become such a characteristic feature of all media discourses that media scholars seem to have a hard time developing a critical distance from that trope (Fickers 2015). Paying attention to newness and 'revolutionary' developments has resulted in a bias in the field of Media and Communication Studies, as well as in Science and Technology Studies and in History of Technology. While processes of technological invention and innovation, as well as phenomena of re-mediation have been analysed in great detail, phenomena of hybridization, habitualization and routinization have received much less attention.

In the conclusions to his remarkable article on the 'new' in media studies, Peters (2009, 24–25) argues that it would be good to go against "the bulk of media history scholarship to treat only one period (usually the first) that a given medium appeared new". He wonders what a new media history conceptualized as a "renewable media history" might look like, suggesting "that the renewable quality of media presents a richer yet significantly underdeveloped framework for understanding media in history than is widely adopted" (ibid.). Thinking of media in terms of their renewability opens up new paths for media historians to look at media history, Peters claims: "(new) media history provides a set of lenses, such as the five stages of media renewability". Accordingly, he presents "a five-step cycle of new media evolution, from obscurity to obviousness and back again", arguing

60 Andreas Fickers and Annie van den Oever

that new media can be understood as *emerging* technologies undergoing a historical process of *contestation*, *negotiation*, and *institutionalization*, and that "[t]hese terms are meant to suggest ways to think through how media arc from social obscurity to invention, innovation, obviousness and obsolescence". In a similar fashion, Gabriele Balbi has proposed a four-step model, starting with a phase of imitation (when the new copies the old); specification (when the new becomes new); reconfiguration (when the old adapts the new); and, finally, co-existence (when the old and the new live together) (Balbi 2015, 231–249).

These proposals are valuable in several ways: as a reminder to media historians and historians of technology that – contrary to the industrial and institutional rhetoric – histories of media are cyclical rather than linear; as an attempt to refocus on such media cycles, and on the middle and last phases thereof, instead of focusing primarily, if not exclusively, on the newness phase; as a pointer at the different technical, cultural, legal, economic, and social powers in play in the history of media use, powers that need to be studied in their own terms. Instead of reproducing the evolutionary logic of linear (technical) improvement and enhancement, we aim to refocus our attention on the processes of 'naturalization' that so often fall under the radar of scholarly attention. When we become accustomed to 'new things', they are interwoven into the fabric of daily life (Nye 2006, 65). Leaving an innovation-centric view behind, we sympathize with David Edgerton's (2006) plea for looking at 'old' technologies in terms of their re-uses and alternative appropriations by offering a specific perspective that we find to be crucial to the understanding of past media practices: that is, the sensorial, perceptual, and experiential dimensions of media use. We want to show their relevance to understanding the individual and collective cultural appropriation and acceptance of media technologies. This article is a plea for a sensorial and tacit approach to media history aiming at a rethinking and a theorizing of media newness and media cycles from the perspective of the user experience.

Sensorial dimensions in media history

In the past, in joint as well as in separate papers, panels, and publications,[1] we have focused on media use and media experiences to be included in the histories of media and technology; our plea was aimed at three specific things:

1. To take media objects from the glass cases of museums to help re-sensitize the researcher to past media objects and to create an awareness of the senso-perceptual and tacit traces left by media in practices of use;
2. To take the materiality of media technologies, as well as the sensorial and tacit dimensions of media use into account in the writing of the histories of media and technology; and
3. To question media history from the perspective of an experimental media archaeology by systematically reflecting upon the value and function of hands-on experiments and the methodology, protocol, and procedures used in such

experiments, from *simulations* of practices of media use under the label of an experimental media archaeology to playfully recreating media experiences by tinkering/thinkering (Huhtamo) with media objects to re-sensitize the researcher, and *reenactments* to play on the historical imagination.

In line with our earlier work, we will take the material object – the technological device – and, more specifically, the sensorial and experiential dimensions expressed in media use as a point of departure for our reflections. Why would the sensorial and experiential dimensions of media use be a relevant point of departure for such reflections? And, by extension: why would such reflections help to theoretically frame media newness? The answer, as we will argue, is that the (media) technologies used for communication and information purposes *work* quite differently on users than, for instance, technologies of transportation. Media technologies stand out amongst the broad range of technologies used by humans, such as trains, aeroplanes, and elevators in as far as media technologies typically use *representation* as a means. *As such*, they affect users in a very specific way, quite different from trains and aeroplanes. Moreover, media technologies stand out among the *media* such as language because of their *technical* make-up, as Kittler has convincingly argued; for this reason, he labelled media technologies, somewhat tautologically as he would admit, 'technical media' (Winthrop-Young and Van den Oever, 2014).

We will first discuss the concept of 'technical media' to address the question of why and how media technologies require special treatment in both media and technology research in terms of the traces they leave in representation – with considerable implications for the user experience. Then, we will address the question as to why the sensorial effects created by technical media would typically be accompanied by a distinct experiential dimension and why this would help create the famous *cyclical* effects in the history of media use. Finally, we will discuss the implications for media historiographical research.

The distortive effect of technical media

In *Gramophone, Film, Typewriter* (1999), Friedrich Kittler introduced the notion of 'technical media' to discuss the specific material and technical make-up of media devices leaving specific traces in media use and needing attention when one studies (excavates) these processes. There were three main sources of inspiration for Kittler to start thinking along these lines: Michel Foucault and his archaeology of knowledge; thoughts on media as the message inspired by Marshall McLuhan (and Harrold Innis); and Rudolph Arnheim's studies of early film and visual perception from the early 1930s onwards.

In his first book, *Film as Art* (Film als Kunst, 2006 [1932]), Arnheim famously discussed a crucial quality of film technologies: technically speaking, they produce a representation of the object, which resembles the object represented, yet they do so *within the limits of the technology used*. This particular line of thinking became a source of inspiration to Kittler, who responded to Arnheim at several places in

Gramophone, Film, Typewriter. In Kittler's words, "(Technical] Media and [technical] media only fulfill the 'high standards' that (according to Rudolf Arnheim) we expect from 'reproductions' since the invention of photography" (Kittler 1999, 12). Here he quotes Arnheim on technical 'reproductions': "'They are not only supposed to resemble the object, but rather guarantee this resemblance by being, as it were, a product of the object in question, that is, by being mechanically produced by it [. . .]'" (Kittler 1999, 12).

This, Kittler argues, implies a radical difference between 'technical media' and other communication media such as language. Whereas language operates by way of a "symbolic grid" that requires that all data "pass through the bottleneck of the signifier" (Kittler 1999, 4, 12), the 'technical media' process the *physical effects of the real* (Winthrop-Young 2011, 59; Winthrop-Young and Van den Oever 2014, 226–228).[2]

However, that is not all there is to it. Technological media, moreover, "operate against a background of noise [or blurs] because their data travel along physical channels; [. . .] According to Arnheim, that is the price they pay for delivering reproductions that are at the same time effects of the reproduced" (Kittler 1999, 45). Now let us reconsider within this context the Kittlerian dictum that "A reproduction [. . .] refers to the bodily real, which of necessity escapes all symbolic grids" (Kittler 1999, 12). The problem is that in the process of production of data (to stick to Kittler's words), engineers and other technically oriented experts clearly identify the 'noise' and 'blurs' that are the by-product of the data traveling along the physical channels. Furthermore, it is clear that technical teams (e.g. engineers, projectionists and broadcasting teams) not only tend to identify such accidental by-products of the production process *as such*, but also to propose technical amendments in line with the use of the medium as envisioned from the production/distribution perspective, as documents indicate.[3]

The dynamic unfolding of invention testing/amendment is in itself a very interesting part of the dynamics in the history of technology, as well as the history of a medium (Turquety 2014). The user perspective, however, provides a remarkably different story. As abundantly shown in reception documents, users may well attribute meanings and emotions to traces made by the machine though they are made accidentally and without any intention.[4] Viewers respond particularly strongly and often even with great excitement to 'distortions' in the visual representation of animated figures (Van den Oever 2011; 2013). *Distortion* is a generic term used by Arnheim for all types of (visual) distortions, be it disproportions, deviations, enlargement, deformation, decolorization, or fusion. Such distortions require attention in the study of media use as they affect users and leave traces in the perceptual process (Van den Oever and Tan 2014). From the start, Arnheim largely marked the limitations of the technologies as a positive thing. Seen from the perspective of the arts and aesthetics, the technical limitations came with a potentially huge advantage: expressive power. In the early essays assembled in *Film as Art* (2006 [1932]), Arnheim elaborately discussed the peculiarities created by the new film technologies during recording and projection, such as low-contrast, black-and-white images, 2D, and the numb world of the movies before the invention of sound in the cinema. Particularly the last feature Arnheim valued: cinema being silent as opposed to reality being full of sounds. The cinema's 'silence' almost automatically and inevitably moved film into the realm of the arts and aesthetics because these 'unrealities' (as Arnheim called them) come with the advantage of a notable impact on the user experience. They affect viewers.

Clearly, Arnheim, a perceptual psychologist, mainly focused on the expressivity of the image and the perceptual effects of the unrealities under discussion; unlike others, he did not focus as much on the powers unleashed by the machine itself. It was Kittler who put this topic of study on the research agenda by coining the term 'technical media' as part of his archaeology of the media. In addition to both Arnheim and Foucault, he developed a focus in research on the material, technical traces of media technologies, which needed to be excavated as they co-shape 'the message' (McLuhan) and the 'regimes' (Foucault). In Arnheimian terms, they create 'unrealities' that have an impact on the perceptual process. We propose labelling the distortions created by a technical medium *technology-instigated distortions* as they constitute interesting aesthetic and perceptual categories in their own right.

Technology-instigated distortions

Technology-instigated distortions are interesting to artists, art historians, and philosophers of aesthetics – but why would they be of special interest to media historians, too? First, we assume that there is a direct connection between the technology-instigated distortions produced by *novel* (mimetic) media and their senso-perceptual and experiential impact on users, the so-called *novelty experience*. It is marked by an experience of a notable 'discontinuity' in the perceptual process: the process is deepened, complicated, and prolonged. Such effects are particularly well-known from first-time experiences with novel media (Van den Oever and Tan 2014). Psychologists speak about arousal symptoms that habituate. Here, in psychology, we find solid ground to theorize media novelty, hence to create the *conceptual constancy* needed for the field of media studies to speak about the 'new' in media history. Media newness can best be studied from the user perspective in terms of arousal symptoms in response to the use of novel (mimetic) media which trigger new/unfamiliar technology-instigated distortions which *momentarily* affect the user experience as a result of a discontinuity in the perceptual process. They are notable as they affect the user's (first-time) experience; and media historians have access to these because they are marked by users in reception documents (the distortions in the representations may be marked as 'new' or 'strange', etc.; the experiences as awesome or amusing or repulsive, etc.). If we know *why* novelty experiences appear (due to novel, technology-instigated distortions in the representation of people and things) and if we know *how* they express themselves in the user experience (in the notably deepened, prolonged perceptual process), then the question is: why do they disappear?

64 Andreas Fickers and Annie van den Oever

In line with psychological studies,[5] we assume, second, that the arousal symptoms disappear due to habituation; that is to say the *effects on experience* of the technology-instigated distortions of a novel medium are smoothened in the successive process of habituation (Van den Oever and Tan 2014). Clearly, the technology-instigated distortions themselves do *not* just disappear – unless the technical medium is technically amended, e.g. by technicians. Interestingly, however, the *effects* of these distortions *on the user experience* do disappear in the process of repetitive exposure to a medium as perception becomes habitual (media habituation). *Repetitive exposure* – as is typical for the use of most (communication) media – creates so-called habituation effects which render the medium 'transparent'. That is the reason media become 'second nature' (Gunning 2003) so quickly and easily.

Following early perception studies, we assume that habituation/de-habituation cycles help constitute the cycles that seem so typical for media use. In "Art as Technique", Viktor Shklovsky spoke about the mechanisms of *dehabituation* and *habituation* respectively; these two key terms are often translated as *de/automatization* and de/*familiarization*. Though his discussion of these twin mechanisms misses psychological precision, we want to draw additional attention to it as part of our reflections on the *experiential* dimensions of *de-habituation* effects – to help researchers recognize references to related experiences in reception documents as typical for first-time and frequent users of media respectively. We assume that moments of so-called *de-habituation* are put in motion by novel media technologies at their moment of introduction; moreover, that such moments typically *sensitize* users to the novel technologies and, at least potentially, make them aware of the material, technical, and senso-perceptual make-up of the novel medium at hand. The sensitivity to the medium exists only momentarily and vanishes over time in the process of habituation. Van den Oever and Tan (2014) proposed calling such *Sensitization Desensitization Cycles*. Accordingly, we propose not to speak of De-habituation Habituation Cycles but, more specifically, of Sensitization Desensitization Cycles. Additionally, we propose to discuss such phenomena as *medium awareness* and *medium sensitivity*, *medium transparency*, and media becoming '*second nature*' in terms of such Sensitization Desensitization Cycles or SDCs, that is to say, in terms of an increase or decrease in sensitivity to a (technical) medium due to first-time or regular exposure to a (mimetic) medium respectively.

Furthermore, we assume that there is a close relationship between habituation effects and the appreciation for and adaptation of media used for communication and information purposes. The relationship (as we provisionally call it) requires further attention with the help of (media) psychology and perception studies to allow for an empirical testing of the habituation hypothesis and the precise effects on media users perceptually, cognitively, and emotionally. However, that is not the primary focus of our attention here. In line with our argument thus far, we assume that there is an interesting relationship between the SDCs as proposed here and the *media cycles* as proposed by Benjamin Peters. We assume that media cycles are only partly institutionally driven; and partly by user experiences shaping user practices (called 'user cascades' by Salehabadi 2016). Correspondingly, we propose a further conceptualization of media newness, with the help of (media) psychology to create the conceptual constancy needed to reconstruct not only the story of novelty experiences appearing and disappearing, but also the histories of 'middle' and 'late' periods of media as Park and others suggested.

This brings us to the topic of media researchers being *desensitized* to the material, sensorial, and tacit dimensions of their objects of study. Unsurprisingly, perhaps, 'media transparency' is at the root of most modern media theories as Lambert Wiesing (2014) has convincingly shown. Therefore, let us take a closer look at the predictable effects of Sensitization Desensitization Cycles on our field of study. First of all, we wonder whether new media researchers, sensitized to the 'new media' of the 1990s, have helped to create an overfocus on newness in the field of media studies, if only because novelty experiences may well spur expert users no less than amateur users to distinct moments of sharpened medium awareness and experiences of *awe, wonder*, and *astonishment*, to use Gunning's favourite terms (Gunning 1995; 2003). Second, we wonder about the perhaps more important and more lasting effects on media research of routine exposure. The question is whether media researchers are not *de-sensitized* to most media, too, and have lost their medium awareness, by and large, just like the amateur users?

Being *desensitized* to a medium normally means that the sensitivity to the medium vanished as the initial arousal effects wear off due to habituation. This inevitably leads to a decrease in sensitivity to the distorting powers of the technology, to the point of users becoming almost fully insensitive to them. It may almost automatically lead to a point where the material presence of technologies in the perceptual process is no longer noted: a quick and swift shift in focus from the medium to the mediated becomes not only habitual, but even natural or 'second nature'. Being perceived as "natural" indicates that once the mechanism of habituation enhances such a smooth shift in the perceptual process from perceptual input to cognition, fully automatic and unnoticed by the percipients, they may altogether stop noticing the ontological difference between say *a pipe* in reality and one on a photo, TV, laptop, smartphone, cinema screen or canvas. This easily leads to an identification of the represented and the 'real thing'. As in the Magritte painting, one must remind the viewer: *Ceci n'est pas une pipe* [This is not a pipe] (The radical irony, of course, also includes the connotation of this painted pipe as overtly phallic).

In general, medium *unawareness* is a predictable and almost inevitable effect of habituation. Once media technologies have become second nature, media scholars easily lose sight of them. As a result, the special ontological status of the image as 'mediated' is easily overlooked and the technical make-up of the medium may simply go unquestioned – even by media scholars. In other words, media research does not necessarily benefit from the Sensitization Desensitization Cycles: long intervals of medium *de*sensitization may straightforwardly facilitate a dominant research focus on the 'real' (an overlooking of the medium itself once habituation has kicked in). This may be referred to as the *realist fallacy* in media-historical research: desensitized to its effects, realists basically leave the medium itself understudied. Therefore, we must conclude that overlooking the medium is not

66 Andreas Fickers and Annie van den Oever

an accidental, but a fundamental and structural phenomenon, also in the field of media research, and that habituation is the mechanism underlying the phenomenon (Van den Oever 2011; 2013).

The re-sensitization of researchers

Where does this leave media historians and their attempts to write the histories of media (technologies)? We assume that *doing* hands-on experiments with media technologies, e.g. in lab situations, helps to reverse the processes of habituation and de-sensitization.[6] Such experiments help to *re-sensitize* researchers to the effects of media technologies (Fickers and Van den Oever 2014). Experimental media archaeology, hands-on, can make historians (at least potentially) aware of the material, technical and senso-perceptual make-up of old and obsolete media technologies and so-called 'dead' media (Hertz and Parikka 2012). As part of a cultural archaeology of (media) technology, such an enterprise seems relevant if not inevitable. As early cinema historian, Tom Gunning, argues in "Re-Newing Old Technologies", new technologies enter culture(s) charged with a utopian envisioning of a future they "radically transformed by the implications of the device or practice". However, he also concludes that the sinking of technology into "a reified second nature" indicates the failure, by and large, of the transformations envisioned: (once) new media end up fitting into, rather than changing, the already existing "grooves of power and exploitation". We need an archaeology of technology to grasp again the (lost) *newness of old technologies* as Gunning states (2003, 56).

On the basis of our own (lab) experiences with colleagues and students, we assume that in general researchers can be made much more medium aware and medium sensitive, not only to the old/dead media, but also to the traces their use left in historical reception documents, among them the cues marking distinct historical user experiences of media newness – mainly *awe, wonder,* and *astonishment,* in the perception of Gunning (1995; 2003): they provide an ideal background to the utopian envisionings in which the launch of novel media can take place. The re-sensitization of the researcher may make him/her more sensitive to the experiential, senso-perceptual and tacit dimensions of media use; moreover, it may help trigger questions concerning novelty experiences and their (mostly) sudden appearance and gradual disappearance as the ebb and flow of media's (de)habituation histories.[7]

Hands-on experiments and reenactments as a research (and teaching) method

One possible way of exploring past media practices is to do reenactments or hands-on experiments with old media devices, which is at the heart of a new approach called experimental media archaeology (Fickers and Van den Oever 2014). At the heart of this is our proposal to open the vaults and glass cases of museums: to make the device collections available to researchers for experiments, *hands-on*.[8] Experimental media archaeology not only aims to sensitize researchers but, beyond that, to 'grasp' media and communication technologies in their concrete materiality and tangibility. *Grasping* is to be understood here as a hermeneutical act in the meaning given to it by Ernst Cassirer (1995): it comprises both the intellectual process of comprehending, as well as the sensory-bodily appropriation of getting a grip on things.

In line with Cassirer and others, we want to argue that *doing* media archaeological experiments in this experimental system of knowledge production turns historians into experimenters who experience the "mangle of practice" (Pickering 1995) of "science in action" (Latour and Woolgar 1979). From this experimental practice flows a series of advantages marked by researchers under a range of different labels: "collaborative thinking" (Corrigan 2012); "thinkering" (Huhtamo 2013); "heuristic groping" (Breidbach et al. 2010); or "bricolage" (Rheinberger 2015), taking place in a "living laboratory" (Arrigoni 2013), a context that fosters a process of "situated learning" (Lave and Wenger 1991) and "learning by doing" (Heering and Wittje 2001). Moreover, the careful documentation and self-reflexive analysis of such an experimental practice will be greatly beneficial for the fields of media archaeology, media history, and material and museum studies (Ludwig and Weber 2013; Byrne et al. 2011; Csikszentmihalyi 1993).

We wish to emphasize that doing experiments with old media technologies – be it with originals or replicas – produces authentic contemporary experiences, but these (lab) experiences can, in no way, recreate 'authentic' historical experiences. As one of the pioneers of sensory history, Mark Smith, has convincingly argued, we need to carefully distinguish between sensory production and consumption. While it is possible to reproduce a particular sound or image of the past by using original hardware and software, the way we understand, experience and 'consume' these sounds and images is radically different from the way in which people interpreted these in the past. "Failure to distinguish between sensory production (something that can, at least theoretically, be replicated in the present) and sensory consumption (something that is hostage to the context in which it was produced) betrays the promise of sensory history", as Smith argued (2007, 841).

Doing hands-on experiments with old media technologies also opens up the way to a reflexive hermeneutical research practice aimed at reflections on the co-constructedness of situated knowledge production. Such a practice of *reenacting*, *re-staging*, *re-doing*, and *re-making* in an experimental setting is geared towards raising the awareness of the participants in the experiment about the functionalities ascribed to the *materiality* of the object (what can and cannot be done with a device), as well as the *symbolic nature* (design, semantics, interfaces). Moreover, such a practice facilitates the explication of implicit inventories of knowledge and ignorance (knowledge that provides a springboard for action); the creative disconcertion of available knowledge (education through failure); the reflective analysis of the per-formative dimension of technical objects (object as medium); and the

68 Andreas Fickers and Annie van den Oever

critical reflections of the situational dynamics in the experimental space (between the object and the experimenter, as well as between different actors).

Although authenticity is "a currency and competency standard within the reenactor's history work", as Stephen Gapps (2009, 398) has put it, the reenactors/ experimenters are charmed *not* by the original, but by its authentic simulation. It is the combination of old and new, the playful practice of locating, embodying, and recalling that make reenactments or media archaeological experiments an authentic mode of communicative memory practices (Dreschke et al., 2016) or, to quote Tilmans, Van Vree and Winter (2010, 7): "Re-enactment is both affirmation and renewal. It entails addressing the old, but it also engenders something new, something we have never seen before. Herein lies the excitement of performance, as well as its surprises and its distortions". Reenactments and experimental approaches open up possibilities that allow history to be unfinished business (Gapps 2009, 207). With a similar appreciation, Simone Venturini (2013) speaks of a "handmade environment for using the technology available and the human and corporal reclaiming of the technology". Such 'aesthetic experimentations' with media devices are described by her as "practical operations on the technology and material of a reflective nature". Interestingly, in his 1977 book *Ricognizione della semiotica*, Emilio Garroni (quoted by Venturini 2013, 202) already typified such practical operations as *mainly meta-operational activities*.

While the heuristic potential of experimental media archaeology has been outlined in detail (Fickers and Van den Oever 2014; Fickers 2015; 2018), the question of how to document and 'translate' the sensorial experiences and perceptions made during such hands-on interactions with past media technologies remains largely unexplored. Within the field of 'sensory studies' (Howes 2013), anthropological and ethnographic approaches have been most explicit in documenting processes of embodiment and the plurality of sensory modes of engagement. Most prominently, Sarah Pink has advocated a 'sensory ethnography' that experiments with multiple media for the registration and communication of cultural facts and practices (Pink 2009). As a reflexive and experiential process through which understanding, knowing, and (academic) knowledge are produced, research on sensory perception and reception requires methods that are capable of grasping "the most profound type of knowledge [which] is not spoken of at all and thus inaccessible to ethnographic observation or interview" (Pink 2009, 4).

By using audiovisual media to document non-verbal communication, behaviour, and emotional reactions of users interacting with media technologies, we can try to open up for research and help make explicit the embodied and implicit forms of knowledge invested in past media usages. Sound and video recordings can work as analytical instruments to document the tacit knowledge of our hands, bodies, eyes, and ears when operating media devices; such recordings help us to grasp the complex and subtle human–machine relations as social interactions in situations of media consumption or use. In the exposure to the aesthetic and performative quality of media technologies, we aim to re-sensitize the experimental historians to their own embodiedness and enhance their awareness of the limitations of speech and written language as primary modes of knowledge production (Serres 2008). Capturing and documenting these embodied forms of implicit or tacit knowledge enables researchers to make explicit what the experimental historian of science Otto Sibum has described as "gestisches Wissen" – *skilled knowledge* (Sibum 1998, 154). Reflecting on his hands-on simulations of 16mm film editing, John Ellis emphasized the limits of using linguistic/textual representations as the most adequate technique for describing implicit forms of expertise or technical skills: "Verbal analysis can go some way to explicating the details, but in the end this is hands-on history where information has to be experienced as well as written . . . or, at least, has to be read audiovisually" (Ellis 2015).

But what will such audiovisual representations tell us about the experiences of the experimenters/reenactors? Will they enable us to get closer to their sensorial perceptions, emotions or performative pleasures when interacting with old or replicated media technologies? Hardly so. Sure, a trained video or sound analyst (or experienced 'sensory ethnographer') might be able to detect specific gestures or emotional reactions, to map the spatial setting and situatedness of the human–machine interactions as well as the social interactions during the hands-on experiments that can help to qualify a reenactment as contemporary historical performance. However, in terms of interpretative evidence, such documentation remains somewhat speculative, unless used as a guide to our own encounters with these technologies. Much more important, it seems, is the added *heuristic* and *meta-reflective* value of doing hands-on experiments (and additionally document them audiovisually): to deconstruct the myth of authentic historical experience, moreover, to turn the inherent contradiction of any such endeavour into a purposefully *distortive* intellectual experience full of creative uncertainty.

Epilogue: some remarks on authenticity, distortion, and the art of failure

Instead of reproducing canonical master narratives of moments of 'media newness' based on discourse analysis of textual, sonic or visual representations of the past, the hands-on experiments with old media devices or replicas we propose aim, first of all, at re-sensitizing researchers and at the human and corporal reclaiming of technology (Venturini, 2013). It means a regaining of a keen, corporal sensitivity to the senso-perceptual, tacit, and experiential dimensions present in practices of media devices, a sensitivity researchers predictably lost in their routine use of media technologies. Second, we aim to nurture a heuristic and meta-reflective attitude towards user practices – including an awareness of the fact that *making things work* (as they should) is most likely to be an experience of failure, breakdown, and disappointment rather than one of immersion, habituation, and routinized pleasure. While our appropriation and use of media technologies – especially since the emergence of so-called consumer electronics since the 1960s – can be

70 Andreas Fickers and Annie van den Oever

negatively characterized by some as an 'inflation of things' ("Dinginflation", Heßler, 2013), which have invaded our domestic and public spaces, the *positive* experience of some new media practices in the mechanical and electro-mechanical era, to some others, is the exposure to extensive intervals of tinkering, learning and, most importantly, repair and maintenance (Krebs, Schabacher and Weber 2018). In other words, habituation and routine use as dominant modes of media consumption are the result of a "ready to use" consumption habit (closely tied to a "ready to throw-away" culture in case of dysfunction), whereas the exposure to ever-new media invites de-habituation and a re-sensitization to (modes of) media use much appreciated by (new) media researchers.

Putting our hands, bodies, and brains to experiments with old media technologies will, inevitably, resensitize us to the fact that user manuals, do-it-yourself handbooks for operators, not to mention advertisements, have little to do with past or present realities of media usage. Just as the act of turning a messy and lengthy process of scientific experimentation into a publication must be interpreted as the first step in a process of canonization of knowledge (carefully subordinating the vitality of the experimentation process to a linear logic of reasoning and conceptual consistency; Rieß 1998), instruction books and leaflets accompanying media devices clearly represent idealized situations of use that have little in common with actual practices of appropriation and use.

> For experimenters, the problem with experiments is that they rarely work according to plan, if they work at all. For historians, the problem with experiments is that scientists' accounts of them naturally reflect the plan or the finished product, rather than actual practice.
>
> (Gooding 1989, 64)

What is true for experiments in science is certainly true for the less codified and structured spaces of experimental media archaeology. The "art of failure" (Aasman 2014) is probably one of the most important learning experiences in this heuristic practice. In his thought-provoking essay "Rethinking Repair", Steven Jackson (2014) pleas for a "broken world thinking" that focuses on moments of breakdown, maintenance, and repair instead of privileging moments of initial encounter and general predilections for the new. In re-orienting our attention to the history of "an aftermath, growing at the margins, breakpoints, and interstices of complex sociotechnical systems as they crack, flex, and bend their way through time" (ibid., 223), Jackson (ibid., 234) argues that we might be able to redirect our gaze from moments of production to moments of sustainability and "the myriad forms of activity by which the shape, standing, and meaning of objects in the world is produced and sustained – a feature especially valuable in a field too often occupied with the shock of the new". Building replicas, taking precious devices from their glass cases, and experimenting with originals will help to dehabituate media historians from their fixation on media newness and authenticity; to produce creative distortions in a field dominated by canonical narratives of technological inventions and innovations; to refocus on cascades of media use (rather than technical

newness); and, lastly, to value the surprisingly capricious and quirky (de)habitua-
tion histories so typical of the experiences of past media practices.

Notes

1 As in our earlier articles written together, our names are presented in a simple alphabeti-
cal order. Fickers mainly contributed to the historiographical reflections; Van den Oever
mainly contributed to the theoretical reflections. Here too, we draw from earlier, joint
work (Fickers and Van den Oever 2014; 2018). Moreover, both of us draw from parts of
our past research projects and publications; Van den Oever draws, in particular, from her
work on distortions in the representation of figures leaping into the grotesque and the
effects on viewers, published in *Image & Text* and in *Leonardo* in 2011 and 2013 respectively;
and a research project she prepared with Ed Tan (in 2014) on sensitization desensitization
cycles. Andreas Fickers builds on his research in the framework of the history of home
movie film making (with Jo Wachelder, Susan Aasman, Tim van der Heijden and Tom
Slootweg), stereophonic recording technologies (with Stefan Krebs) and transnational television transmissions (with Andy O'Dwyer).
2 Geoffrey Winthrop-Young is Kittler's most solid bridge between the German and English-
speaking world. Winthrop-Young translated parts of Kittler's work, originally written in
German, into English and wrote illusive introductions to his work, clarifying in passing
Kittler's complex relations to Foucault, McLuhan, Arnheim, and others (see Winthrop-
Young 1999); with ironic precision, Winthrop-Young characterizes and clarifies Kittler's
cryptic terminology and provocative phrasings (see Winthrop-Young 2011); see also our
dialogue on Kittler and Arnheim (among other things): Winthrop-Young and Van den
Oever 2014.
3 There are many examples (e.g., the amendments discussed by David Bordwell in his *Poetics
of Cinema* from 2007), but in this article we mainly restrict ourselves to some references to
Tsivian (1994), to be discussed below and in note 4.
4 Remarkable examples have been excavated in an exemplary way by Yuri Tsivian in his
illusive study of *Early Cinema in Russia and Its Cultural Reception* (1994). This study has
inspired research in this field ever since. Today, many good examples are to be found
in the phase of very early cinema and many particularly interesting discussions are to
be found in the field of early cinema studies, a classic being the debates concerning
Maxim Gorky's response to a Lumière "filmshow" in 1996: "Last Night I was in the
Kingdom of Shadows"; for the full text, see: https://www.mcsweeneys.net/articles/
contest-winner-36-black-and-white-and-in-color.
5 Habituation is defined in standard studies as a dissipation of a target-psychological
response, e.g. psychophysiological activation at the presentation of a novel stimulus due to
repeated exposure only; see Thompson and Spencer 1966.
6 In his 2003 article, Tom Gunning speaks of reversing the cycle of wonder.
7 There are signals that not all the novelty/arousal symptoms (fully) disappear due to habituation, for example, the question is whether the arousal effects triggered by the famously
huge IMAX screens positioned above the seated cinema audience who is made to look up
at them disappear: though the impact of the screens on experience is clearly designed by
IMAX technicians to *not* fully disappear, the effects seem to be diminishing gradually. This
is just one among many examples where further research is needed to explain the effects of
habituation and user appreciation and acceptation (Van den Oever and Tan 2014).
8 For a range of examples and a further explication of the strategy, see also the "Introduction" by Fossati and Van den Oever to *Exposing the Film Apparatus* (2016, 13–43) and the
examples provided by 29 authors in each of the successive 29 chapters. See also the historical, hands-on work done by BBC teams under the supervision of John Ellis and his
research team studying the BBC television production practices of the 1960s: John Ellis,
"16 mm Film Editing. Using Filmed Simulation as a Hands-on Approach to TV History",
in: *VIEW Journal of European Television History and Culture,* 4(7); Available from: https://
vimeo.com/123212931

Bibliography

Aasman, S. (2014) Staging the Amateur Film Dispositif. A Report. [Online]. Available from: https://homemoviesproject.wordpress.com/report-staging-the-amateur-dispositif/.

Ahrens, S. (2011) *Experiment und Exploration. Bildung als experimentelle Form der Welterschließung.* Bielefeld: Transcript.

Arrigoni, G. (2013) Innovation, Collaboration, Education: Histories and Perspectives on Living Labs. xCoAx 2013: Computation Communication Aesthetics and X, Bergamo.

Arnheim, R. (2004) *Art and Visual Perception: A Psychology of the Creative Eye.* Berkeley, CA: University of California Press.

Arnheim, R. (1977) Systematik der fruhen kinematographischen Erfindungen. In H. H. Dietrichs. (ed.). *Kritiken und Aufsatze zum Film.* Munich: Lizenzausg. der Ausg.

Arnheim, R. (2006) *Film as Art.* [*Film als Kunst*, 1932]. Berkeley, CA: University of California Press.

Balbi, G. (2015) Old and New Media. Theorizing Their Relationships in Media Historiography. In Kinnebrock, S., Schwarzenegger, C., and Birkener T. (eds). *Theorien des Medienwandels.* Köln: Halem, 231–249.

Bordwell, D. (2008) *Poetics of Cinema.* New York: Routledge/Taylor & Francis Group.

Breidbach, O., Heering, P., Müller, M. and Weber, H. (2010) Experimentelle Wissenschaftsgeschichte. In Breidbach, O., Heering, P., Müller, M. and Weber, H. (eds). *Experimentelle Wis-senschaftsgeschichte.* Munich: Wilhelm Fink Verlag, 13–72.

Byrne, S., Clarke, A., Harrison, R. and Torrence, R. (eds) (2011) *Unpacking the Collection: Networks of Material and Social Agency in the Museum.* New York: One World Archaeology.

Cassirer, E. (1995) Form und Technik. In Orth, E. W. and Krois, J. M. (eds). *Symbol, Technik, Sprache. Aufsätze aus den Jahren 1927–1933.* Hamburg: Meiner, 39–89.

Chateau, D. and Moure, J. (2016) *Screens: From Materiality to Spectatorship – A Historical and Theoretical Reassessment.* Amsterdam: Amsterdam University Press.

Corrigan, K. (2012) Collaborative Thinking: The Challenge of the Modern University. *Arts & Humanities in Higher Education,* 11(3): 262–72.

Csikszentmihalyi, M. (1993) Why We Need Things. In Lubar, S. and King-ery, W. D. (eds). *History From Things: Essays on Material Culture.* Washington/London: Smithsonian Institution Press, 20–29.

Dreschke, Anja et al. (eds) (2016) *Reenactments: Medienpraktiken zwischen Wiederholung und kreativer Aneignung.* Bielefeld: Transcript Verlag.

Edgerton, D. (2006) *The Shock of the Old: Technology and Global History Since 1900.* London: Profile Books.

Ellis, J. (2015) 16 mm Film Editing. Using Filmed Simulation as a Hands-on Approach to TV History. In *VIEW Journal of European Television History and Culture,* 4(7): 2015. [Online]. Available from: https://vimeo.com/123212931 (Accessed: 11 September 2018)

Fickers, A. and Van den Oever, A. (2014) Experimental Media Archaeology: A Plea for New Directions. In Van den Oever, A. (ed.). *Technē/Technology.* Amsterdam: Amsterdam University Press, 272–278.

Fickers, A. and Weber, A-K. (2015) Towards an Archaeology of Television. Editorial. *VIEW Journal of European Television History and Culture,* 4 (7). DOI: 10.18146/2213-0969.2015.jethc076.

Fickers, A. (2015) Hands-on. Plädoyer für eine experimentelle Medienarchäologie. *Technikgeschichte,* 82(1): 67–85.

Fickers, A. (2018) How to Grasp Historical Media Dispositifs in Practice. In Aasman, S., Fickers, A. and Wachelder, J. (eds). *Materializing Memories. Dispositifs, Generations, Amateurs.* New York: Bloomsbury, 85–91.

Fickers, A. and Van den Oever, A. (2018) Doing Experimental Media Archaeology: Epistemological and Methodological Reflections on Experiments with Historical Objects of Media Technologies. In Roberts, B. and Goodall, M. (eds). *New Media Archaeologies*. Amsterdam: Amsterdam University Press, 45–68.

Fossati, G. and Van den Oever, A. (2016) *Exposing the Film Apparatus. The Film Archive as a Research Lab*. Amsterdam: Amsterdam University Press, 13–43.

Gapps, S. (2009) Mobile Monuments: A View of Historical Re-enactment and Authenticity from Inside the Costume Cupboard of History. *Rethinking History*, 13(3): 395–409.

Gitelman, L. (2008) *Always Already New: Media, History, and the Data of Culture*. Cambridge, MA: The MIT Press.

Garroni, E. (1977) *Ricognizione della semiotica. Tre lezioni*. Rome: Officina.

Gooding, D. (1989) History in the Laboratory: Can We Tell What Really Went On? In James, F. (ed.). *The Development of the Laboratory. Essays on the Place of Experiment in Industrial Civilization*. Basingstoke/London: Macmillan, 63–82.

Gunning, T. (1995) An Aesthetic of Astonishment: Early Film and the Incredulous Spectator. In Williams, L. (ed.). *Viewing Positions: Ways of Seeing Film*. New Brunswick, NJ: Rutgers University Press.

Gunning, T. (2003) Re-Newing Old Technologies: Astonishment, Second Nature, and the Uncanny in Technology from the Previous Turn-of-the-Century. In Thorburn, D. and Jenkins, H. (eds). *Rethinking Media Change: The Aesthetics of Transition*. Cambridge: MIT Press, 39–59.

Heering, P., Markert, M. and Weber, H. (eds) (2012) *Experimentelle Wissenschafts-geschichte didaktisch nutzbar machen. Ideen, Überlegungen und Fallstudien*. Flensburg: Flensburg University Press.

Heering, P. and Witje, R. (eds) (2011) *Learning by Doing. Experiments and Instruments in the History of Science Teaching*. Stuttgart: Franz Steiner Verlag.

Hertz, G. and Parikka, J. (2012) Zombie Media: Circuit Bending Media Archaeology into an Art. *Leonardo*, 45(5): 424–430.

Heßler, Martina (2013) Wegwerfen. Zum Wandel des Umgangs mit Dingen. *Zeitschrift für Erziehungswissenschaft*, 16(2), S. 253–266.

Howes, D. (2013) The Expanding Field of Sensory Studies. Version 1.0 (August 2013). [Online]. Available from: https://sensorystudies.org (Accessed: 8 September 2018)

Huhtamo, E. (2011) Thinkering with Media: On the Art of Paul DeMarinis. In DeMarinis, P. (ed.). *Buried in Noise*. Heidelberg: Kehrer, 33–39.

Huhtamo, E. (2013) *Illusions in Motion. Media Archaeology of the Moving Panorama and Related Spectacles*. Cambridge, MA: MIT Press.

Ihde, D. (1986) *Experimental Phenomenology: An Introduction*. New York: State University of New York Press.

Jackson, S. J. (2014) Rethinking Repair. In Gillespie, T., Boczkowski, P. and Foot, K. (eds). *Media Technologies: Essays on Communication, Materiality and Society*. Cambridge MA: MIT Press, 221–239.

Kittler, F. (1999) *Gramophone, Film, Typewriter*. Translated, with an Introduction, by Geoffrey Winthrop-Youg and Michael Wutz. Stanford, CA: Stanford University Press.

Krebs, S., Schabacher, G. and Weber, H. (eds) (2018) *Kulturen des Reparierens*. Bielefeld: Transcript.

Latour, B. and Woolgar, S. (1979) *Laboratory Life: The Construction of Scientific Facts*. Princeton, NJ: Princeton University Press.

Lawson, C. and Stowell, R. (1999) *The Historical Performance of Music: An Introduction*. Cambridge: Cambridge University Press.

Lave, J. and Wenger, E. (1991) *Situated Learning: Legitimate Peripheral Participation*. Cambridge: Cambridge University Press.

Ludwig, D. and Weber, C. (2013) A Rediscovery of Scientific Collections as Material Heritage? The Case of University Collections in Germany. *Studies in History and Philosophy of Science*, Part A 44(4): 652–659.

Marvin, C. (1990) *When Old Technologies Were New: Thinking About Electric Communication in the Late Nineteenth Century.* Oxford: Oxford University Press.

Nerone, J. (2007) The Future of Communication History. *Journal Critical Studies in Media Communication*, 23(3): 259.

Nye, D. E. (2006) *Technology Matters. Questions to Live With.* Cambridge MA: MIT Press.

Park, D., Jankowski, N. and Jones, S. (2011) *The Long History of New Media: Technology, Historiography, and Contextualizing Newness.* [Online]. Available from: http://thelonghistoryofnewmedia.net/toc/introduction-history-and-new-media (Accessed: 15 June 2018)

Peters, B. (2009) And Lead Us Not into Thinking the New is New: A Bibliographic Case for New Media History. *New Media & Society*, 11(1/2): 13–30.

Pickering, A. (1995) *The Mangle of Practice: Time, Agency, and Science.* Chicago, IL: University of Chicago Press.

Pink, S. (2009) *Doing Sensory Ethnography.* London: Sage.

Rheinberger, H-J. (2015) *Die Farben des Tastens. Hans-Jörg Rheinberger im Gespräch mit Alexandru Bulucz.* Frankfurt am Main: Edition Faust.

Rieß, F. (1998) Erkenntnis durch Wiederholung – Eine Methode zur Geschichtsschreibung des Experiments. In James, F. (ed.). *The Development of the Laboratory. Essays on the Place of Experiment in Industrial Civilization.* Basingstoke/London: Macmillan, 157–172.

Salehabadi, D. (2016) The Scramble for Digital Waste in Berlin. In Oldenziel, R. and Trischler, H. (eds). *Cycling and Recycling. Histories of Sustainable Practices.* Berghahn: New York, 202–214.

Serres, M. (2008) *The Five Senses. A Philosophy of Mingled Bodies.* London: Continuum.

Sibum, O. (1998) Die Sprache der Instrumente. Eine Studie zur Praxis und Repräsentation des Experimentierens. In Heidelberger, M. and Steinle, F. (eds). *Experimental Essays – Versuche zum Experiment.* Baden-Baden: Nomos, 141–156.

Smith, M. (2007) Producing Sense, Consuming Sense, Making Sense: Perils and Prospects for Sensory History. *Journal of Social Sciences*, 40(4): 841–858.

Thompson, R. F. Spencer, W. A. (1966) Habituation: A Model Phenomenon for the Study of Neuronal Substrates of Behavior. *Psychological Review*, 73: 16–43.

Tilmans, K., Van Vree, F. and Winter, J. (eds.) (2010) *Performing the Past. Memory, History, and Identity in Modern Europe.* Amsterdam: Amsterdam University Press.

Tsivian, Y. (1994) *Early Cinema in Russia and Its Cultural Reception.* Translated by Alan Bodger. Chicago, IL: University Press Chicago.

Turquety, B. (2014) Toward an Archaeology of the Cinema/Technology Relation: From Mechanization to 'Digital Cinema. *Technē /Technology*, 50–64.

Van den Oever, A. (2010) Ostrannenie, "The Montage of Attraction", and Early Cinema's "Properly Irreducable Alien Quality". In Van den Oever, A. (ed.). *Ostrannenie. On "Strangeness" and the Moving Image. The History, Reception, and Relevance of a Concept.* The Key Debates. Mutations and Appropriations in European Film Studies, 1: 33–60.

Van den Oever, A. M. A. (2011) The Prominence of Grotesque Figures in Visual Culture Today. Rethinking the Ontological Status of the (Moving) Image from the Perspective of the Grotesque. *Image & Text*, 18: 100–123.

Van den Oever, A. (2013) The Medium-Sensitive Experience and the Paradigmatic Experience of the Grotesque, 'Unnatural', or 'Monstrous'. *Leonardo*, 46(1): 88–89.

Van den Oever, A. and Tan, E. (2014) *Settling the Unsettling: Medium Sensitization and Desensitization Cycles and the Adaptation to and Acceptation of Novel Media by Viewers.* Project Proposal RUG/UvA 2014.

Van den Oever, A. (ed.) (2014) "Introduction". In Van den Oever, A. (ed.). Technē/ Technology. Researching Cinema and Media Technologies, Their Development, Use and Impact. The Key Debates. *Mutations and Appropriations in European Film Studies*, 4: 15–26.

Venturini, S. (2013) Technological Platforms. In Hediger, V., Saba, C. G., Le Maitre, B. and Noordegraaf, J. (eds.). *Preserving and Exhibiting Media Art. Challenges and Perspectives.* Amsterdam: Amsterdam University Press, 201–202.

Wiesing, L. (2014) What are Media? *Technē/Technology*, 93–104.

Winthrop-Young, G. and Wutz, M. (1999) Translator's Introduction: Friedrich Kittler and Media Discourse Analysis. In Kittler, F. (ed.). *Gramophone, Film, Typewriter.* Translated, with an Introduction, by Winthrop-Young, G. and Wutz, M. Redwood City CA: Stanford University Press.

Winthrop-Young, G. (2011) *Kittler and the Media.* Cambridge: Polity.

Winthrop-Young, G. and Van den Oever, A. (2014) Rethinking the Materiality of Technical Media: Friedrich Kittler, *Enfant Terrible* with a Rejuvenating Effect on Parental Discipline, a Dialogue. *Technē/Technology*, 219–239.

5

(UN)CERTAIN GHOSTS

Rephotography and historical images

Mary Agnes Krell

This chapter is borne of days walking the streets of St Malo, stacks of photographs in our arms as we looked for traces of the past in buildings and streets. It attempts to articulate multiple sites of encounter in the viewing and, crucially, making of a rephotographic image. While there has been some scholarly exploration of the nature of rephotographic images and the promise they offer viewers, far less has been written about the photographic acts involved and the new knowledges that might emerge from those. The ghosts in the title refer simultaneously to the original photographers and to the people and places who have disappeared from the spaces and places we inhabit.

On Lee Miller

Lee Miller was the first female photographer to enter Normandy with troops during the Second World War. She was working in a freelance capacity for *Vogue* magazine in England during that time. She was also one of a small number of female photographers officially accredited by the Allies. Miller was an American expat and was therefore able to obtain permission to work as an actual war correspondent, making her the first woman to write and photograph her own stories from that time. In her capacity as a reporter for *Vogue* she produced a series of reports on her experiences. For each, she provided the magazine with photographs and her own written accounts of activities. Not long after returning from the war, those images, notes and ephemera were boxed and placed in an attic only to be rediscovered decades later by her son.

This chapter emerges from a project exploring those materials and focusing on Miller's own words, images and marginalia. She was a photographer and author whose life was often framed through her proximity to famous men with whom she lived, worked and loved. She is sometimes included in discussions of surrealist art both because her early work shows surrealist influences and because she worked

FIGURE 5.1 Screenshot from the project, 'Traces of Lee Miller: Echoes from St. Malo'.

and associated with many famous individuals from the period. Such a narrow reading of her life and work is problematic. For that reason, the project at the core of this article consciously focused on her own work, and not her work with Man Ray or her collaborations with her husband Roland Penrose and others.

Miller's war photography presents a unique and personal account of war. It warrants further study and, as such, we chose to focus on her time in St Malo in Normandy, the place at which she first saw battle, to begin our work. Miller was sent to St Malo but, as a result of misinformation, arrived not after but in the midst of the city's siege. Women were not supposed to see combat but Miller landed at the heart of it. During the following week or so her life and her photographic practice would change significantly. This period in Miller's life, and – I would argue – this very moment in St Malo changed her work from the somewhat surrealist (almost playful) early images to darker and more complex material.

In light of those experiences and that notional moment of transition, we produced a project with rephotography at its core. Alongside the rephotographs is a wide range of materials including Miller's contact sheets, captions, personal notes and the original manuscript as submitted to her editor at *Vogue*, Audrey Withers. We also included the revised manuscript (as printed) and interviews with war survivors, one of whom was actually a French soldier in one of Miller's photos. In writing about her work from this time, McLoughlin describes how Miller's writings, "provide pointers missing from her photographs" (McLoughlin 2010). In our project, we presented the user with a range of visual, textual and interactive objects which, together, create a series of possibilities for exploring and constructing readings of Miller's work and life.

On rephotography

Rephotography is a practice that offers novel opportunities for engagement with archival materials for both the creator and the viewer. It is sometimes called "repeat

78 Mary Agnes Krell

photography" in the fields of geology and anthropology or referred to as "then and now images" in contemporary press. The rephotographic method has become a tool used to study change in communities, landscapes and built environments.

In this chapter, both the creation and reception of rephotography are of interest. Rephotographic images, when discussed, are often described in terms of how a viewer responds to the images presented. Much has been said about how one might interpret rephotographic material and the possibilities afforded by interacting with work that simultaneously contains both a notional past and a present. While that simultaneous present and the various readings afforded are touched on in this chapter, it is the rephotographic act – that of making a rephotographic image – that bears more consideration.

The act of making a rephotograph

Rephotographic practice is, in many ways, doubly hands on. It is, at the point of creation, an act of physically reenacting the moment of taking a picture belonging to someone else and of conjoining the two in a single final form. The rephotographer is responsible for undertaking research to determine the precise location and framing of the original in order to create the new image and layering the two. This merging of images can lead to the creation of work which evokes strong reactions. It is described by Kalin in his work on memory and rephotography as, "a style of engagement with the past, a visual style and aesthetic, that reorients the time and place of memory" (Kalin 2013, 172).

In an interview about the act of rephotography Mark Klett, founder of the Rephotographic Survey Project (RSP), describes the act of creating rephotographic images as one which "increased our ability to visualize space and time relationships". (Rothman and Klett 2011). Klett's project included restaging images originally shot by land surveyors in late nineteenth century North America, more than one hundred years after they were originally made. Having trained as a geologist, Klett's work began largely with landscape images but has expanded in recent decades to include urban environments and other subjects. Cultural historian Rebecca Solnit accompanied Klett during the process of making rephotographs of work by Eadweard Muybridge and others in Yosemite. She describes the feelings she experienced as a result of taking part in those acts of creation by saying that

> afterward each place had imprinted on me – it wasn't that I could recall the place with some sort of photographic accuracy, but that it had become part of me, that when I thought of it there was a definite feeling, not an image of place but a sense of place.
>
> (Solnit 2004)

Solnit's articulation of feeling a sense of place is eerily similar to the ways that members of my own team described their experience of rephotographing Lee Miller's work in St Malo. That articulation of the sense of a place as somehow larger than the image that was taken there suggests that the creators of the rephotographic image were having the same kind of experience as the viewers. Both seem to be engaging in some kind of temporal drift where the real and imagined places exist simultaneously. Later in this chapter, I will return to exploring the act of rephotographing Lee Miller's work in St Malo and this notion of place. That project employed interactive rephotography. There are, however, many ways of presenting rephotographic material. The primary forms of rephotographic practice one might encounter are touched upon below.

Types of rephotography

Standard formats for presenting rephotographic work have emerged over the past few decades. They range from the wholly static side-by-side images to fully interactive overlays, with a range of styles in between. The most common of these formats and their differing qualities are described below.

Side-by-side

Side-by-side presentation is a comparative style of repeat photography in which the original image and contemporary image are, as described, placed side by side. While both images are visible, viewers can only focus on one at a time when looking at an image in any great detail. This format is the one commonly employed in geographic studies and has been used for decades as a tool to measure change within landscapes. This is perhaps the most common format for presenting rephotography.

Embedded

An increasingly popular method for presenting rephotographic material is that of holding an historic image up in front of a contemporary place so that both can be photographed together. This can be seen commonly in the "Looking Into the Past" Flickr group. This style, like the split style, shows past and present within the same frame. A crucial difference is that the older image actually hides or masks part of the newer. While this style is aesthetically pleasing, it is also problematic in the way that the past effectively obliterates the present.

Split

Another common form for the presentation of rephotographic images is the split image showing past and present on either side of a vertical axis within the same frame. These can be presented as static or interactive images with the most common being to present the image with a static split. Some forms of split rephotography contain degrees of photo manipulation and interactivity described below.

A variation on the split image is the selective inclusion of elements of the past where, for example, people or other elements may be placed in the present, rendered in black and white but without significant borders or other lines around them. It is implied that the photo-manipulation in these images is used only to draw and soften the boundaries between the two but that the contents of both original and newer image remain intact.[1]

Interactive split

An increasingly popular format for presenting rephotography is the interactive split model. In this, a vertical line in the image can be dragged to the left and right, changing the point at which the old image and new image meet. The National Park Service has produced the *Klondike Gold Rush* project in which this method is used to present rephotographic images. Though interactive split images allow increasingly active engagement on the part of the viewer, they still struggle from the problem that only part of each image is visible at any one time.

Interactive overlay

The most interactive format for presenting rephotography sees the images overlaid and includes an interface for users to fade back and forth between the two, either by scrolling left and right or through some other means of interactivity such as the use of a touchscreen or other interface. The interactive overlay allows viewers to see both the original and the rephotographic images simultaneously fading into and emerging from another. It is this format that we employed in *Traces of Lee Miller* and it can also be seen in David Levene's project *The American Civil War Then and Now* (Levene 2015). This interactive overlay allows a viewer to actively interact, giving her the freedom to reconfigure material within a frame exploring new forms of both content and meaning-making. This format gives the viewer an opportunity to engage with the relationship between space and time in much the same way as

FIGURE 5.2 This image is interactive on the National Parks Service Klondike Gold Rush Site (https://www.nps.gov/klgo/learn/nature/repeatphotography.htm).

Klett described when discussing the act of actually creating rephotographs. It is this form of rephotography that often leads viewers to describe the presence of ghosts or to talk of a kind of daydreaming or temporal drift taking place as they interact with the images. It is these type of interactive rephotographic images that I wish to discuss in the most detail.

Tracing footsteps

This chapter builds upon my previous work, including *Traces of Lee Miller: Echoes from St Malo*, a rephotographic project that focused on Miller's photos of and experience in St Malo during the Second World War. While not my only rephotographic project it was the most expansive and it saw the largest number of people interacting with it around the world. It was produced as a DVD available for purchase and was also shown around the world including alongside an exhibition of Miller's work at the Victoria and Albert Museum in London, as part of a touring exhibition in New Zealand and Australia, and as part of an exhibition entitled *Curating Knowledge* in England.

Creating rephotographic images requires careful planning and close study of the original materials. Rephotographers must analyse images for the visual cues provided by buildings and other environmental elements. Architectural details and pronounced features of the landscape in an original can be used to help determine the point from which to take the rephotographic image. In studying Miller's material from St Malo, change (and specifically, the destruction and later reconstruction of the city after the War) presented serious challenges. In developing our project, we devised an interface that included access to Miller's original images alongside a range of relevant materials. These included her contact sheets which provided context and her own commentary on the images. Other items of hers including maps and her own handwritten notes were also available to users. The project was navigable via multiple pathways each with its own interface. One was a simple timeline allowing people to explore the rephotographs and related materials chronologically. The other was a map showing the location of each image set. The final pathway was presented as a series of themes that emerged from studying the material as a whole. They included topics such as everyday life in war, the experiences of soldiers, the act of being a journalist and the challenges of actual physical movement. Users could explore the rephotographs along thematic lines.

Each element of the project's interface was driven by what we learned in the process of rephotographing Miller's work. The act of creating the rephotographs forced us to study Miller's images and associated writings closely and to follow in her footsteps as we recreated them. While we expected the process to reveal details about how the world, and specifically the built environment, changed, we were surprised at the other things we learned about the spaces we inhabited. We learned that the framing of the original image, when recreated at the location in which she stood to take it, told us rather a lot about the original photographer. As we retraced Miller's steps through St Malo, pointing our cameras where she once pointed hers, we began to see her stance change. As she experienced the war in St Malo, Miller seemed to hold her camera differently. Through physical positioning a kind of embodied knowledge began to emerge from the rephotographic act.

What we learned about the act of rephotography through the process of staking out and re-shooting each of the images from Miller's time in St Malo was that the movements of the photographer and the framing of the images themselves told a story. Having arrived in St Malo amid active combat, Miller's photographic process was affected by the space around her. As she spent more time in the war-torn town, her images were shot from increasingly lower points of view, suggesting that perhaps she was shooting from a tenser or less visible space. The focal points within the images varied, and contact sheets revealed that the images were shot rapidly and often in a way that suggested a photographer on the move. The images Miller chose to shoot in the spaces between locations, perhaps en route from one to another, suggest her path through the city and the encounters she might have had. These paths, as retraced when creating the rephotographs, show surprising patterns of movement which, when considered alongside her own notes from the period, highlighted Miller's concerns. She often commented on how the details of everyday life became complicated and regularly used her camera to capture them. The life of the GI himself and the notional everyday nature of his existence emerged as an analogous but different concern. She followed people, looking not for large moments of conflict but for the moments of pause, of rest: lingering in an archway to look at the light; resting on the stoop outside of a building; sitting quietly at a desk lost in thought.

Traces of Lee Miller utilizes rephotography to highlight the impermanence of the world we inhabit. A viewer's presence causes the images to merge and fade. By being there, viewers cause the images to retreat into one another. Their very presence interacting with the work creates instability within the frame of the image. The project itself includes a large number of interactive rephotographs of Miller's work as well as hundreds of images of her own notes, contact sheets and other ephemera from that time. When creating the project, we chose to build it around rephotography as the form offered both artists and viewers the opportunity to come to new understandings about that period in Miller's life through the reframing and recontextualization rephotography allows. The project allowed users direct engagement with Miller's work whilst navigating existing and new narratives emerging from it.

Participation and exchange: the rephotographic impulse

There has been much debate about how the digital age is reshaping photography. While it may be simpler to accept more pessimistic views regarding changes in both the material form and reception of photography, digital media also brings with it a distinct potential for expanding photographic practices. The act of creating rephotography could be seen as an example of a kind of expanded photographic practice which, through its very form encompasses acts of both participation and exchange.

In his introduction to *The Art of Participation* exhibition at the San Francisco Museum of Modern Art, Rudolf Frieling highlights the importance of systems of exchange between artist and viewer. While these are relationships we rehearse in various ways across media, his comments bear consideration. Frieling asks whether "new modes of communicating and distributing information change a museum's policies and attitudes" (Frieling 2008). While we are not exploring curatorial practice, his comments remain relevant precisely because he highlights the nature of certain exchanges between creators and audiences that can be seen across rephotographic practice. Frieling suggests that "the process of mutual exchange between visitors, users, artists, curators, and collectors is essential" (Frieling 2008).

It is that process of mutual exchange that we see in the rephotographic image – not least because these images are built on an assumption that viewers are encouraged to interact with them literally or imaginatively, leading to a consideration of the effects of change. In rephotographic practice the original photographer, rephotographer, viewer and other members of the team involved in the project engage in a kind of mutual exchange as they engage with the creation and viewing of images that hold multiple simultaneous moments of the present. That strategy of considering the exchange informed the process of creating *Traces of Lee Miller*.

The roles of the rephotographer and the viewer are separate, and, for each, distinct discoveries can be made. In the case of the rephotographer, the act of retracing the footsteps of the original photographer and of recreating the framing can lead to an understanding of, among other things, the space she occupied. For the viewer encountering a rephotograph, there is much to be learned about what has changed between the two images both in terms of what has gone but also in terms of what is new. In images where people or buildings are present, the viewer may find herself wanting to know more about who or what has disappeared or emerged within the images. The rephotographer chases the ghost of the photographer while the viewer chases those who may or may not have come before.

While rephotography has its roots in the landscape images of geological study, the choice of image and the distance in time between the original and its rephotograph can reveal a range of different types of knowledge. In urban spaces or war-torn regions where much has occurred, details emerge that speak largely to absence, change and decay. In geological contexts, when rephotographing landscapes that change more slowly over time, the information revealed within the image may show small changes which relate to more significant events. In both instances, the possibility of knowledge discovery exists for both the photographer and the viewer as each is forced to contend with the changing spaces in which the image is taken and with the actual change which emerges within the frame between the two images. In his writings about rephotography as encountered by viewers, Kalin proposes a kind of ghostly ontology or hauntology inside of which the multiple times and places represented in the images coexist and are complicated by our own present readings of them. He suggests a kind of becoming or an emergent state in the work: "Rephotography as hauntography produces a different style of engagement with memory that disrupts the linear flow of time by circulating and accumulating many times and places" (Kalin 2013, 177).

These multiple possible readings of rephotographs that engage with memory and can be disruptive present interesting challenges when considering the indexicality of the image. Doane (2007) directly addresses the tendency, in a digital era, to highlight the problematic state with photography. She explores how the wholly digital image, lacking in its chemical processes, is difficult to locate in a specific time or place in the same way as a more traditionally produced photograph could be seen to have come into being in the moment it was taken, therefore linking it to the moment of its creation. Through her work, however, she arrives at a suggestion that in many ways describes the state of rephotography. It effectively privileges the materiality of the photochemically produced image over the ephemerality of the digital image. She suggests that the former offers a promise that, "is that of touching the real" (Doane 2007). In rephotography, however, the act of constructing a rephotograph itself creates an interaction between the notional real and the digital which could be seen in some ways as touching the real.

When deriving meaning from context we are activating a kind of indexicality. Consequently, it becomes useful to consider the rephotographic act as an indexical statement. Rephotography is unique in its insistence that the audience simultaneously read multiple images as one. It could be described as polysemic in the way that rephotographs encourage close readings which invite viewers to engage in multiple simultaneous readings. In her work on rephotography and witness, Miles describes how the past and present converge, describing how "rephotographs challenge historical distanciation" because "the 'then' of past and the 'now' of the present become entangled with one another" (Miles 2016, 65).

Encounters and disappearances

I regularly create opportunities for viewers of my work to share their experiences. As my work has toured the world, people have regularly reported feeling as if they'd seen ghosts, or that interacting with the rephotographs had caused them to "daydream" or "think about what was missing". Rephotographic practice creates the conditions for that kind of temporal drift that often leads users to express feelings of nostalgia. They repeatedly asked questions about what happened to the children playing on the tanks in the middle of a road within a picture from the Second World War. They wondered why once-bustling streets now seemed empty. In an image taken within a hotel that served as a command point, they often spent significant time watching the soldiers appear and disappear within the images.

In observing people interacting with the images, we would regularly see them slowly explore what has changed in each. The amount of time spent on each image was longer than we anticipated in nearly every instance. After interacting with the rephotographs, people seemed eager to talk about their experience and to wonder aloud about disappearances. They often commented on the changes they have seen in their own lives and world in the time roughly represented by the images.

FIGURE 5.3 An image from the project *Traces of Lee Miller: Echoes from St. Malo*.

In the same way that Miles describes an entangled then and now in her writing about rephotography, viewers seem to articulate a space where then, now and the personal become entangled. As Solnit described the way that the place of the rephotographic act imprinted on her, one could argue that the moment of actively interacting with rephotographs had a similar effect on viewers.

In the early twenty-first century, rephotography has become increasingly popular. Once a tool used largely by geologists, photographers and artists, the practice of creating repeat photographs has become more widespread. Through a combination of the rise of web-based sites where people share their images and institutions including newspapers and museums producing rephotographic projects, they have become more visible in a number of areas. Writing about the work of Argentinian photographer, Gustavo Germono, Miles suggests that this trend represents acts of reconciliation. "Rephotography has become a particularly popular trend in recent years, as amateurs and professional alike seek to represent change in their personal lives and environments, and reconcile an aspect of the past and with the present" (Miles 2016, 54). In the Appendix to this chapter, a number of rephotographic projects are described. They represent a range of work spanning the personal, the geographical and the historical. The projects employ a range of practices discussed here and offer the potential for further engagement.

Conclusion

Rephotography provides unique opportunities for discovery to both photographers and audiences. The simultaneous reading of multiple images necessitated by rephotography creates the condition for audience members to construct meaning from a range of possibilities. Current writing about rephotography has tended to focus upon the experiences of viewers as they engage with the images, highlighting the ways in which they interpret the work. Few, however, have explored what can be learned from the act of creating rephotographs.

86 Mary Agnes Krell

Rephotographic practices are by their very nature 'hands on'. In making them we combine the 'then' of the original image with the 'now' of the rephotograph to create new work. By using rephotographic practices, we might gain new insights into the images, their creators and the spaces in which they were taken. As we discovered when creating *Traces of Lee Miller: Echoes from St Malo,* the embodied practice of retracing the steps of the original photographer and of recreating the framing of the original image lead to new insights about the work and its wider context. When shared with audiences, those insights could open even more possibilities when interacting with the work. In creating and interacting with rephotographs, we occupy a space between the moments of the original image and its rephotograph. In it we find disappearances, appearances and change. In that space the distance between then and now is different, and in that difference I believe there are still discoveries to be made.

Appendix

The American Civil War Then and Now

David Levene's project rephotographing American Civil War sites in 2015.
https://www.theguardian.com/artanddesign/ng-interactive/2015/jun/22/american-civil-war-photography-interactive

The Desert Laboratory Repeat Photography Project

Perhaps the largest collection of its kind in the world, these images are created to help researchers understand the effects of changes in climate and land use in deserts across the world.
https://pubs.usgs.gov/fs/2007/3046/fs2007-3046.pdf

Exploring Land Cover Change Through Repeat Photography

A project cosponsored by the University of Alaska and the National Parks Service, it is similar to other repeat photography projects and it also encourages citizen scientists to get involved in documenting landscape changes in the Denali National Park and Preserve.
http://denalirepeatphotos.uaf.edu/

Klondike Gold Rush: Capturing a Century of Natural Resource Change Through Repeat Photography

In this project, repeat photography is used to show change in a national park. The interesting or novel thing about this is that is used the more contemporary central slider allowing people to position the point of distinction between the two images at any point across the image. They can slide the differentiating line between past and present back and forth. These can be seen in the National Parks Service Klondike website.

https://www.nps.gov/klgo/learn/nature/repeatphotography.htm

The Repeat Photography Project

A United States Geological Service project that uses rephotography to showcase forestry-related sequences of images.

http://www.repeatphotography.org/intro/

Thomas P. Peschak

Peschak, a *National Geographic* photographer, uses rephotographic practices to highlight environmental change.

https://www.worldpressphoto.org/collection/photo/2018/environment/thomas-p-peschak

Vincent Zénon Rigaud

Rigaud has produced a wide range of rephotographic images showing past and present, often with a central blurred line between the two.

http://vincentzenon.com/rephotography-repeat-photography

Note

1 For an example of the selective static split technique, see Danielle Cadet's *Huffington Post* article about 'then and now' images of significant moments in American history (Cadet, 2014).

Bibliography

Anon (n.d.) *Capturing a Century of Natural Resource Change Through Repeat Photography* [online]. Available from: https://www.nps.gov/klgo/learn/nature/repeatphotography.htm (Accessed 11 November 2017)

Anon (n.d.) *Looking Into the Past* [online]. Available from: https://www.flickr.com/groups/lookingintothepast/ (Accessed 12 December 2017).

Cadet, D. (2014) *Then And Now Photos Recall The History In Places We See Every Day* [online]. Available from: https://www.huffingtonpost.com/2014/02/21/then-and-now-photos-black-history-month_n_4826565.html (Accessed 4 December 2018)

Doane, M. A. (2007) The Indexical and the Concept of Medium Specificity. *Differences*, 81(1): 128–152.

Engelmann, T. (2007) Who Are Our Fathers? *Journal of American History*, 94(1): 163–171.

Frieling, R. and San Francisco Museum of Modern Art (eds.) (2008) 'Introduction', in *The Art of Participation*. New York: Thames & Hudson.

Kalin, J. (2013) Remembering with Rephotography: A Social Practice for the Inventions of Memories. *Visual Communication Quarterly*, 20(3): 168–179.

Levene, D. (2015) *The American Civil War then and Now* [online]. Available from: http://www.theguardian.com/artanddesign/ng-interactive/2015/jun/22/american-civil-war-photography-interactive (Accessed 8 November 2017)

McLoughlin, K. (2010) Glamour Goes to War: Lee Miller's Writings for British Vogue, 1939–45. *Journal of War and Culture Studies*, 3(3): 335–247.

Miles, M. (2016) Rephotography and the Era of Witness. *Photographies*, 9(1): 51–69.

Rothman, A. and Klett, M. (2011) Views Across Time. *Places Journal*. [Online] Available from: https://placesjournal.org/article/views-across-time/ (Accessed 4 November 2017)

Solnit, R. (2004) Slow Seeing: How a 'Rephotography' Project Taught Me to Go Beyond Looking. *The Utne Reader.* (May/June).

Winter, J. (2001) The Generation of Memory: Reflections on the "Memory Boom" in Contemporary Historical Studies. *Canadian Military History*, 10(3): 57–66.

PART II
User communities

6

PHOTOGRAPHY AGAINST THE ANTHROPOCENE

The anthotype as a call for action

Kristof Vrancken

The online digital photo archive grows daily at an increasing pace. Contributing to the digital visual overload are not only the thousands of selfies or hundreds of sunsets that are uploaded every second, but also the automated images created by security cameras, satellites, and Google Streetview. Almost every moment and street corner is digitally captured, documented, and shared (Shore 2014, 7–11). This digital hyper-documented world raises a question: how can photography still be useful and how can an image maker can bring his or her message across?

Disciplines like photography and film attempt to respond to this digital dominance, and are experiencing a growing suspicion of the digital process. It cannot be denied that the digital revolution is a tremendous step forward in terms of speed, quality, and convenience. It has changed our way of seeing, thinking, and acting enormously, but now that digital technology has become so firmly embedded in our lives it is perhaps time to consider what we have lost.

This sense of loss is acknowledged by a recently established group of artists, photographers, and filmmakers, whom Jonathan Openshaw describes as post-digital artisans (2015, 7–9). They use digital technology, but also fall back on old techniques and examine how they can combine these to arrive at a new and modern version of the profession. They are looking for something that digital technology cannot offer, namely tactility and authenticity: the feel of the material, the experience, the magical moment when craftsmanship and non-reproducibility develop something unique. This is not so much a nostalgic vision of history as a critical stance towards the digital era.

Regarding photography from this perspective made me doubt the evidence of my own predominantly digital work process and prompted me to look for alternatives. I have experienced the transition from analogue to digital personally during my studies. I therefore see myself as part of what Openshaw calls the "connector generation" (2015, 9). This means that, like many other contemporary image makers, I combine different styles, methods, and media: photographing with analogue large and medium format cameras, developing negatives with alternative methods, scanning, experimenting with emulsions, old procedures, 360° recording techniques, video, digital image recordings, and processing. This opens up a range of possibilities, both on a technical and a content level. I feel that an image maker today must almost necessarily examine cross-disciplinary methods in order to revive photography and make it useful again. These experiments strengthen the message of the photographic image to communicate in an innovative visual way that prevents the image from sinking away into the everyday, fleeting, visual digital mush (Shore 2014).

Dark ecology

In an online world in which truths and untruths are intertwined, in which main affairs and additional ones cannot be separated and in which the fight for attention usually is more important than the message, it is difficult to reach a mass audience (Rushkoff 2015). There are, however, stories that require our supreme attention. One story that urgently needs to be told and retold, is that of the human era, or how humanity became a geological force. How we increasingly pressured the earth and nature and how we therefore urgently need to redefine our thinking and acting to keep the planet liveable for future generations (Bonneuil and Frezoz 2017).

In contemporary academic literature this story is usually referred to as the Anthropocene or the Capitalocene. The discussion about which terminology is most suitable, and what the starting point of this era would be, is ongoing (Haraway 2016; Moore 2016). Apart from this theoretical discourse we should however be afraid of the consequences and weirdness of climate change, writes Timothy Morton in his book *Dark Ecology* (2016). We should be standing on the barricades to call for structural action to limit the unforeseen effects of the

FIGURE 6.1 *Transit*, slag heaps of Winterslag, Genk, 2017. (Kristof Vrancken)

destruction of ecosystems, mass extension, and growing social inequality. All too often, however, we click away and continue to lead our lives as if nothing is going on and the cited problems will resolve themselves. Proponents of the *Degrowth* movement have been urging for some time now for a gradual transition toward a reduced or at least smarter consumption, to the construction of a society that is alert to the imbalance between human and planet and which is not solely directed to short-sighted economic growth margins and power relations (D'Alissa, Demaria and Kallis 2014).

If we don't act now, the ecological reality will soon overtake us. We are at a point of no return for the survival of our species and life on earth. Politicians, scientists, philosophers, historians, and artists – and in fact everyone – should dare to bet on a new narrative and vision. We too quickly lose sight of the urgent current problems, the complexity of big stories and their mutual cohesion because we constantly want to be entertained by easily to understand digital distraction, determined by our likes (Rushkoff 2015). We need action and awareness in addition to academic discourse. According to Bonneuil and Frezoz, this means freeing ourselves from repressive institutions and from alienating dominations and imaginaries. (2017, 288–291). T. J. Demos asks how we can convert into image and narrative the disasters that are slow moving and long in the making, disasters that are attritional and of indifferent interest to the sensational driven technologies of our image-world (2017, 13). One of his conclusions is that more activism, not neutrality, is needed: "We need a revolt against brutality against the violence of climate change" (2017, 81). There is an urgent need for a global call to action.

Call for action

My artistic PhD research, carried out at the LUCA School of Arts, responds to this call in an unconventional, visual manner. To shape the vital transformation to a sustainable world we need new streams of thought and design processes, as well as a new visual language in order to understand, document, and spread them. My research is based on the methodology of Sustainist Design. This is a recent movement within social critical design that argues in favour of sustainable design processes. In *Sustainist Design Guide* (2013) Schwarz and Krabbendam define four pillars for sustainable design. The first is *Sharing* – exchanging knowledge, materials and tools, both online and offline, instead of hiding them, leads to greater efficiency in development and production. The second pillar, *Localism*, stands for returning to and upgrading the local. Our focus should be locally rooted but globally connected. The third pillar, *Connectedness*, exceeds the principle of sharing in development and manufacturing. It underlines the importance of offline and online interpersonal contact. This pillar also refers to the connection with nature and argues in favour of restoring our bond with it. Finally, *Proportionality* stands for bringing production into balance and introduces custom designing to suit the social and local context. Proportionality also incorporates the aspect of time. In a world in which everything must go faster it is a relief to build in slowness. By daring to stand still there is more time to discover and to reflect. Sustainist design no longer designs for a society; it starts a new movement from within.

Central to my research are the following questions: What effect does applying sustainist design principles in the photographic process have on visual language, method, material use, and photographic techniques? This interdisciplinary approach creates a new hybrid method of visual storytelling in which not only the image is important but also the process, context, and social interaction. In addition to the relationship with design, my research questions photography as a discipline. By analysing and opening up the entire photographic process new lines of reasoning about forming and experiencing images arise. The anthotype image is a key tool in this process.

The anthotype process

Regarding photography from the perspective of postdigital artisans, dark ecology and sustainist design prompted me to return to the roots of the discipline, which are located in the middle of the nineteenth century, the same period as one of the turning points of the Anthropocene.

The anthotype is a traditionally analogue process. This photographic technique was first described by the prominent scientist, mathematician, botanist, and experimental photographer Sir John Herschel (1792–1871) in 1842. Herschel's significance in the development of photography is incalculable. He invented a way to fix photographic images using hyposulfite, which is still used today. He also discovered the cyanotype process, in which the print eventually becomes cyanogen, and worked closely together with the well-known pioneer Henry Fox Talbot (1800–1877) on the first negative-positive process (Batchen 2016; James 2016). The anthotype process is an organic contact printing process that affects the discolouration of natural pigments exposed to ultraviolet light (James 2016). An anthotype is created by applying a photosensitive emulsion made from the colour pigments of plants to a carrier and exposing it to sunlight for several days or weeks. Ultraviolet rays break down the colours, slowly creating an image. The organic emulsion undergoes a chemical change or photo-destruction during this process and the pigments become lighter. Not only does each plant respond differently to light, the harvesting point, freshness, pollution, and additives are also parameters that affect the discolouration.

In order to extract the colour of plants the organic fibres must first be crushed. Adding alcohol is sometimes necessary to help plants to give off their chlorophyll pigments to the liquid. The emulsion can be applied to all kinds of surfaces. Every surface will change the look of the print and emphasizes the handmade characteristics of the process. When the coating is dry the carrier is ready to be illuminated. Most photographic techniques require a negative that gives a positive image after illumination, as was the case with Herschel's and Talbot's photographic experiments. The anthotype process, however, requires a positive. It can either be an analogue positive (glass plate or film) or a digital one (transparent). To illuminate the image it must be placed in sunlight. Ultraviolet rays break down the colours, slowly creating an image by selective destruction of the colour pigments. The unexposed parts of the image will retain their colour, while the exposed parts will slowly lose their colour and intensity.

The plurality of the anthotype printing process proved to be endless. Each plant responds differently to light, and the harvesting point, freshness and additives also affect the discolouration.[1] Light sensitivity can vary greatly from plant to plant, even within the same species. For example, my experiments with a poppy emulsion showed some results after only a few days, while the exposure time of blackberries took a few weeks or even months. I did some tests by using an anthotype sheet in a large format camera to expose it directly in the camera, but after an exposure time of more than two months in full summer there was no visible result. For the time being, the possibilities of the anthotype process seem limited to contact printing.

Since pigments of vegetable origin are used the landscape forms an essential factor in creating an anthotype. Not only does it provide the setting for the photographic image, it also provides the ingredients for the photographic emulsion that is used to print the image. Even the *an sich* invisible aspect of the photographed landscape, the soil composition, plays an important role because it partially determines which plants grow in that specific spot and therefore which pigments can be used for the photographic emulsion. Moreover, a combination of the soil composition and external environmental conditions, such as the quantity of sunlight that the plant receives and the air-soil contamination, has an impact on the chemical composition and, consequently, on the progress of photosynthesis (Ahmad 2002).

I experienced first hand how much our society is accustomed to speed when it comes to obtaining results during my initial experiments with the anthotype technique. It required a *lot* of patience and a completely different approach than that of a solely digital recording. Collection of materials, preparation of emulsion, coating of paper and development of prints turned out to be time-consuming activities.

FIGURE 6.2 Harvesting ingredients on a contaminated area, 2016. (Kristof Vrancken)

FIGURE 6.3 Cameraless photograph: dune pansy, abandoned Ford grounds, 2016. (Kristof Vrancken)

I literally had to follow the pace of the seasons and had to adapt my agenda to the harvest times of the different plants. The entire process also came to a halt in winter due to a lack of materials and sunlight. It made me realize how little we actually know about these plants and how our lives have become disconnected from nature (Rushkoff 2015, 66–129).[2]

The anthotype print is saturated with time, much more so than the fleeting digital image. Not only does it require time to make the photographic emulsion, but the time that the print must be exposed to sunlight depends upon the light sensitivity of the species. Once the anthotype print is formed the time aspect continues to play a role. Although each anthotype is unique – only one print can be made – it is at the same time ever-changing.[3] If the print is exposed to light it will continue to fade. This has interesting consequences. Because the anthotype image fades over time it does not necessarily have to be seen as a static image with a limited shelf-life. Its constant degradation can also be interpreted as a slowly moving image. The contours of what was photographed are not permanent, and after some time has passed the original image also transforms. Recent tests I performed in a simulated lab environment as part of the exhibition *The Artist's Studio* in Z33 – House of Contemporary Art, have shown that an anthotype print with an emulsion of elderberry and alcohol needs more than 130,000 lux hours to form a well-exposed image.[4] Further tests will be undertaken in my studio to investigate the relationship between the appearance and reappearance of an anthotype image. When placed on a timeline, the inherent gradient of the print adds a valuable and meaningful element to the anthotype image: entropy as an essential part of the photographic work.

Due to the temporary aspect of the image, the imperfections, the amount of work involved and the long exposure times, this procedure never became popular.[5] Yet, for me, this transitoriness is precisely where the poetry and power of the image lie. It is precisely the aforementioned characteristics that make the anthotype

FIGURE 6.4 The appearance of an anthotype print – lab test, 2018. (Kristof Vrancken)

process relevant today, as a counter reaction to the sterile digital image. It forms a critical counterbalance against the current obsession with the eternally enduring or an unnatural denial of the ephemeral (Rushkoff 2015, 159).

The vulnerable side of the anthotype image is also closely connected to its tactility. Contrary to the fleeting digital image, which can often only be seen on a computer screen and is not always printed (Openshaw 2015, 4–9), an anthotype cannot exist without a physical medium. This essential physical existence, combined with the fact that the print was made with an emulsion of vegetable origin, emphasizes how much this type of image is linked to the tangible world and, above all, to nature. Its tactility renews attention on experiencing photographic images. While digital photos only serve the eye, an anthotype also appeals to one's sense of smell (the image smells like the plants that were used) and sense of touch (small plant fibres are often visible and perceptible). Even one's sense of taste can be involved when the emulsion is drunk by the viewers.[6]

The anthotype print has a final and very special property related to this connection with nature. By actually using plants originating from the depicted landscape to create the photographs, an interesting relation is established between the physical landscape and its photographic representation. The anthotype print not only *represents* the landscape, it *is* the landscape since it is made from the flora that grows there. The multisensory organic and tactile anthotype image that carries the landscape within itself is a response against today's Anthropocene visualizations which are mainly dominated by scientifically framed imagery, digital high resolution images and data visualization (Demos 2017, 13).

The time aspect, the entropy, the tactility, the connection with nature, the importance of the experience and the ability to incorporate what was photographed in the print, enable the anthotype to open up a number of layers of meaning that remain irrevocably closed to digital photography. Because plants are increasingly affected by environmental stresses, especially by the devastating consequences of pollution and global climate change (Ahmad, et al., 2002), the anthotype, in which plants are used in the preparation of a photographic emulsion, acts as a suitable tool

98 Kristof Vrancken

to illustrate the narrative of the Anthropocene. The technique is also a means of raising awareness of it and of reacting against it. One of the oldest photographic methods becomes paradoxically an appropriate instrument for approaching a contemporary topic and to relive history. I would like to illustrate this on the basis of two artistic projects: *Transit* and *MijnKOOL*.

Transit

The project *Transit* started in 2016. It resulted from a collaboration with the C-Mine Cultural Centre, the Emile Van Doren Museum, and the City of Genk, Belgium.[7] The main focus of this photographic series is the history and evolution of the landscape of the former mining city Genk in Belgium.

The waves of change in Genk, currently the third largest industrial city in Flanders, can be unmistakably linked to the pre-industrial era and the effects of two Industrial Revolutions. The history of Genk illustrates on a micro-scale the development of the Anthropocene. The area around the city changed drastically, from a wide-open landscape loved by late nineteenth-century painters such as the Brussels artist Emile Van Doren (1865–1949), to an industrial city. Van Doren fell in love with the idyllic landscape, marked by infertile sandy areas, vast heathlands with ponds, and marshland (Figure 6.6). He gathered a group of artists around him who painted the landscape extensively in open air. In imitation of the Barbizon school of painters in France, the Genk school of painters became one of the most important artist colonies in Belgium around 1900. In 1901 André Dumont (1847–1920) found coal in the Genk area, and large-scale coal exploitation started in 1917 (Reulens 2015).

Emile Van Doren was sad to see the industrialization of Genk and in his paintings hung on to the romantic landscapes, in which he completely ignored the emerging mining industry. In some panoramic views, he eliminated mine shafts and dumping grounds to not disturb the romantic quality (Reulens 2015). Armand Maclot (1877–1959), on the other hand, took a more activist stance and sketched an ominous view of a mining landscape suffocated by smoke plumes, with the ironic title *Villégiature* or refuge (Reulens 2010).

The artists based around Genk, and especially Van Doren and Maclot, played an important political role in the fight for nature conservation. They, for instance, opposed for a long time the construction of roads and industry in their beloved area around the steel ponds. In the beginning of the twentieth century there were, thus, already active counter voices that felt the necessity to protect ecosystems and nature. Unfortunately, economic interests prevailed. Because of the flourishing coal industry – at its peak there were as many as three coal mines in Genk – pollution increased as well. In the 1960s and 1980s coal exploitation was no longer a profitable industry and the mines closed down one by one, leaving their marks on a radically transformed landscape (Reulens 2010).

The city proceeded to attract other industries. For example, car manufacturer Ford – historically seen as the founder of standardized mass production with

FIGURE 6.5 *Transit*, slag heap of Zwartberg (black-mountain), Genk, 2017. (Kristof Vrancken)

FIGURE 6.6 *Transit*, slag heap of Waterschei and parking lot, Genk, 2017. (Kristof Vrancken)

FIGURE 6.7 *Transit*, Waterschei, Genk, 2017. (Kristof Vrancken)

assembly lines (Bonneuil and Frezoz 2017, 229) – established a factory in 1964 that was shut down permanently in 2015. At its peak the factory made almost half a million cars each year and employed over 14,000 people (Kloostermans 2014). After the closure, the company sold its grounds to Genk for a symbolic one euro. The costs involved with cleaning up the polluted site, however, were estimated at 12 million euros (Figure 6.10) (Lenaerts 2015). The establishment of metal-processing companies and other heavy industrial branches brought economic development to Genk but it also had severe ecological consequences. A study into internal exposure to pollutants and their early effects in 14- to 15-year-olds in the period 2007 to 2011 showed that young people from South Genk, where the industrial estates are located, had higher concentrations of heavy metals and polycyclic aromatic hydrocarbons in their bodies. Higher levels of DNA damage and hormonal disturbances, which increase the chance of developing cancers, were also detected (Vrijens et al. 2014).

The city of Genk has worked hard to reduce pollution but a lot of work still needs to be done. The city is currently making efforts in nature conservation. Although the population of Genk grew to 66,000 inhabitants it is still one of the greenest regional cities in Belgium. Heathlands are being maintained, burned, and levelled to restore a piece of the authentic – albeit cultivated by human hands – landscape. The endless and undisturbed horizon that appealed so strongly to Emile Van Doren has, however, been lost for good. Chimneys, steel constructions, apartment buildings or windmills always come into view.

For *Transit* I made a series of artistic work portraying Genk's landscape using the anthotype method, looking in 2017 for the muse found there by Emile Van Doren. The title *Transit* refers both to the many evolutions – from nature to industry – that the landscape of the mining town of Genk has undergone since the introduction of the first Industrial Revolution, as well as to the type of van which was manufactured in the Genk Ford factory between 1960 and 2000.

Each image is about how human action cultivates the landscape and how this landscape yields to it or resists (Notteboom 2013). The Genk landscape changes so fast that it almost sits in a continuous transition. It happened more than once during the preparation of this project that a location that was to be photographed had disappeared on arrival. Geographically and via Google Earth it would still exist, but it had in reality been transformed into an unrecognizable, churned, almost surreal place. Often these areas are waiting for a new destination in the contemporary economic reality. Sand is supplemented and taken away.[8] Roads are constructed to be deserted. Woods are planted while others are wiped away. Buildings are constructed on the dumping grounds of the mines. The landscape is continually managed while the landscapes that for the moment are unmanaged are most attractive to me.

I used plants from the area that I photographed to display Genk's biodiversity and soil quality to create my anthotypes. In doing so, the landscape is not only captured on camera but it is also literally incorporated and preserved in the print. In this way, the print, in fact, becomes a physical piece of Genk. The choice of a plant to make an emulsion is, thus, not based on some coincidence, but declares something about the history and the current state of the photographed location.

The series *Transit* comprises 11 anthotype prints made from different kinds of plants that grew at the photographed locations. A greenhouse was built next to the Emile Van Doren Museum to be able to expose the different images and to enable the prints to be exposed all summer long despite the changeable rainy Belgian weather. The month of August 2017 had relatively few sunny hours, which caused problems for the print production. The prints based on poppy were exposed in about two weeks, while the elderberry emulsion needed an exposure time of three to four weeks, just like the emulsion based on marigold. As earlier tests had already shown, the emulsion based on blackberry was the least light-sensitive. Some prints needed an exposure time of at least 8 weeks.

Plants are not only capable of generating an image. Research proves that some plants are excellent receptors and collectors of heavy metals and fine dust, and that anomalies in growth and flowering of certain plants in a certain area could be an indicator of pollution. Therefore, they are not only extremely suitable as research tools in exact sciences, but also in my work. Because these plants collect these toxic substances in their systems, these also end up in the anthotype prints.[9] The traces of pollution are literally encapsulated in the print. This causes the anthotypes of the polluted landscapes of Genk to have a disturbing undertone, despite their romantic appearance.

The Anthropocene is a difficult and abstract concept. It could easily remain invisible to the general public until it is too late to act. The consequences of a global ecological catastrophe happen too slowly for our human perception even though they become more and more apparent. The delay between cause and effect of our human activity on this earth is too large in order for us to see the big picture. Morton therefore sees the Anthropocene as a hyper-object, something that

FIGURE 6.8 *Transit*, Genk-South, 2017. (Kristof Vrancken)

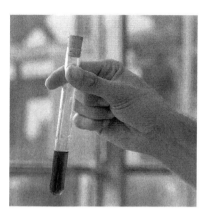

FIGURE 6.9 The potable and light-sensitive Anthropocene elixir. (Kristof Vrancken)

stretches out endlessly in time and space, making it impossible to fathom (2016, 47–49). I think that we need to make the problematic of the Anthropocene more apparent and personal in order to bring the message across.

In an attempt to make the Anthropocene more tangible, I created for the *Transit* series, in addition to the photographic prints based on the anthotype process, a drinkable photographic emulsion based on the plants in the documented polluted areas. For the creation of this emulsion I followed historical liquor and anthotype recipes by Sir John Herschel. With this knowledge in hands I created a somewhat sinister, organic, photographic emulsion that was both light-sensitive and nice, both sweet and wry.

The sanguineous elixir is made on the basis of sloe berries and elderberries, harvested on the seriously polluted sites of the closed Ford factory at Genk. The berries can contain increased levels of nickel, chrome, manganese, and zinc, but the potion itself tastes deliciously sweet as these metal parts are as good as odourless and tasteless. They don't impact on the taste and thus can enter unnoticed into our system on a daily basis. We are not conscious of the fact that we daily absorb harmful substances by driving in heavy traffic in the morning, living in busy cities alongside industrial areas and consuming food polluted by pesticides and antibiotics. But consciously drinking this toxic emulsion makes you an active bearer of the Anthropocene. The elixir reveals things we don't see, and possibly also don't want to see. Drinking this 'unheimliches' elixir thus almost becomes a political act.

I presented the Anthropocene elixir and the photographic images for the first time during the *A–Z Night #5: Dark Ecology, Artistic Encounters in the Anthropocene* organized by Z33 House of Contemporary Art.[10] I toasted to the Anthropocene and to my surprise most of the audience emptied their glass. There were only a few that resolutely refused to do so, but the hesitation that was palpable in the room before and after the toast was a sign that the elixir definitely caused an intrinsic unrest and that the Anthropocene is hard to digest. According to Benjamin Verdonck, the most constructive thing to do as an artist is to take the

FIGURE 6.10 *Transit*, abandoned Ford grounds, Genk, 2017. (Kristof Vrancken)

darkest elements from reality, transform them into an object or a performance and enter into a dialogue with an audience.

The sweet taste of the dark elixir mirrors the call to give in to the lure of laziness, doing nothing, and continuing our lifestyles and the current consumption model. Luxury and abundance after all taste sweet. The pollution is a free addition. *Degrowth*, although essential to tackle the consequences of climate change and pollution, tastes rather wry. Or as Morton puts it eloquently: "Dark Ecology is ecological awareness, dark depressing. Yet ecological awareness is also dark-uncanny, and strangely it is dark-sweet" (2016, 18). Ironically, Morton refused to drink this dark emulsion when I offered it to him during a brief encounter in Nijmegen on the occasion of his talk about his book *Being Ecologic* in January 2018.

Translating the different layers of meaning of an image – from an impression of a forever-lost pristine landscape to pressured ecosystems due to industrial superiority – would not have been possible with a digital picture. The literal and figurative multi-layeredness could only be achieved through the anthotype process. This shows how one of the oldest photographical techniques is, ironically, better able to visually communicate the urgency of a contemporary topic than more recent ones.

MijnKOOL (myCABBAGE)

Next to the artistic series *Transit*, there is a second track in this Genk project that involves a partnership with design studio SOCIAL MATTER.[11] In order to stimulate awareness about the Anthropocene on a larger scale we organized several workshops with local Genk residents. In these workshops, we shared the anthotype process and the opportunity to relive the wonder of this historical photographic process. The main ingredient for the photographic emulsion was in this case red cabbage. Thanks to its anthocyanins, red cabbage could function as a bio-indicator and proved to be an interesting ingredient in the anthotype process (Chalker-Scott

1999; Szczygłowska et al. 2011). If red cabbage is grown in pure soil it will turn out more blue, and in alkaline environments it will turn more green and yellow. If the red cabbage is grown in acidic soil, it will yield a red colour. An erratic pH value can point to contamination. I carried out two experiments to test this method in May 2016 and 2017. A dozen cabbage plants were planted in contaminated and uncontaminated areas in Genk, and in pure potting soil (Figure 6.14). Four months later the cabbage pants were harvested and documented. Although some plants had trouble surviving due to the city's poor subsoils, shortage of rain and damage from caterpillars and slugs, there was enough basic material to carry out pH tests. For this test I added three grams from each red cabbage plant to 50ml distilled water and brought it to the boil in order to dissolve the anthocyanins in water. This resulted in clearly perceptible colour differences in the final liquids, varying from light to dark blue and from light to dark purple. The diverse colours in the test tubes show that red cabbage really does react to the pH value and soil quality of the subsoil that it grows in. At the same time, my test illustrates and confirms that this method is suitable for making a visual map of the diverse, historically formed soil compositions of an area.[12]

Every participant in the *mijnKOOL* workshop received a red cabbage plant grown in pure compost and was asked to plant it in his or her garden. After a few months the group came together again and brought their harvest. The participants used their plant to create an emulsion that would serve as a basis for their anthotype portrait and their print of the planting area. Everyone had to follow the protocol as strictly as possible in order for the experiment to succeed. Each participant made an emulsion by weighing 100g of leaves of their red cabbage and boiling it for 30 minutes in 400ml of distilled water. In order not to affect the test results alcohol was not added to the photographic emulsion. Depending on the acidity of the soil in which the cabbage was grown the final prints clearly showed different colours, bringing forth a participative sample card of the Genk surface – and thanks to the anthotype process – of the subsurface as well.

A map of the City of Genk was created to illustrate this. It was made with organic ink from local raw materials and drawn by illustrator Jenny Stieglitz. The map consists of two layers. On the lower layer the soil samples of the different locations are resting in small petri dishes which allow you to discover the diverse soil structures of Genk. On the higher layer you can find the different emulsions made by the participants that are clearly different in colour. By comparing the colour of the anthotypes with those of the emulsions you can find the growing place of the cabbage on the map.

In the context of *MijnKOOL* I also experimented with red cabbage to develop photographic films. During one of the workshops I made portraits of the participants using my analogue large format camera. I used a Sinar F2 with a Rodenstock 150mm lens with a maximum aperture of f/5.6 and a copal shutter. This camera was made by Swiss camera manufacturer Sinar in 1986 and was as an advanced modular lightweight professional large format field view camera. I usually use this camera to photograph landscapes. The slow, fully manual method of handling the camera results in a more thought-out image strategy, but photographing a portrait with a large format camera is an experience in itself. Not only for the photographer but also for the person portrayed. The workshop turned out into a historical reenactment instead of a standard portrait shoot. The participants reacted with amazement about the use of this old analogue camera. Young children looked with disbelief at the large strange device where the image on the frosted glass is swapped left-right and displayed the other way around. The fact that the image was not immediately visible also caused astonishment among the youngest participants. Due to the large film format of 4×5 inches, there is little depth of field and manual focusing therefore needs to be done with extreme precision. It takes five to ten minutes to fully prepare the camera for recording, which is an eternity in today's digital age. Unlike photographing a landscape, it is not only the photographer who has to concentrate on large-format shooting, but also the person portrayed who needs the necessary concentration not to move. A small movement to the back and the head disappears from the sharpness plane. Due to the slowness of the entire photographic process, both the photographer and the person portrayed become more aware of every small gesture and the tension is built up. The 'click' of the Sinar Copal shutter is loud and fills the entire space with one clear stroke. The negative is exposed, the photographer and the person portrayed breathe again. "Can I have a look at the picture?" one man asked.

The photographic large format film was not developed using the standard chemical products of industrial manufacturers, but with a self-made developer of red cabbage juice, vitamin C and soda. To develop my 4×5 inch Ilford FP4 film I used 32g of water-free soda, 10g of pure vitamin C and the juice of 400g of red cabbage in a solution of 600ml distilled water. I got the best results with a developing time of 15 minutes at a temperature of 23°C. This process – related to the caffenol process – considerably reduces the quantity of harmful chemicals normally used during the photographic development (Williams 1995; Bendandi 2015).[13] Not only can red cabbage develop negative film, but it also causes a shift of contrasts which makes the image harsher and less even than a traditionally developed image. The negatives developed with red cabbage juice formed the basis of the anthotype prints that the participants of the workshops made with the emulsion of their home-grown red cabbage

FIGURE 6.11   Portraits *mijnKOOL*, Genk, 2017. (Kristof Vrancken)

FIGURE 6.12 *Transit*, Winterslag, Genk, 2017. (Kristof Vrancken)

MijnKOOL, the title of this participatory project, alludes, on the one hand, to the red cabbage plants that participants grew in their own gardens. On the other hand, it alludes to Genk's industrial past via the words 'mine' and 'coal'. By adopting the anthotype process as a participatory research method, we intended to bring people together through open communication and to raise awareness about the unbalanced human-nature ratio. The anthotype technique was effectively used as a call for action as inhabitants of Genk were informed via the workshops about the potential uses of wild plants, soil quality and local problems with pollution. They were directly addressed because they and their habitat were implicated and united in the photographic process and the final image. This participatory method provided a strong local context as well as a wider reach. The project not only connected the usual photography and culture enthusiasts, but also engaged a wider network of participants. Combining knowledge and strategies from exact sciences, social design, history, and photography in a transdisciplinary project thus created new possibilities to inform and activate people. At the same time it enabled them to relive and experience the magic and possibilities of historical photographic processes.

Conclusion

My research shows that it is important to explore the possibilities of old techniques in the light of contemporary and future technologies. Media archaeology can thus play a crucial role in developing ways to visually capture the world and society in a meaningful way and to also understand them better. In my search to make the problem of the Anthropocene visible and contribute to a greater consciousness of the problematic state of our planet, I deliberately chose to use the nineteenth-century anthotype technique in artistic photography as a participatory research method. The application of this method is not purely an aesthetic choice. The organic anthotype technique has special characteristics that are in danger of being lost in the digital era, such as incorporating time, entropy, and tactility, the connection with the landscape and nature, and the importance of sensory perception. As the photographic emulsions for the anthotypes are plant-based they not only form a good indicator of the state of the increasingly disturbed and polluted landscape in which the plants have to survive, but they also incorporate this information as critique in the photographic image. The ability to embed what was photographed in the print itself is almost impossible in digital photography. One of the oldest photographic techniques thus becomes one of the most appropriate tools to visually and multisensorial translate the urgency of a current topic and to call for much needed action. At the same time it also allows us to relive photographic history through experimentation and, in combination with today's digital technologies, opens up new possibilities and avenues of thought in imaging.[14]

Notes

1 Steve J. Appleyard (2012) Experimenting with Cameraless Photography using Turmeric and Borax: an Introduction to Photophysics. *Physics Education*, 47(4): 423–428.

2 "Most of us today live in cities and spent most of our time indoors, where the cues that used to alert us to the changing days, moon phases and seasons are largely hidden from us". About our contemporary digital culture and alienation from the seasons (Rushkoff 2015, 107).

3 This uniqueness of an anthotype image is reminiscent of Walter Benjamin's aura of a not mechanically reproduced work of art: "This unique existence of the work of art determined the history to which it was subject throughout the time of its existence. This includes the changes which it may have suffered in physical condition over the years [. . .]" (Wells 2003, 43).

4 See my project Latency Hasselt 2018, http://kristof-vrancken.com/project/latency

5 Over the last few years, there has been increased interest in the technique thanks to the remarkable qualities of the anthotype. The work of Christine Elfman and Binh Danh illustrate this evolution (James 2016, 43, 50, 56–59).

6 See my project Manufactuur Hasselt in 2016, http://www.sustainistgaze.com/tag/hasselt/.

7 See http://www.c-minecultuurcentrum.be/; http://www.emilevandorenmuseum.be/.

8 For instance, I found seashells in a vast sand plain in South Genk at more than 200km distance from the coast. This infertile layer of sand caused the withering of many of the trees.

9 At the same time, some plants can also be used to clean grounds. This method is called phytoremediation. The research group of Environmental Biology of the University of Hasselt had poplars planted on the Ford grounds in Genk that can partially break down the present oil pollution (Barac et al. 2009).

10 See: http://www.a-znights.be/event/a-z-night-5/

11 SOCIAL MATTER, founded by Giacomo Piovan, is looking for ways to return abandoned and polluted industrial areas to the local population by means of social and participating design. See http://www.socialmatter.eu/.

12 Further scientific research, however, will have to show the level of concentrations of heavy metals that nest within the photographic emulsions made from the red cabbages and in the final anthotype image and/or whether there are actual colour differences between the emulsions of polluted and non-polluted plant species. With the results, we could make a visual mapping of the possible pollution and quality of the soil. After completing this Genk project I would like to apply this methodology to other cities and polluted sites.

13 This open-source developing process was developed in 1995 by Scott A. Williams at the Rochester Institute of Technology. Caffenol is a developer made of coffee, vitamin C and soda. See <https://people.rit.edu/andpph/text-coffee.html> [Accessed 11 November 2017].

14 I would like to thank Jan Boelen, Dr Leen Engelen, Dr Leen Kelchtermans, Prof Dr Jean Manca, Dr Dirk Reynders, Dr Veerle Van der Sluys and Prof Dr Roland Valcke for their valuable remarks and Edith Doove for the translation.

Bibliography

Ahmad, P. (ed.) (2002) *Environmental Adaptations and Stress Tolerance of Plants in the Era of Climate Change.* New York: Springer.

Barac, T., Weysens, N., Oeyen, L., et al. (2009) Field Note: Hydraulic Containment of a Btex Plume using Poplar Trees. *International Journal of Phytoremediation*, 11(5): 416–424.

Batchen, G. (2016) *Emanations. The Art of the Cameraless Photograph.* Munich, London and New York: DelMonico Books-Prestel.

Bendandi, L. (ed.) (2015) *Experimental Photography. A Handbook of Techniques.* London: Thames and Hudson.

Bonneuil, C. and Fressoz, J.B. (2017) *The Shock of the Anthropocene: The Earth, History and Us,* Translated from French by David Fernbach. London: Verso.

Chalker-Scott, L. (1999) Environmental Significance of Anthocyanins in Plant Stress Responses. *Photochemistry and Photobiology*, 70(1): 1–9.

D'Alissa, G., Demaria, F. and Kallis, G. (2014) *Degrowth: A Vocabulary for a New Era.* London and New York: Routledge.

Demos, T.J. (2017) *Against the Anthropocene: Visual Culture and Environment today.* Berlin: Sternberg Press.

Hallmann, C.A., Sorg, M., Jongejans, E., et al. (2017) More than 75 Percent Decline over 27 Years in Total Flying Insect Biomass in Protected Areas. *Plos One*, [e-journal] 12(10). https://doi.org/10.1371/journal.pone.0185809.

Haraway, D.J. (2016) *Staying with the Trouble: Making Kin in the Chthulucene.* Durham: Duke University Press.

Herschel, J. (1842) On the Action of the Rays of the Solar Spectrum on Vegetable Colours, and on Some New Photographic Processes. *Philosophical Transactions of the Royal Society of London*, 132: 181–214.

James, C. (2016) *The Book of Alternative Photographic Processes.* Boston: Cengage learning.

Kloostermans, G. (2014) Einde van een tijdperk. *Het Belang van Limburg*, 9 Nov., p. 4.

Lenaerts, X. (2015) Sanering vervuild Fordterrein kost Vlaamse regering 12 miljoen euro. *Het Laatste Nieuws*, 15 Oct., p. 17.

Moore, J.W. (2016) *Anthroposcene or Capitalocene? Nature, History and the Crisis of Capitalism.* Oakland, CA: PM Press/Karios.

Morton, T. (2016) *Dark Ecology. For a Logic of Future Coexistence.* New York: Columbia University Press.

Notteboom, B. (2013) Drie keer de mijnstreek. In: K. Reulens and D. Lauwaert, ed. 2013. *Citygraphy #03*. Brussel: Eferma. 31–45.

Openshaw, J. (2015) *Post Digital Artisans, Craftmanship with a New Aesthetic in Fashion, Art, Design and Architecture.* Amsterdam: Frame Publishers.

Reinold, G., Overs, M., Roberts, E., et al. (2012) *The Caffenol Cookbook and Bible.* [pdf] Baden-Württemberg: Community Spirit Publications. Available at: <http://caffenol-cookbook.com> [Accessed 11 November 2017].

Reulens, K. (2010) *Genk door schildersogen. Landschapsschilders in de Limburgse Kempen, 1850–1950.* Leuven: Davidsfonds.

Reulens, K. and Lauwaert, D. (eds) (2013) *Citygraphy #03*. Brussels: Eferma.

Reulens, K. (2015) *Emile Van Doren (1865–1949). Biografie van een schilder en zijn landschap*. Oostkamp: Stichting Kunstboek.

Ripple, W.J., Wolf, C., Newsome, T.M., et al. (2017) World Scientists' Warning to Humanity: A Second Notice. *BioScience*, [e-journal], bix125. https://doi.org/10.1093/biosci/bix125.

Rushkoff, D. (2014) *Present Shock: When Everything Happens Now*. New York: Current.

Schwarz, M. and Krabbendam, D. (2013) *Sustainist Design Guide: How Sharing, Localism, Connectedness and Proportionality are creating a New Agenda for Social Design*. Amsterdam: BIS Publishers.

Shore, R. (2014) *Post Photography. The artist with a Camera*. London: Laurence King Publishing Ltd.

Szczygłowska, M., Piekarska, A., Konieczka, P., et al. (2011) Use of Brassica Plants in the Phytoremediation and Biofumigation Processes. *International Journal of Molecular Sciences*, 12(11): 7760–7771.

Vanhellemont, M., Verheyen, K., Staelens, J. and Hermy, M. (2009) Factors Affecting Radial Growth of the Invasive Prunus Serotina in Pine Plantations in Flanders. *European Journal of Forest Research*, 129: 367–375.

Vrijens, J., Leermakers, M., Stalpaert, M., et al. (2014) Trace Metal Concentrations Measured in Blood and Urine of Adolescents in Flanders, Belgium: Reference Population and Case Studies Genk-Zuid and Menen. *International Journal of Hygiene and Environmental Health*, 4(5): 515–527.

Wells, L. (2003) *The Photography Reader*. London and New York: Routledge.

Williams, S. (1995) *A Use for that Last Cup of Coffee: Film and Paper Development*. [online] Imaging and Photographic Technology Department, School of Photographic Arts and Sciences, Rochester Institute of Technology. Available at: <https://people.rit.edu/andpph/text-coffee.html> [Accessed 11 November 2017].

7
ON THE PERFORMANCE OF PLAYBACK FOR DEAD MEDIA DEVICES

Matthew Hockenberry and Jason LaRiviere

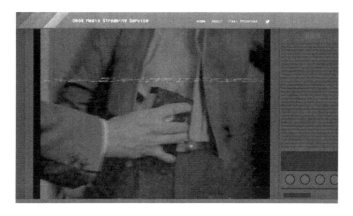

FIGURE 7.1 Performance of *Videodrome* (1982) on the Dead Media Streaming Service.

David Cronenberg's 1982 masterpiece *Videodrome* depicts a very peculiar act of media consumption. After viewing a televised sermon from Brian O'Blivion, the film's McLuhan-esque techno-profit, protagonist Max Renn (played by master of postmodern smarm, James Woods) develops a rare condition: a large slit opens in his abdomen for access to the wetware of Max's internal organs. The high concept gambit of Cronenberg's film is typically read by cinema scholars as a symptom of his overarching concern with "body horror" – an investigation into the uncanny permeability of the human body explored in films such as *Scanners* (1981) and *The Fly* (1986). But here it is media *itself* that has the ability to interpenetrate the body's soft exterior. As Steven Shaviro puts it, "Video technology is no longer concerned merely with disembodied images. It reaches directly into the unseen depths, stimulating the ganglia and the viscera, caressing and remoulding the interior of the body" (Shaviro 1993, 142). The strategy of *Videodrome*, he explains, is to take theorists like McLuhan and Baudrillard at their word, to "overliteralize their claims for the ubiquitous mediatization of the real" (Shaviro 1993, 138). At a crucial moment in the film's final act, Max has a videotape inserted into his body that brainwashes him into going on a killing spree, eventually resulting in his own suicide. Perhaps, the viewer is meant to assume, he is just another victim of too much media exposure.

If most critics agree about the moral of Cronenberg's ending, what is not often remarked upon is the *format* of the tape that brings about the bloody denouement: Betamax, Sony's entry in the home video format wars that began in the late 1970s (Benson-Allott 2013, 70–101). One might imagine that by making a Betamax cassette – the "late lamented Betamax," as Cronenberg puts it – the "preferred Videodrome format," the director was suggesting something significant. After all, Max's death prefigures the "death" of this media format at the hands of VHS only a few years later. The truth is more material. "It was smaller", Cronenberg explains, a better choice to fit into "strange places" (Cronenberg 2004). When the Dead Media Streaming Service screened a Betamax copy of *Videodrome* at the end of July 2017, it was again forced to fit into a "strange place". The service, which streams obsolete formats to the web from original hardware, seemed to permit a similar act of parasitic interpenetration to take place. The Betamax tape was remediated, transformed into something old and new – strange and mutated.

The analogue undead

What does it mean to press play? There was a moment before the advent of digital video where this process was the culmination of some careful preparation, and this nostalgic history of the salad days of the video store – along with its attendant cultural rituals – has become something of a scholarly genre (Herbert 2014). It begins with walking the shelves of the store. Making the selection. Popping popcorn after the long drive home. Dimming the lights. Freeing the film from its clamshell case. Finally, there is the familiar resonance of the VCR's tape head moving into place. Click. Whrr. Action. Even then, there were countless rites that consumed the night. Adjust the tracking. Fumble for the remote. Pause. Play. Rewind.

The first showing on the Dead Media Streaming Service, with no advance notice and only a little fanfare, was 1980's infamously bad rock opera, *The Apple*. The copy in question – the Betamax home video release from Cannon Film – was a poor recording of what is already considered an unwatchable movie. Nothing as transformative as *Videodrome*. Still, when the play button was pressed on the 30-year-old player an entirely obsolete format was brought back to life: its crackling audio and fuzzy images streaming out to any viewer who might have happened to follow the link. Presenting a home video in this way was intended only as a technical demonstration, a proof-of-concept for a web-based video service we had developed. We had no idea how well the tape would perform, if anyone would tune into the broadcast, or, indeed, if the system would come together at all. This performance, this media archaeological experiment, was not without its problems. The tape constantly fell out of sync, and the continuous tracking adjustment required proved especially tedious over the course of multiple showings. But it was not without some measure of success, an undeniable tremor of transformation. Indeed, since that impromptu opening dozens of films have been screened for the community gathered around the service, with a mandate to not only present at least two each month over the regular academic term, but to incorporate them into courses in media archaeology and media history as we develop our own sort of parasitic pedagogy out of the performance of the obsolete.

The sort of programs that are performed on the service vary. Some are meticulously planned, requiring considerable time and effort to acquire the appropriate movie on the appropriate format. It took more than a year to obtain *Videodrome* on Betamax, but no other copy would do. Other screenings, like our memorial presentation of *Night of the Living Dead* on VHS for director George Romero, *Aliens* on Laserdisc for Bill Paxton, or *Purple Rain* on Betamax for Prince, had to be assembled in response to more unexpected circumstances. Most are organized thematically, either as compilations such as our "creature feature" of the cult-classic *Hardware* and the campy *Saturn 3*, series like our "cyberpunk" summer of *The Net*, *Strange Days*, *Hackers*, and *Blade Runner*, or for specific events – *Halloween* on Halloween, *Ladyhawke* coinciding with a solar eclipse. Over the "life" of the service we've programmed everything from *The Last Dragon* on Betamax and *The Peanut Butter Solution* on VHS, to *Battle Royale* on VCD and *Lady Snowblood* on Laserdisc. The only requirement for a selection is that the format on which it will be presented is obscure, obsolete, or otherwise *dead*.

The question at the heart of this practice is what it once meant to press play on these obsolete objects – and, perhaps, what it could still mean. There was a moment when it seemed that cinema *itself* could be contained in plastic shells,

FIGURE 7.2 Custom posters for some of the home video releases screened on the service.

made manifest on magnetic tape. But with video streams encoded for almost every device imaginable, an isolated apparatus for the reproduction of outdated electrical signals has become an unthinkably archaic appliance. Heaps of discs, tapes, cassettes, and cartridges sit idly by, mouldering in dusty attics and damp basements. As Jonathan Sterne has suggested, our expectation of technology's eventual obsoleteness brings with it a painful truth: new media always becomes old (Sterne 2007, 16–17).

Media archaeology must always begin from what Wolfgang Ernst calls the "media assemblage," a device that is technologically – and therefore historically – "operational". But the effort to excavate these remains brings with it, he muses, a surprisingly "haptic taste" for the "mouldy, decaying fragments" that constitute the "mummies, parchments, [and] remnants" of media technology (Ernst 2005, 589). Perhaps as a consequence, our attempt to instil a new means of meaning has fallen victim to what Garnet Hertz and Jussi Parikka have called "zombie media." Less dead media, more "media undead". With these "living dead of media history," we are not concerned with media *in use*, but media "resurrected to *new* uses." No wonder the stream of Romero's *Night of the Living Dead* was one of the most successful! By "probing, exploring and manipulating" consumer technologies beyond their natural life spans, our analogue undead stagger into unexpected and entirely unfamiliar contexts (Hertz and Parikka 2012, 427–429).

Programs for streaming software

Rather than Romero's cemetery in western Pennsylvania, we turn to a website in Manhattan's Greenwich Village. Through it, we watch the reanimation of early video formats for life in the digital age. Despite the uncertainties that accompany these phenomena in the movies, the happenings here aren't quite so mysterious. Indeed, from a purely technical perspective, they require only a modest amount of hardware. Some off-the-shelf, some in the junkyard. From the latter, a media capture station to interface with otherwise derelict media players, converting their analogue audio/video formats to contemporary digital signals. From the former, a relatively standard media server managing the published stream. Through this arrangement, we are not limited to already receptive spaces like those of Max Renn's Toronto. More remote geographies with more limited infrastructural resources – the flea markets and thrift stores that will constitute the grave-sites of most media – become equally viable sources for dissemination. A veritable horde of dead media devices.

Working with these formats in the current moment, acquiring the "haptic taste" it requires, is a more difficult proposition than it might seem. Contemporary video practices revolve around software for editing high definition digital signals – not magnetic tape decks and specialized effects boxes. Students rely on ports prepared for compliant HDMI and SDI interfaces, not the unmediated electrical connection of RCA-style composite video jacks, BNC connectors, or SCART-style plugs. The material world of analogue video has not only fallen by the wayside, it is rotting there. Circuits necessary to process the curiosities like composite and component video are out of production, discontinued. Ancient artefacts of an earlier era.

The transition to digital video was marked by signs of sacrifice. New forms of content control were carried along with unfamiliar connectors and cables, complete with compression artefacts, evidence of over processing, and an entirely new set of errors and irritations. "Squeezed through slow digital connections, compressed, reproduced, ripped, [and] remixed," Hito Steyerl opines, "only digital technology could produce such a dilapidated image" (Steyerl 2009). But, like most moments of transition, the past isn't easy to see from the other side. It is now the analogue image that is in disrepair, and the gap between the past and the future cannot be kept open indefinitely. Modern devices are tuned for capturing 4K and VR, not comparatively primitive DV streams. The very image of current day HD televisions can seem out of focus for filmmakers who are actively appropriating a retro look and feel for their productions. Matt and Ross Duffer, creators of the Netflix series *Stranger Things*, have been outspoken in their criticisms of the default "motion smoothing" of most contemporary screens. When watching their show – a self-conscious mélange of 1980s horror tropes attributable to icons of the genre like John Carpenter, Stephen King, and Steven Spielberg – they encourage viewers to turn off features like "TruMotion" or "smooth motion" (Sternbergh 2017). But it is a futile request. Like modern televisions, streaming services like Twitch and YouTube expect pure digital signals at the highest frame rates, pure digital production for pure digital playback – the output of digital devices intended as the inputs for yet another digital device.

The result is that it can seem like we are struggling to speak analogue in a digital world. But we should not forget its basis in that ancient dialect. Before releases were described with generic ubiquity as media (or worse, *content*), industry sources referred, quite simply, to "software". While this might evoke a sense of the always-already digital, at the time this was just a way to suggest "something that went into a machine", marking their suitability for playback on the comparatively hardware of a turntable or tape-deck. While Joshua Greenberg suggests that distributors "were marking out a specific relationship between pre-recorded tapes and video recorders" that had the consequence of ignoring video cassette's materiality, *this* might be the very metaphor that allows us to recover the *implications* of that materiality (Greenberg 2008, 55–56). In a moment where everything already seems to be software, it may be just the right kind of language for bringing the dead back to life.

It opens avenues to some other metaphors as well. Emulators and field-programmable gate arrays are only some of the means by which software's old incarnations still persist, alive and "running" on new devices. Retrocomputing enthusiasts will speak about having a "tweener" – a computer that is "in-between", as it were, the truly old and obsolete. They support prior disk formats and drives, previous card interface and ports, but they feature more accessible networking, more flexible storage solutions, and more recent operating systems (see, for example, Vintage Computer Federation 2011; Lineback 2017). The most useful are often the last generation of a system to support certain capabilities, and – while its Thunderbolt support positions it partially toward more recent cameras and capture devices – the most obvious benefit for obsolesce from our mid-2011 Mac Mini is found here. Firewire, the high-throughput serial interface designed to replace the aging SCSI standard, prefigured the oncoming ubiquity of digital video. "It wasn't long ago that video on the desktop was more fiction than fact," *PC Magazine* wrote in 1997. It was only through technologies like Firewire that it had finally become "reality" (Ozer 1997, 159). As the first widely implemented standard for working with digital video, Firewire became a fixture on the final generations of tape-based digital camcorders that had begun to store digital, rather than analogue, video. As a consequence, a wide range of consumer devices were produced with analogue inputs and digital outputs capable of reliably converting the formats used by tapes, cartridges, and discs to the early digital video (DV) codec. Indeed, we make use of Canopus AVDC converters precisely because of their support for DV over Firewire. But it is a temporary solution. Most computers that support this workflow have, themselves, become period pieces – back from fact, to fiction.

While the conversion to digital video is a complex requirement for any non-analogue transmission of dead media, the requirements for constructing a streaming server capable of delivering the results remain relatively modest. While there is some irony in the fact that our only hardware failure has been with the new, rather than the old, in practice nearly any computer will suffice. For our service, we have symbolically set a RaspberryPi into an otherwise ordinary Betamax cassette case. The Nginx server running on this box allows the contents of this cassette to be "played" over an RTMP stream or through the HTML5 video player loaded into the site. It also provides the basic software structures required for operating the community around the service – both its web presence and the storage necessary to collate archived video files from prior performances.

Our Betamax box is a rogue media server. Though consumer-facing streaming services have become increasingly commoditized for players of video games,

FIGURE 7.3 Betamax streaming server.

both retro and recent, they have proved problematic when applied to other media objects, with the terms of the largest services, Twitch, YouTube, and Facebook, prohibiting these broadcasts in compliance with the legal requirements of the DMCA (see Jenkins, Ford, and Green 2013, 49). Policies remain highly contingent, with much of the vernacular traffic in dead media archives falling victim to digital fingerprinting and copyright protection technologies (with YouTube channels like Techmoan and Oddity Archive, both of which regularly demonstrate obsolete media formats and technologies, offering valuable insights on the amount of content one can safely show and what countermeasures are necessary to avoid triggering these automated responses). While we have no illusions about the legal status of the works we broadcast, it seems reasonable to differentiate when they are no longer, for most definitions of the term, *playable*. If this was more conventionally credited software, we might describe them as "abandonware". The fact that we can't stems largely from the extensive back catalogues of modern media companies. Almost everything will be re-released. That they come to us as digital remasters, special editions, and deluxe features suggests that the objects we are interested in reanimating have not always been left behind. They've been replaced.

Forms and formats

Every screening on the service begins the same way. A particular title is selected and the format is found. The object – tape, disk, cassette, or cartridge – is tested and tuned. Any details necessary for playback are noted. At the scheduled time, the appropriate equipment is prepared. Hitting play on the deck begins the broadcast, converting the original object to a digital signal streamed out on the service. Adjustments to tracking, the switching of tapes or discs, and any other operations necessary for viewing must be performed, live, over this initial broadcast. As a result of this process, a recording – for our purposes, an "archival" representation of the event – is created by the streaming software. Despite the reproductive promise of the recording, each event is an individual performance, with a unique set of constraints and demands. While entire boxes of VHS tapes may require only a few adjustments over the course of playback, the more venerable Betamax can require multiple machines, with multiple, misaligned, tape-heads, to produce any image at all. Laserdiscs, with their manual movement between the sides of a disc and awkward assembly of special features, exact their own concessions in the sorting of sleeves. For our students, this software "programming" reinforces the particular temporality and materiality of these objects. Magnetic tapes are formed and formatted by the players they get played on. The split sides of laserdiscs are gaps in the continuity of presentation, just as they are openings to unexpected places. Just as long-lost images have been recovered in the margins of film leaders, Tromo collaborator Richard W. Haines recalled that the technical constraints of laserdisc manufacture required signal on the side not intended for playback, with this "dead side data" accessible to those pioneering media archaeologists willing take a chemical solvent to their discs (Haines 2003, 135).

Relatively early in our process we made the decision to limit the more mechanical aspects to the initial screening, to allow "reruns," so to speak, from the video file produced by digitization. While one consequence was that we were able to make screenings available in a rotating "video on demand" feature, the primary motivation was that for most movies it was overly tedious to manage the particulars of a "live" performance for an extended period of time. For some it was almost impossible. The ideal circumstance for streaming a laserdisc, for example, requires only that one is fully committed to the presentation – watching the program carefully to respond to the request to flip discs and restart playback, noting the timing of each transition for when a manual procedure will be required. But a poorly preserved Betamax tape requires almost continuous active adjustment. While this might be a reasonable hazing activity for a new programmer, it is unreliable as part of a regular practice. Automation is possible, of course. Algorithms can be written, mechanical intermediaries constructed. Playback can be triggered by networked infrared emitters (for devices equipped with remote controls), but even this requires the media be physically present (though more popular formats might offer multiple-device systems – multi-disc CD players or dual-tape VHS decks, for example). It seems that these media always require a little bit of fiddling alongside their particular presence in space and time. Always messier and more material than we might imagine.

This materiality is something that becomes almost immediately clear to any viewer of the stream. Or rather, it doesn't. For those used to the high-resolution imagery, crisp and complex audio encodings, or smooth movement and perfect frame rates on Blu-rays and digital download services, the differences of older formats can come across as deficiencies. They are copies, imitations, and poor ones at that. But this comes from a very particular way of looking, one premised on the idea that there is some *original* that this copy stands against. Before the days of digital cameras, films were shot on *film*, and so it is certainly true that there did exist a single material object that was, for all meaningful purposes, *the* film. The existence of a "master" carries with it the understanding that there was some ideal to which all iterations must be compared. But despite the perfection of its appearance, a digitally "remastered" release of an analogue artefact is no more materially like the original than any other. It has been re-encoded, re-presented, and re-animated for an entirely different format – one with entirely different capabilities and curiosities. The transition to the digital brings with it an embrace of a digital aesthetic, with pixels, rather than lines, of resolutions; with frame rates intended for LCDs and OLEDs, not projectors and cathode rays. While this new regime of visual fidelity is taken to present a superior picture from the media of analogue mediums, this sort of fidelity is no more faithful than any other. Nor does digital production imply an exact duplicate. Encodings and compression ensure that few will see the same sequence of ones and zeros that defined the original. They all just pieces of software, each just another format. To embrace the "economy of the multiple," Erika Balsom writes, is to recognize how meaning shifts to the channels through which these copies will flow (Balsom 2017). In the history of home viewing, most consumers before the 1980s settled for Super 8 reproductions, "highlight reels" that were compressed down to a few scenes and which ran at less than ten or twenty minutes. When the end of the 1970s brought the opportunity to see a film in full, it did so with the seemingly obvious and inconsequential caveat that they were, indeed, no longer *films*.

As Jonathan Sterne has put it, the dominant mode of media history depends on the imagination of a particular sort of verisimilitude, where progress can only be imagined as "progress in terms of greater and greater definition" (Sterne 2015, 35). Certainly the logic of this paradigm was familiar to manufacturers in the home media industry, and companies like Sony and JVC readily declared the heightened fidelity of many of the components they released. But they rarely applied this language to home *video*, where the emphasis was largely on the capability to *move* media from one place and time to another. The only claim to quality was to the length of the feature – an entire film rather than the edited selections that had been available on formats like Super 8. "Watch whatever, whenever", as Sony suggested in 1978.

But media forms, Sterne counters, "are not like suitcases; and images, sounds, and moving pictures are not like clothes". There is no definitive edition to be found. There are only different *definitions*, and despite the claims of early video sales that cassettes could put "Hollywood in a box", Sterne reinforces that media objects have "no existence apart from their containers and from their movements – or the possibility thereof" (Greenberg 2008, 55–56; Sterne 2015, 35–36). Different formats are not interchangeable; they cannot be played just anywhere. At best, they are "ports", alternative instantiations for the subtleties of the systems on which they are released. Anyone who has listened to *Sgt Pepper's Lonely Hearts Club Band* on 8-Track or played *Assassin's Creed* on their mobile phone can attest to the fact that the limitations of these platforms impose demands on their porting practice.

These new demands call for new ways to conceptualize them. The turn to a focus on formats, in other words, ought to give rise to *format theory*. "If there is such a thing as media theory, there should also be format theory", entreats Sterne (2012, 7). Figured in this way, the Dead Media Streaming Service can be taken as an attempt to put something of this into practice. By foregrounding the format specificity of each individual stream, by emphasizing the *historical and material contingency* of a particular remediated experience of an obsolete format, the service's programs resist the teleology of verisimilitude that Sterne locates in a traditional account of communication history that "outlines a quest for definition, immersion, and richness of experience" (Sterne 2012, 4). By refusing the "a priori hierarchy of formations of any given medium", and recognizing that communication has a "network reality" – not a binary relationship of mediated transmission, but rather "an ensemble of relations that only produce the moments of transmission and reception after the fact" – format theory invites us "to ask after the changing formations of media". We begin to consider not only the "contexts of their receptions", but "the conjunctures that shaped their sensual characteristics", and even "the institutional politics in which they were enmeshed" (Sterne 2015, 35–35;

2012, 11). To pursue this alternate path, as we wish to do, is to explore the intriguing swerves, the missed opportunities, and the outright failures that have piled up as the angel of media history backs itself into the increasing ubiquity of digitalization.

Optical media

Laserdisc is only one example of the persistence of the service in following this path. Students struggle to make sense of these strange and mysterious "oversized CDs". Indeed, quite unlike CDs, DVDs, and most other formats that are read optically, laserdiscs are largely analogue objects. Though they seem to share some perceptual connection to DVDs, they have no native capability for "menus", for "soft" removable subtitles, or the other programmable video features that debuted with that format. They aren't defined by the sampled sources of the DVD codec, but by a composite video stream inscribed on plastic pressed 12" aluminium platters. At its release, laserdisc held a justifiable claim to a superior video format, with a staggering 425 lines of horizontal resolution compared to VHS's 240. But while it began with an advantage over the mechanical complexity of video cassettes, a combination of economic and technical limitations (it was a read-only format), relegated it to the margins of mediation. Marketed to cinephiles, it struggled to compete even with expensive – but more reliable – film prints.

The format not only persisted, it pioneered features that became permanent fixtures for the future. The capability for multiple audio tracks (both analogue and digital) not only permitted multiple language imports, it allowed distributors like Criterion to experiment with commentary tracks. Its position outside the mainstream allowed it to stretch the limits of analogue television's 4:3 aspect ratio, with countless widescreen releases over the format's life. While the format held no more than 60 minutes of video per side, many included a frame-perfect, 30-minute, constant angular velocity (CAV) encoding on the second disc – presenting the dramatic climaxes common to blockbuster action films with the potential for frame-by-frame follow through, slow-motion, or reverse tracking trick-plays. The availability of a "fourth side" on these releases led to the inclusion of special features like trailers, production art, and making-of documentaries, while clever uses of chapter markers and automatic pausing prefigured the more sophisticated menuing of later optical formats. The result was that laserdisc became a connoisseur format (Klinger 2006, 54–90). At the height of this phenomenon acrylic platters proliferated. Special editions could include as many as six discs, and multiple versions of a particular film, with alternative editors and director's "cuts". Copies of copies for a cinephile's delight.

It is remarkable how many of the unique features of laserdisc emerged because of the peculiar properties of the format. Late in its life, VHS began to mimic traits that had become common to laserdisc and DVD, including widescreen editions and special features. But even though these formats came to copy the conventions, they'd never had the same technical constraints – the extra sides to fill – that laserdisc had. While Betamax cassettes were more constrained, VHS distributors had rarely been limited by the amount of tape they could spool inside their shells. For the few features that did come on two (or more) tapes, divisions were set at entirely arbitrary points. But there were exceptions. When *Gone With The Wind* was designed to break at the same point that the theatrical release had its intermission, the recording media seemed to have captured a material reminder of the previous format. As Wolfgang Ernst notes, media archaeology, "is both a self-reflexive method and an archival object of research". For a digital culture of "apparent, virtual, immaterial realities" this sort of reminder – of the "insistence and resistance of material worlds" – is, he writes, "indispensable" (Ernst 2005, 589).

Our media formats will always come burdened with their own limitations. But even overcome by technological development, they give rise to entirely new ones. In cinema, directors were originally constrained by the physical size of the film reel that could fit on the camera. When Alfred Hitchcock, to offer one prominent example, wanted to make his *Rope* a one-take, uninterrupted, single shot, the ten-minute maximum provided by a standard reel of 35mm forced the director to find creative ways to "hide" his cuts – moving the camera behind a character's back, lingering on a dark prop, and so on (see Bordwell 2008). At the exhibition stage, this constraint was marked, quite literally, by the "cigarette burn" in the corner of the frame that signalled a reels' end (a feature immortalized by Brad Pitt's anarchistic projectionist in *Fight Club*). When the dream of the single-take feature finally became a reality through the storage capacity of digital cameras, in "films" like Alexander Sukorov's *Russian Ark,* it was accompanied by the oncoming ubiquity of digital *projection*. Seeing celluloid became a boutique cinephile practice. The need for a break between reels all but disappeared.

But not all interruptions were the result of technical limitations. The intermission is a break, a stoppage in a performance. For a time in the twentieth century, the roadshow theatrical presentation was the ultimate mark of a "prestige" production. Epics like *Gone with the Wind* or David Lean's *Lawrence of Arabia* included intermissions, along with overtures, exit music, elaborate lobby ephemera, and souvenir programs – all of which contributed to the special sense of the experience. These films were typically longer than the average feature, upwards of four hours, and these breaks were no doubt welcomed. Be it for dramatic effect or for comfort, the *entr'acte* is a cultural technique that can be traced across a number of historical contexts and performance practices – from the act breaks of eighteenth century opera to flipping a laserdisc to play the other side. By "cultural technique" we have in mind the German concept of *Kulturtechniken* that has emerged as a key approach in continental media studies. As Bernhard Siegert explains, "The concept of cultural techniques highlights the operations or sequences of operations that historically and logically precede the media concepts generated by them" (Siegert 2011, 15). Figured in this way, the interruption of performance becomes a recursive historical operation that has always already preceded our current media theoretical conception of it. And some, at least, might be creatively remediated, from the public time of the roadshow intermission to the private time of the disc flip and the pause button.

This sort of remediation is all the more necessary in a media landscape where the proliferation of digital files has served to mask the differences between formats. Not that digital distinctions are any less significant. After all, two digital music files, alike in representation save for the .MP3 or .WAV appended to their names, nevertheless stand at the end of processes of production with little else in common. The former is a lossy data compression format founded on psycho-acoustically modelled samples; the latter is a "raw", uncompressed, bitstream. Even this description neglects the multitude of differences that lurk within files of the same supposed type. Break them open and a whole host of encodings and corresponding codecs start to spill out. These are distinctions that have become remarkably less distinct. While there was a point in the heyday of the MP3 where at least one feature – filesize – was readily apparent to any bandwidth-bound user, that day is long past. Even the idea of the file, itself, is fading. Nearly everything seems to play inside the same sorts of apps, lost somewhere out in the stream.

Through our return to the more obvious artifactuality of analogue media forms, we hope to find ourselves better able to see the crystallizing conditions for the "social and material relations" that give form to *all* of our formats (Sterne 2006, 826). As we do, we come to all sorts of remarkable realizations about the logics that structured them. We see, for example, that despite the perception of physical incompatibility, analogue formats were sometimes more forgiving than their digital counterparts. Digital files cannot open outside their expected applications, but Betamax tapes will "play" a haunting magnetic motion inside a VHS shell. PAL formatted video will display strange signals when NTSC devices work to process them. The flexibility of these formats, the shock of our students reminds us, has been lost somewhere along the way. Our media objects, it seems, can no longer fit into quite as many strange places as they could before.

Pedagogy of performance

While the service has been utilized in a number of undergraduate and graduate contexts, including in our Dead Media Research Studio and by students studying in the Technology, Culture, and Society department, we are particularly invested in its ability to provide a "hands on" experience for media studies students new to media archaeological practice. While many of those interested in media archaeology come from backgrounds with some degree of technical skill, few occupy quite the same celebrated position of Friedrich Kittler's "technological bricoleur" who writes on media theory by day and works with "soldering gun in hand and DOS screen in view" at night (Peters 2010, 7). Coupled with the demanding expertise of foundational media archaeological theorists like Kittler, Ernst, and Siegfried Zielinski, media archaeology presents a formidable front. "Programming" for the software of the service offers a practical entry point for those for whom Assembly Code and C++ are not native languages. *This* sort of programming not only presents an opportunity for students to learn about dead media forms and formats, it

FIGURE 7.4 Curriculum for use with the Dead Media Streaming Service.

provides them with a crash course in the basic techniques necessary for their acquisition, exploration, and preservation. Students learn to recognize the unfamiliar and unexpected sites of media archaeological investigation, cataloguing an ever-changing list of flea markets, vintage shops, and dumps. They become familiar with the vernacular traffic in old media formats, developing connections to communities where practitioners discuss techniques and equipment in vintage electronics forums and perform them in the course of creating retro-nostalgia video series. Students have the opportunity, in other words, to get something of the "haptic taste" for old media formats *before* they are asked to start cutting things open (for more details on this curriculum, see the Center for Analog Humanities at http://www.analoghumanities.com).

While the Streaming Service is not, in itself, intended as an archival preservation process, it utilizes much of the same technological workflow that those processes require. The difference being that we operate at a far more cursory level – the same specialized sorts of equipment, but with less of a concern for a process's results. For example, the service uses tools like a time base corrector with a full frame synchronizer (and background signal generator) to ensure that there is no signal loss during a stream, but we are not necessarily concerned with flaws in the transmission *per se*. We only need to have the appropriate equipment in place to prevent the stream from terminating unexpectedly when the digital capture detects a signal loss. Archivists working with video formats tend to be concerned about output quality – carefully monitoring for noise, interference, and dropped frames. The programs we have screened on tape have degraded visual playback, tracking lines, or mild to moderate tape damage. Some of the laserdiscs are even experiencing symptoms of laser rot. We are interested in mummies, after all, not statues. Nevertheless, the actual mechanics of preparing a release rests on some of the same skills and considerations that would be employed in archival preservation.

Even here, particularities of playback force programmers to confront sometimes significant differences between the material meaning of various formats in their viability for remote representation. Students are often surprised to learn that Betamax, though often lauded as the superior format in its confrontation with VHS, presents far more difficulty for streaming. Though it has not necessarily aged worse, it has aged. The format wars may have started to Beta's advantage in 1976, but it took only four years for VHS to control 70% of the market. The rapid decline of the format by the early-1980s ensures that not only are there fewer home video releases, both in the number of tapes produced and titles available, but – more significantly – the median point of obsolescence falls significantly earlier (it wasn't until 1990 that the VCR finally reached a 70% market penetration in consumer households, see Coplan 2006, 9). VHS technology, whatever its condition at the start of the 1980s, had advanced significantly by the end of the format's life. When Sony shifted to VHS in 1988, dozens of companies were producing high quality VHS decks. The few non-Sony Betamax decks, in comparison, were junk (Digital FAQ 2012).

Acquisition itself presents insights into the afterlife of video formats. Laserdisc, one of the most expensive formats in life, has become one of the cheapest in death. While rare or historic titles retain significantly more value than their videotape counterparts, the bulk of the laserdisc library can be had for next to nothing. In a bit of a historical quirk, the common size they share with vinyl LPs ensures that they turn up, unwanted, in the bulk sale of music collections. There are few record stores that actively advertise their availability, and fewer still that are interested in maintaining them. As students begin to excavate, we have come into a substantial cache of laserdiscs from crate-digging in local brick and mortar stores in New York City – most notably the now-shuttered Bleeker Street Records where several boxes could at one time be found haphazardly arranged next to the world music section in the basement. Gems from the Criterion Collection, some of which have never made the transition to DVD and Blu-ray, sat rather incongruously next to pornographic relics from a bygone era of the West Village.

The existence of the service, and its place as a regularly recurring site of dead media research, offers the opportunity to explore broader media archaeological topics related to the history of home video in an active, situated, context. This has resulted in a number of additional projects, including the performance of 8mm, Super-8, and 16mm footage on telecine boxes, and an exploration into VHS "games" like *Action Max* (1987), *VCR 221 B Baker Street* (1987), and *Nightmare* (1991). In one of the more extensive, we've coupled the digital stream of the service with a more conventional broadcasting technology: analogue television transmission. Connecting the service's server to an agile modulator allows us to take the NTSC composite video source and generate a broadcast RF signal (a popular solution for vintage television collectors, see Nelson 2017). While the range is somewhat limited (the transmission covers the building floor where the server is housed), simulcasting the service on analogue television allows students to compare a contemporary "broadcast" medium with a historic one.

The psychic life of dead media

Why do we remain so enamoured with these dusty formats, what draws us back to a diminished way of watching that, by all current consumerist logics, could be seen as radically perverse? Worse, why do we want to visit this strange habit on others? Perhaps the answer lies in a revanchist desire to return to an earlier period of cinematic culture, a time before the instant availability of video-on-demand and the constant stream of content. Between iTunes, YouTube, Netflix, and Amazon (to name just a few) it can *feel* like just about any film is available to view at home at the touch of a few buttons. In defiant resistance to the many epitaphs for the "death of cinema", we are overwhelmed by a glut of entertainment choices. Jeffrey Sconce has diagnosed this particular irony:

> Rather than witnessing a cinema in evaporation, then, we are now increasingly buried under a cinematic avalanche. And therein lies the problem for the older cinephiliac order. Nothing is more frustrating to desire than satiation, of course, and continuing satiation must ultimately lead to torpor.
>
> (Sconce 2004, 71)

Is the Dead Media Streaming Service a baroque reaction to this contemporary laziness? Are we just making it hard on ourselves? If this banquet of entertainment must eventually result in a decline of symbolic efficiency, then what? What happens after the orgy, as Jean Baudrillard famously asked? As Dominic Pettman notes, there is more than a little resting on our answer (Pettman 2002). Again, Sconce is instructive: "'After the orgy' of absolute cinematic access and obscenity through new distribution technologies, who knows what paraphilias cinephiles will have to devise to maintain their celluloid libidos?" (Sconce 2004, 74–75). If cinephilia is an erotics, then the Dead Media Streaming Service may seem almost necrophilic. But the objects of the past are not quite dead, and we not mired in nostalgia, but in "revival" (Parikka 2012, 3). No longer bound and buried in their old meanings, the "media undead" are put to the performance of entirely new ones.

Bibliography

Balsom, E. (2017) *After Uniqueness: A History of Film and Video Art in Circulation.* New York: Columbia University Press.

Benson-Allott, C. (2013) *Killer Tapes and Shattered Screens: Video Spectatorship from VHS to File Sharing.* Berkeley, CA: University of California Press.

Bordwell, D. (2008) *The Poetics of Cinema.* New York: Routledge.

Coplan, J. (2006) Diagnosing the DVD Disappointment: A Life Cycle View. *The Leonard N. Stern School of Business*, April 3.

Cronenberg, D. (2004) *Videodrome* [Director's Commentary] New York: Criterion.

Digital FAQ (2012) Is there a Betamax VCR Buying Guide? Digital FAQ Forum [Online]. Available at: http://www.digitalfaq.com/forum/video-capture/5557-betamax-vcr-buying.html (Accessed: 10 November 2017)

Ernst, W. (2005) Let There Be Irony: Cultural History and Media Archaeology in Parallel Lines. *Art History*, 28(5), November: 582–603.

Greenberg, J. (2008) *From Betamax to Blockbuster: Video Stores and the Invention of Movies on Video*. Cambridge: MIT Press.

Haines, R. (2003) *The Moviegoing Experience, 1968–2001*. London: McFarland & Company.

Harris, M. (2008) *Pictures at a Revolution: Five Movies and the Birth of New Hollywood*. New York: Penguin Press.

Herbert, D. (2014) *Videoland: Movie Culture at the American Video Store*. Berkeley, CA: University of California Press.

Hertz, G. and Parikka, J. (2012) Zombie Media: Circuit Bending Media Archaeology into an Art Method. *Leonardo*, 45(5): 424–420.

Jenkins, H., Ford, S. and Green, J. (2013) *Spreadable Media: Creating Value and Meaning in a Networked Culture*. New York: New York University Press.

Klinger, B. (2006) *Beyond the Multiplex: Cinema, New Technologies, and the Home*. Berkeley, CA: University of California Press.

Lineback, N. (2017) What Do I Do with an Old Computer? *Toastytech* [Online]. Available at: http://toastytech.com/about/vintagecomputing.html (Accessed: 10 November 2017)

Nelson: (2017) Creating a Home TV Transmitter. *Phil's Old Radios* [Online]. Available at: https://antiqueradio.org/HomeTVTransmitter.htm (Accessed: 10 November 2017)

Ozer, J. (1997) The Complete Video Desktop. *PC Magazine*, October 7.

Parikka, Jussi (2012) *What is Media Archaeology?* Cambridge: Polity Press.

Peters, J. D. (2010) Introduction: Friedrich Kittler's Light Shows. In Kittler, F. (ed.) *Optical Media*. Cambridge: Polity.

Pettman, D. (2002) *After the Orgy: Toward a Politics of Exhaustion*. Albany: SUNY Press.

Sconce, J. (2004) The (Depressingly) Attainable Text. *Framework*, 45(2), Fall: 68–75.

Shaviro, S. (1993) *The Cinematic Body*. Minneapolis: University of Minnesota Press.

Siegert, B. (2011) The Map *is* the Territory. *Radical Philosophy* 169, September/October.

Sternbergh, A. (2017) "Turned Upside Down," *Vulture,* August 20.

Sterne, J. (2006) The MP3 as Cultural Artifact. *New Media & Society*, 8(5): 825–842.

Sterne, J. (2007) Out with the Trash: On the Future of New Media. In Acland, Charles R. (ed.). *Residual Media*. Minneapolis, MN: University of Minnesota Press, 16–31.

Sterne, J. (2012) *MP3: The Meaning of a Format*. Durham: Duke University Press.

Sterne, J. (2015) Compression: A Loose History. In Parks, L. and Starosielski, N. (eds). *Signal Traffic: Critical Studies of Media Infrastructures*. Champaign, IL: University of Illinois Press.

Steyerl, H. (2009) In Defense of the Poor Image. *e-flux* 10, November.

Vintage Computer Federation (2011) Networking a 5150 to a Modern PC. *Vintage Computer Forum* [Online]. Available at: http://bit.ly/vcf-tween (Accessed: 10 November 2017)

8

THE ARCHAEOLOGY OF THE WALKMAN

Audience perspectives and the roots of mobile media intimacy

Maruša Pušnik

When du Gay et al. (2013/1997) made a cultural study of a material device, the Sony Walkman,[1] in the late 1990s, with clear observations about the symbolic meanings of culture, nobody realized that it would become the most famous book in its field. Moreover, at the time, nobody realized that the Walkman already predicted a dramatic extension of the era of media that had first been identified as 'mobile privatization' by Raymond Williams in 1974. Therefore, present concerns must be projected precisely onto that past to understand the rise of mobile and privatized, intimate, online mediatized worlds. In their preface to the 2013 edition of *Doing Cultural Studies: The Story of the Sony Walkman*, the editors write that while the media landscape has changed greatly since it was first published, the book's analysis of the material cultural artefact that was the Walkman can help us critically reflect the past

> in relation to examining the practices attached to the mobile devices we use now; in other words, their place in how we live now, and just how new and different that 'now' is (or is not) from the 'now' of the Walkman.
>
> (du Gay et al. 2013/1997, xiv)

Most studies of the Walkman have concentrated on the producers or marketers; however, my intention in this chapter is to emphasize the mass users of the Walkman. To understand the social construction of the Walkman, it is crucial to include its consumers in the analysis.[2] This chapter investigates the archaeology of a portable media player, the Walkman, and its development from a portable audio cassette player to the Discman, from the perspective of audiences – real users of portable entertainment devices. The Walkman boomed all over the world in the 1980s and represents the beginnings of mobile intimacy. My intention is to seek the roots of contemporary mobile media (MP3 Player, iPod,

The archaeology of the Walkman **127**

mobile phones/app music players) in a now archaic media technology. I treat the Walkman as a portable medium and as a material artefact that functions as a site of memory (see Nora 1996). When put in the hands of users, the Walkman can aid in understanding and historicizing trends towards 'mobile intimacy' within contemporary cultures of mediatization. The study of such media devices through evoking people's memories with the help of hands on historical research, combined with oral history interviews, can help build a new kind of cultural history of mediatization. This new history reveals hidden aspects of these media technologies and explains a contemporary epoch that no longer holds these past experiences and practices.

Since the introduction of the Walkman in the early 1980s in Slovenia, portable media devices have gone through many technological, cultural, and social changes. Because the perspectives of production and consumption are intertwined, many authors suggest that to understand the culture surrounding portable media technologies we must pay attention to audiences and their uses of media, which affected the ways in which technologies were invented and how they evolved (see Geraghty 2000; du Gay et al. 2013/1997). This chapter focuses on people's memories and their dealings with the Walkman, and studies past uses of the Walkman to understand Walkman users in their broader social and cultural contexts. My study is based on an investigation of the history of Walkman technologies through hands on simulations to observe how our informants (born in the 1960s and 1970s) reacted when being faced with this old or even dead media technology. Our research reveals how these users identified with the deep material structure of this media technology, or in other words, how this technical media has transmitted and processed culture (see Parikka 2012).

This research was carried out during a Media History course in 2015–2017. I am grateful to students who helped me gather hands on history participant observations, interviews, and evidence about historical uses of the Walkman. In most cases, they interviewed their own parents or their parents' friends. They reported this as a provocative and thought-provoking experience. They had little previous conception of idea how media structured everyday life in the past. They were fascinated by how much time their parents spent on outdoor activities and on socializing with their friends in face-to-face communication, and how media took a secondary place in their lives. In most cases, they reported how they were fascinated about the "innovative ways" that they parents found when using this "cumbersome and outdated technology", as they described Walkman. They called Walkman a "old big box", tending to see it as a predecessor of their iPods or MP3 Players. They argued that their parents used media in a similar way as students use media today – they hid in their rooms and escaped from the outer world with the Walkman or they walked around engaged in media practice. They argued that their parents' media world did not differ significantly from their current media world, using similar media technologies to isolate from the world and to be mobile. The principal difference lay in how little time their parents spent with the Walkman and media in comparison to their present time spent with media.

128 Maruša Pušnik

We gathered 114 personal testimonies of female and male users of the Walkman from urban and rural areas of Slovenia. We asked these informants to search for their old Walkmans, and many found them in their basements, closets, and attics; if they were unable to find their old devices, we placed a Walkman in their hands, and throughout the interview they carried it in their hands, played with it, demonstrated, and explained how they used it in its heyday. The method of the hands on history of the Walkman helped us to observe how people used this technology, what they did with it, and how the changes in music listening habits were introduced by allowing people to carry music with them through the development of portable devices. In addition, with portable media technologies in their hands, we were also evoking their (hi)stories regarding the contexts of uses of mobile media devices.

People's reconstructed uses and memories of media when directly faced with old technologies can help us to analyse the transformations of (portable) media in history and understand the historical roots of contemporary mobile and intimate mediatized and digitalized worlds. Such a critical attitude towards the history of the Walkman as a portable media reveals that ritualized media uses have profoundly changed, and new mobile media rituals have been invented which are nevertheless historically anchored in the first uses of portable media devices such as the Walkman (see Rothenbuhler 1998).

Reflective nostalgia for past media spaces and experiences also needs to be taken into account when discussing hands on historical approaches (see Boym 2001). I observed that all our informants who were owners/users of old equipment started to build emotional and nostalgic historical narratives the moment they started to use these old portable media devices. However, this nostalgia was not restorative or collectivist, but rather individual – they cherish the memories of the good old days or of their childhood and youth. This does not signify a desire to restore the obsolete media system, but it rather shows the feelings of people who cannot identify with new transcultural and extremely privatized mobile and on-line spaces. Most of the informants reported nostalgic and pleasant feelings when they held the Walkman in their hands. As one among many cases shows:

> I have to admit that the Walkman brings beautiful memories of my youth and my socializang with friends on the basketball court, where we listened to the Walkman. I miss this. I remember how in school I used the Walkman together with my friends when we met at the playground.
>
> (Tjaž, 39 years old)

We have to take into account that precisely such nostalgic feelings have driven the informants' recollections of the usage of the Walkman.

The case of local uses of the Walkman within the hands on historical approaches in Slovenia helps to discover the development of mobile media devices in different historical settings; how these media were used, preserved, subverted, or discarded. It also investigates the technological and cultural roots of the global mobile digital

The archaeology of the Walkman **129**

world order through the practical uses, subversions, and meanings of the Walkman for the first users of portable media. This paper attempts to answer the question of how the media that predate today's interactive, mobile, privatized digital forms were, in their time, contested, adopted, and embedded in everyday life (see Huhtamo and Parikka 2011).

This hands on history project is very nation-specific. The research was conducted in a specific geographical area, in Slovenia, which was a part of the broader Yugoslav socialist state in the 1980s. The Walkman entered Slovenian society under a Communist political system. These socio-political and economic circumstances represent unique or unusual ways in which the Walkman was introduced to Slovenia in the 1980s. Specifically, in the socialist economic system, there was a relatively high average well-being, but there was a shortage of technical goods and Western products (Luthar 2010). Slovenian users thus experienced the Walkman in a different way from users in Western Europe and the rest of the world. For them, the Walkman represented a Western product and the promising idea of Western capitalism, which was something that Slovenian audiences longed for (Pušnik 2010). All our informants described how they obtained Walkmans in the 1980s. In most cases, there are interesting stories about the lack of these goods in the Slovenian stores and about trips to western Italy or Austria to buy these products. Almost all informants reported how there were only one or two 'outdated' types of the Walkman in Slovenian stores, which were also very expensive.

> We travelled to Austria to buy the Walkman. When I saw all these Walkmans on the shelf, it was a new world that opened to me. At that time in Slovenia in Yugoslavia, you couldn't buy all these technological innovations. We were very backward in this sense. I had to convince my parents to go to Austria to buy all these new media. I didn't want to lag behind my friends and I bought a completely new Walkman in Austria.
>
> (Katjuša, 48 years old)

Strict customs controls on the borders between the capitalist Western world and the socialist Eastern world required audiences to smuggle this media technology into Slovenia/Yugoslavia in the 1980s. As Luthar (2006) notes, these were specifically socialist surveillance techniques, which disciplined subjects through their desire of Western goods and through consumption. Longing for the West in socialist Slovenia/Yugoslavia was connected to the peculiar practice of smuggling goods through the border, and socialist individuals were very skilful in this tacit practice. Most of our informants described the smuggling of Walkmans as a normal practice of acquiring this media technology at that time.

> We went to Italy to buy me a new Sony Walkman. Sony was a real brand and it represented a Mercedes among Walkmans. My mother was scared that customs officers would discover it, but I was smarter, I hid it in my pants

because I knew they wouldn't look there. This is the story of my first Sony Walkman, but later I was a hero in the village for having a Sony Walkman.

(Peter, 42 years old)

When our informants were reintroduced to the Walkman and when holding it in their hands and playing with it, in almost all cases they recalled two general trends. The first was their excitement over the possible portability of media technology. They realized that for the first time that they were able to be mobile and to use media technology. The second was their enthusiasm about the possibility of strictly individual, personal, or even intimate usage of that media technology. These two trends were already noticed in the late 1990s: "[. . .] the Walkman was a device that both facilitated and expressed an increasing mobility and privatization of cultural experience" (du Gay et al. 2013/1997, 19–20). The Walkman boomed in the 1980s; it presented new trends of media usage in the environment of the then mainstream mass media (like TV and radio), and it started to drastically change people's lives and especially their ways of connecting with media technology. The Walkman changed the way we listened to music and how we connected with media technology and, in a way, it represented the dawn of a new age of technology.

Increasing mobility: the Walkman's portability as the predecessor of present mobile media

Westlund (2013, 6) argues that the present mediascape is increasingly expanded, fragmented, privatized, digital, and mobile. Like cars, mobile media technologies have become a taken-for-granted part of present society (Ling 2012). Goggin (2011, 2–5) talks about cell phones as global mobile media: all old traditional media, from TV, radio to computers, went mobile on cell phones. Goggin examines how current mobile communication is transforming media and how mobile technology is used for reinventing place or community. Some authors argue that mobile communication has become mainstream and even omnipresent with mobile phones; it certainly is the most rapidly adopted new technology in the world, which has quickly come to seem ordinary and even necessary (Katz 2008; Goggin 2011). As Sutko and de Souza e Silva (2011) argue, mobile media require us to rethink our understanding of urban sociability, particularly how we coordinate and communicate in public spaces. What is important is their ability to increase one's spatial awareness and to encourage one to meet more people in public spaces (Sutko and de Souza e Silva 2011, 815–818).

These mobile media technologies have their roots in the past media devices. The mobile phone is a descendent of the fixed telephone, but has undergone extensive technological transformations. This device now also enables the processing of communication and information through audio, video, graphics, text, and animation (Westlund 2013, 6). Wei (2008) reasons that from early mobile media devices it has been transformed into a mobile media-rich platform that enables the dissemination of information, entertainment, and news. Moreover, its transformation has been influenced by many media, from the Walkman to messaging services, such as the pager (Leung and Wei 1999), and convergence processes that have involved accommodating functionalities such as the camera, GPS, and music player. Although mobiles have roots in the not-so-distant past, they have become deeply embedded in contemporary social life.

Goggin (2011, 102) points specifically to the late 1970s and early 1980s as a significant starting point of mobile media with the appearance of the Sony Walkman. The results of our hands on history analysis also support this thesis. All the informants stressed the importance of the portability of this medium at that time when they engaged with the Walkman device. This was actually the first thing to be noticed when we placed a Walkman in their hands and asked them to describe their feelings and memories of this technology. They reported that this technology was the first one to have drastically changed their media-communication practices in comparison to other old media, communication with which was more static. In this manner, many informants compared it to their present uses of mobile phones. As this statement illustrates:

> I took my Walkman with me with a special device that I attached to my trousers. What was revolutionary with the Walkman was independence, I could listen to whatever music I wanted to, and it offered me mobility. For instance, radio meant society and adaptation, but the Walkman meant independence and solitude. For me, the only problem was when I ran down the batteries when I was travelling, although I always carried spare batteries with me. First, I was afraid of using the Walkman as mobile media, because I was afraid I would damage it, but with time it became true mobile media for me.
>
> (Uroš, 48 years old)

Or, as another informant explained: "For me, the essence of the Walkman was its portability, it was resistant to steps and body motion, more than the Discman was later, which I used more when I was lying in bed and reading" (Simona, 39 years old).

Informants told us about their feelings of freedom when using this technology: suddenly they were not bound to a specific point in space, but they could use this media technology wherever they wanted to. They also stressed the limitation of other old media, which the Walkman overcame:

> What I found the most important with the Walkman in comparison to other media was that that you could carry it around with you and that you didn't need to be connected to the electric cable. I had a Sony Walkman. I liked it very much, and I liked it that I was mobile that when listening to music I could walk around. I could clean or play and jump around with the Walkman stuck to my trousers.
>
> (Nataša, 48 years old)

Our informants connected the Walkman not only with entertainment, but also with work. Precisely because of its portability, this medium also entered the workspace: "I grew up on the farm and with my Walkman the work there got faster for me. My mother made a small pouch for me where I put my Walkman and I tied it up with a belt" (Miha, 49 years old).

In many cases, informants compared the Walkman to the radio, although they stressed a great difference in their usage, the radio was perceived as a more community medium and a static one, while the Walkman as a more individual medium and, most importantly, as a portable medium. Moreover, when showing us how to use this technology, many of the informants argued that the problem with this technology was its batteries and that the mobility of media at that time was severely limited to a couple of hours because the batteries quickly ran down:

> I carried my Walkman in the inside pocket of my jeans jacket. We used it in the way that we could carry it around outdoors. The only thing that was problematic was its batteries. For example, one had to be very careful when using the rewinding function because the batteries ran down even quicker.
>
> (Elena, 46 years old)

I observed that there was a generation gap in the usage of the Walkman. Older generations avoided using a Walkman as they were not familiar with mobile media use:

> I listened to my Walkman at the beach and at work. When I went out, I carried it in my hands. The only problem was its batteries; they were not so cheap as they are today, and they quickly ran down. It was important because you could listen to music everywhere, although not for a long time, because the batteries ran down, but still. My parents listened to the radio more often; they didn't use the Walkman because they were not used to carrying it around with them. It was something too technologically sophisticated for them, but with my sister, we constantly listened to it. You could carry and listen to the music when you were not at home, but somewhere outdoors. Later, I also used an MP3 player, but today I use my smartphone in practically the same manner.
>
> (Vesna, 49 years old)

However, some of the informants also lamented that it was not so easy to adapt themselves to the Walkman's portability because they were used to the stationary uses of the then mainstream media. The portability of the Walkman was something so innovative for them that they needed some time to realize that this medium was a portable one. To illustrate:

> At the beginning, it was not self-evident to me that you can carry music around with you. At that time, I first saw an advantage of the Walkman

more in its ability to put headphones on and to disconnect from the world. Mostly at home, in the bed, that you listened to audiocassettes and to have your own peace. At the beginning, it was not obvious that music could come around with me. It was a super technological toy, and it was cool that I was able to listen to music in peace privately at home. Then, I slowly changed my mind, and I realized that the Walkman could come with me wherever I go, I listened to it at the beach. This was a real advantage, although it took me some time to discover how nice it was to listen to music during some boring activities. The Walkman had only one pair of headphones, and listening to it was not a social activity; it was less social, I used it more for listening to music and to disconnect. And brains off. It was a black box, Sony I think, with bass and treble buttons at the top. At that time, it seemed so little to me, but today I laugh at how big it was.

(Marko, 52 years old)

The Walkman represented a real revolution in comparison to the mainstream media of the 1980s, especially radio, television, and the conventional telephone, which were stationary media and which required sedentary usage. It suddenly brought more active, mobile uses of media since it was freed from the network and electricity cable, although it still had some disadvantages (batteries with a limited charge capacity, impracticality of carrying many audiocassettes, etc.).

Privatization of media experience: intimacy with the Walkman

Okada (2005, 43) explains that the dimension of personalization and privatization of media began in the late 1970s. From the mid-1980s, cordless and extension phones were commonly placed in bedrooms as the telephone found its way into

 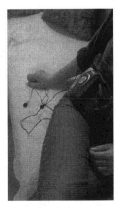

FIGURES 8.1 AND 8.2 Examples of mobile uses of the Walkman. (Photographs by Melisa Lozica and Domen Valjavec)

the private rooms of each family member (Okada 2005, 46). The process of the personalization and privatization of media developed decisively with the popularity of the Walkman with its shift away from products used by the whole family to those used by individuals. Later, throughout the 1990s, during the adoption of mobile media, the original business and official uses of the pager were extended into individual and personal purposes. Okada (2005) describes this sequence of events as the shift from household media to individual media.

In the late 1980s, Beniger discussed the personalization of mass media by disguising the size of mass audiences, targeting messages, and contriving intimacy in content (1987, 354). Beniger argues that this change constitutes a transformation of traditional community into an impersonal association that we might call 'pseudo-community', which has especially been strengthened with new media-communication technology. Nowadays, new media like the mobile phone are so deeply embedded in our personal lives that some authors call these new media intimate technologies (Bell 2006). Wilska (2003) talks about the privatization of the consumption of mobile-phone technology. Livingstone and Bovill (2013, 327) argue that privatization supports individualization and vice versa, when showing how children and youth use media technologies, which transforms more traditional communities (like family) into individual associations: "Within the home the multiplication of personally owned media may facilitate children's use of individual, privatised space, as opposed to communal family space" (Bovill and Livingstone 2001, 17).

In the modern era, we can observe a significant personalization of media and the shift to the use of media in privacy and in intimacy, enabled by the use of smart-phones and personalized mobile smart applications. Spiegel (in Morley 2007, 200) transforms Williams' concept of mobile privatization (1998/1981, 284), which was brought about by television and automobility years ago. Many authors point out that modern media-communication technologies create private media bubbles in the crowd, which results in forms of ghettoization and entrapment in media bubbles, whereby media technology helps individuals to build a barrier with the outside world and, thus, enables an individual to separate his/her internal impulses from the impulses of the outer world (Boyd 2014; Morley 2007; Burchell 2015; Ling 2008; Wellman 2001; Krajina 2014; Pajnik 2015).

Hjorth and Lim (2012) presuppose that these new trends of intimacy with media already have roots in the history and in the historical forms of media:

> Technologies such as mobile media re-enact earlier co-present practices and interstitials of intimacy: for example, SMS (Short Message Service) re-enacts nineteenth-century letter writing traditions [. . .] and sharing vacation photographs via Facebook are a digital analogy of the time-honored 'Wish you were here' postcard. [. . .] new forms of telepresence such as email are linked to earlier practices of intimacy such as visiting cards. In this way, the intimate co-presence enacted by mobile technologies should be viewed as part of a lineage of technologies of propinquity.
>
> (Hjorth and Lim 2012, 478)

The archaeology of the Walkman 135

They go even further when arguing that with the 'intimate' turn in the contemporary era of new media impacting various facets of cultural practice and politics, notions like emotion are no longer defined individually or psychologically but must be seen as an integral part of social life (Hjorth and Lim, 2012, 481). In this respect, intimacy with the Walkman in the 1980s – with headphones on users' ears – resembles the modern practices of listening to an iPod or using apps on a mobile phone. In all cases, users are in an intimate relationship with media technology, remote from the outer world and locked into personal space.

With the hands on history approach, we observed two trends of personalization and privatization of the Walkman experience, when our informants reported their intimate connection with the Walkman device and their individual uses of media. First, this enabled them to move in the solitude of their personal or even intimate space, that they could disconnect from the communication with other people and from the outside world. Second, these privatized and personalized uses of the Walkman enabled them to create their own personal content; they reported that, in comparison to the radio, when listening with a Walkman they were free to listen to whatever they wanted.

The first trend of personalization and privatization of the Walkman, moving to personal, intimate space, also indicates that the users' connection with technology began to be tighter. For example: "I used my Walkman when I was alone; I locked myself with my Walkman in the solitude. It was an analogue technology, but it was reliable as long as the batteries were working" (Uroš, 48 years old). The results also show that the Walkman was a device of intrapersonal communication; with the use of the Walkman, users could escape interpersonal communication and started to communicate with themselves. Many informants reported this: "I remember whenever my parents were giving me a hard time I went out with my bike with my Walkman on my ears" (Elena, 46 years old). The Walkman entered deep into the personal and intimate space of its users, not only because it represented an escape from the real world, as our informants were claiming, but also because it replaced communication and communion with other people with communication with oneself. Hardt (2004) observes that this was already a characteristic of television media in the twentieth century, which started to attack dialogue with other people, substituting it with communion with the screen.

The Walkman also substituted communion with sound for dialogue with other people:

> I disconnected from the real world with the Walkman. When I was young I shared my room with my two sisters – our apartment was crowded, and there was not a lot of privacy. The Walkman was my personal escape, if I may say so.
>
> (Mojca, 50 years old)

Or: "For me, the Walkman was also an escape from the conversation with parents" (Tomaž, 38 years old). There were at least two advantages of the Walkman in comparison to the then mainstream mass media for the informants: the first was an escape to the intimate world and the second was a non-disturbance of an outer world during media activity – like listening to the Walkman: "You did not disturb your neighbourhood with your Walkman. Whenever it was something wrong or when I wanted some peace. I put on my Walkman and closed myself into my own world" (Nataša, 48 years old).

The Walkman allowed its users to escape to a private media bubble in a social space, a characteristic of contemporary media technologies:

> I was obsessed with music and I wanted to listen to it on my way to the school, on my way home, on the way to my friends, everywhere and any-time. The Walkman allowed me all this, and it gave me a feeling that the outside world is not important. Immediately when I left my home, I put headphones on and I used it until I came home. Sometimes, when I felt like a real rebel, I put my headphones on during the class in the school, when the teacher had oral exams, I sat in the rear bench and I listened to my favourite songs. At home, I turned the volume up, and I couldn't hear if parents called me, and they were really nervous about that. The Walkman made music more accessible, because you could carry the device with you wherever you wanted to. This gave the music and the device a touch of freedom. You could enjoy it in private with the Walkman.
>
> (Tine, 48 years old)

In many cases, the Walkman also represented a physical barrier from the rest of the world, with the Walkman acting as a kind of their personal room:

> To me, the Walkman represented an escape to my own world. Together with my two brothers, there was no peace at my home – we were shout-ing, fighting. And the Walkman brought me the five minutes of peace that I needed in the day so that I could think about my future, about girls, and some other things. To carry music around with you and to listen to it when-ever you wanted to was a totally new thing. The purpose of use of mobile phones is similar to that of the Walkman. As we used the Walkman to escape from reality, the same way you use your phones today.
>
> (Matjaž, 42 years old)

Or: "I didn't have my own room, so I put my headphones on and, in the moment, I was all alone and could listen to music all by myself" (Alenka, 44 years old).

Moreover, in the case of personalization and privatization of the Walkman, I noticed a generation gap: younger informants escaped to the intimate communion with the Walkman, older ones required more communal and group uses of media:

> The coming of the Walkman totally changed my habits of listening to music. I could listen to my favourite singers whenever I wanted to. We younger

The archaeology of the Walkman **137**

ones were separated from older ones by the Walkman. I remember that my mother and father were very angry with me and told me that I was too often alone in my room listening to music and that I should spend more time with them in the living room watching television or listening to radio.

(Barbara, 50 years old)

Or another example:

The advantage of the Walkman was that you could listen to what you wanted to. You put in an audiocassette, pushed "play" and listened to music, freed from the rest of the world; you were in your own world. However, radio was a device of the older generation, and the Walkman of the younger generation. The Walkman meant independence for me at that time, also because there often was no electricity in the evenings. The Walkman meant a great leap – MP3s and iPods are not revolutionary at all, it is only a new form of technology for listening to music. I still remember my Walkman often, and I miss those times. I still keep a collection of audiocassettes, around 500 of them.

(Dejan, 40 years old)

The Walkman isolated people from one another; instead of bringing them into contact with other users, users of technology were in contact with the Walkman. Fang (1997, 139) similarly argues for the TV and for the mass media culture in the twentieth century that conversations were slowly displaced from the rooms, where TV communication was going on, and the connection with the TV set was further strengthened. What started with TV was strengthened by the Walkman. In contrast, most media of the twentieth century, especially radio, are more communal media, as our informants also recognized, while the Walkman strictly sharpened these trends of isolation from others:

Radio was not so intrusive as the Walkman was. You can put it in a corner, turn down the volume and still listen to it, but at the same time drink coffee and talk with other people. Meanwhile listening to the Walkman, you cannot do that, with the Walkman you are closed with yourself into your own world. Like you were a part of some other world, into which you do not allow anybody else to enter.

(Andrej, 57 years old)

Or: "We always listened to the radio together, during lunch, for instance, but you could listen to the Walkman all by yourself at your own discretion" (Mojca, 46 years old). And:

With the Walkman, listening to music became more intimate because only you could hear the music. I mostly listened to it in my room, all alone, this was one to one moment – me and my Walkman/music. Radio was more community media, we listened to it together, but the Walkman was more my own media, more intimate.

(Eva, 35 years old)

The privatization and personalization of the Walkman meant also a kind of escape for its users, to escape from their everyday routines, from their obligations:

Many times, I listened to my Walkman in my room, when I needed a bit of relaxation. I shut all the windows and doors, rolled down the shutters, and I lied down on the bed in the darkness and listened to music in peace. The Walkman meant relaxation and escape from the outer world for me at the moment when I needed this. I also used it when jogging or riding a bike. I stitched it to my belt or simply on my t-shirt.

(Petra, 47 years old)

And again:

The Walkman was important because it was more a personal experience, that you could live in music. Especially if I was nervous or something bothered me, I closed myself into my room and put on the headphones. The best therapy.

(Marija, 53 years old)

The second trend of personalization is the individualization of content, processed according to personal wishes, tastes, ambitions, and interests. Informants started to prepare their own repertoire of media contents. Rando (2017) and Stock (2010) call his phenomenon the birth of the 'mixtape' with personal

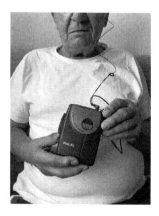

FIGURE 8.3 Privatization of the Walkman experience. (Photograph by Vita Vlašič)

curating of users' own compilations from the radio on audiocassettes. Stock defines the mixtape thus:

> The mixtape is a conglomeration of songs compiled typically by a single individual; however, some tapes are produced in tandem or groups for specific purposes. The mixtape emerged out of the improvement and affordability of recording equipment in the 1980s combined with the availability of the cassette tape released in the seventies.
>
> (2010, 283)

This characteristic of the Walkman resembles the modern media on demand (TV or video on demand, etc.). The key new function of the Walkman that the informants remembered when playing with the Walkman in their hands was recording, which enabled this personalized content. They started to massively prepare their own repertoire of music, which individualized their usages of mass media – radio listening, for example. As one informant described:

> I chose music on the radio, and then I recorded what I liked. This was a great art for me at that time. In most cases, we recorded music from the radio. The good old audiocassettes . . . we were so excited about recording. I asked my parents to request some music for me on the radio for my birthday that I liked, and then I recorded it. We had to be totally silent when recording. The Walkman was a true miracle in this respect, what was the most fascinating was that you could carry it with you and listen to whatever you wanted to. When listening to the radio, you needed to adapt to others and their tastes; with the Walkman, this was different. Thus, I was in love with my Walkman.
>
> (Tatjana, 38 years old)

The most common reason that our Walkman users made recordings of the radio was a shortage of recorded music in the 1980s in the then-socialist Slovenia/Yugoslavia. As informants recalled, there was a "poor choice of audiocassettes in our stores": either they were expensive, or you could not buy the Western releases of popular music on cassettes at that time in Slovenia at all. There were only two ways to get Western popular music: either to travel to Austria or Italy and buy audiocassettes or to record music from the radio. According to the analysis of interviews, our informants became experts at curating compilations from the radio according to their own wishes. In this regard, Rando (2017, 65) calls mixtapes 'wish tapes', 'a heterotopic space' and explains different techniques for curating people's own compilations of music: "The wish image of the mixtape is also invested in reordering, restoring, and translating the commodified fragments of music back into an unalienated musical whole or totality".

Another significant reason for the mixtape was that a certain kind of male teenager wanted to compile it for courting girls. According to Stock (2010, 284), the mixtape was "a courting tool for adolescent and young adult males". Many of our male informants mentioned this trend:

> I was in love with one girl from the neighbouring village, and every week when we met I recorded a new cassette with love songs in English for her because I wanted to impress her. Then we both listened to these songs together on the Walkman, each with one headphone on. I was a real stud with all these brand-new songs.
>
> (Miro, 50 years old)

A mixtape might also be a gift, as Stock (2010) argues. A mixtape is a compilation of individual songs often presented to someone else as a gift or to denote a specific event. In this regard, the Walkman was most often compared to radio, which did not allow for such an individualized and personalized listening to music or a programme: "The Walkman was a first device that enabled you to be a master of your own music wishes, and you didn't depend on others' choices, as was the case with radio" (Žiga, 38 years old).

The mixtape was a kind of "wishful expression of the new" (Rando 2017, 11). Stock (2010), in another sense, argues that such a mixtape, which is created using other artists' songs and music for a specified purpose, is an art-based act of creativity; for him, this is a type of creative imagination. Evidence from our informants supports this theory; almost all noted that they felt free and emphasized their fantasy and imagination when they were compiling their own music together. The following informant precisely described the function of recording, which was so crucial for individualized listening with a Walkman:

> I still remember that there was a show with foreign music on Mondays, and every Monday we waited with fingers on the 'record' and 'play' buttons, to record a new single. These were real events. We waited for an exact song. Many times, it happened that you recognized your favourite song too late and then you didn't have the beginning of the song, or that the speaker still spoke when the song was already on, or that he started to talk when the song was not yet over, or that there was some noise during the song. You recorded all this on your tape.
>
> (Polona, 47 years old)

Another informant recalled: "One of my favourite activities of that time was recording audiocassettes for my Walkman. I could sit for hours listening to the radio and waiting for a certain song so that I could record it then" (Tanja, 43 years old). The testimonies of our informants reveal that they had certain rules for recording on the cassettes, which are also mentioned by Stock (2010) as important art-based rules.

Another recollection of the recording function on audiocassettes emphasized the importance of personalized content:

> We mostly recorded music from radio for listening to it on the Walkman, especially the show "Top 20". If something went wrong, we rewound the

cassette with finger or pen and recorded the new song on the tape again. It was the best that you could re-record the old song with the new one when you got bored with the old song. But then, it was a problem if the old song was longer from the new one because at the end of the new song than you could still hear the end of the old song. The Walkman represented a jump into the advanced society. It definitely changed our lives. It was a technology that certainly influenced individual's state in the society.

(Simon, 41 years old)

This example demonstrates that there were specific art-based techniques of how to prepare the mixtape and users were real craftsmen masters of this recording practice. In this regard, today's 'playlist', created by Napster, iTunes, or other computer software programmes to organize and create playlists, lacks an art of imagination that was so characteristic of mixtapes: "today, with CD burners and online servers with hundreds of thousands of songs at their fingertips, people are losing the art of making a really great mixtape" (Stock 2010, 285).

When showing us different functions of usages of the Walkman, informants specifically mentioned the rewinding/fast-forwarding function as a great advantage of this technology, because they could listen to whatever they wanted to in comparison to radio where they could not choose.

With radio, there was always a compromise what we would listen to. My word was nothing, and I couldn't listen to my favourite songs. The Walkman gave me the freedom to listen to my songs in the moment I wanted to.

(Simona, 45 years old)

It is worth mentioning that a kind of cultural nostalgia, which Rando (2017) also observed regarding the mixtape, is seen in the informants' testimonies of recording functions, which they describe as a real art and observe as unrepeatable in time.

FIGURES 8.4 AND 8.5 Examples of handling the Walkman. (Photographs by Lea Plut and Ema Kranjc)

Conclusion: the Walkman and mobile intimacy

The adoption of the Walkman in Slovenia influenced the media practices of its users and introduced them to uses which over the years have slowly become the prevailing communication practices in society. As I observed with the hands on history approach, our informants were very nostalgic about the uses of the Walkman; they were all very positive about that technology, and they mostly remembered it as a kind of freedom in comparison to the then-mainstream media. They revealed mobility, intimacy with technology, personalized content, and isolation from others. What Hjorth and Lim describe as characteristic of this century's media practices therefore has roots in the history of the Walkman:

> That is, the ways in which the various forms of mobility (across technological, geographic, psychological, physical, and temporal differences) and intimacy infuse public and private spaces is spearheaded by the increasing role of personalization by mobile media to both blur and reinstate boundaries between online and offline worlds. This has allowed for multiple cartographies of space in which the geographic and physical space is overlaid with an electronic position and relational presence, which is emotional and social. This overlaying of the material-geographic and electronic-social is what can be called mobile intimacy.
>
> (2012, 478)

It is precisely in this sense of mobile intimacy that I understand the Walkman as shaped by the social construction of its users. The process of mobile and intimate media reception became the dominant one with a new medium in the 1980s – the Walkman. A hands on historical perspective, in which users of mobile phones are faced with this old technology, can help us to understand how minor or subversive media uses evolved and transformed into mainstream media uses through time. To understand the role of the Walkman in the history of media we must understand this popular cultural device of that time as the main transformer of younger generations' trends of communication in the 1980s and 1990s. Furthermore, as Okada argues, "we must analyze how these changing media forms both grow out of and shape trends in communications. [. . .] We need an even clearer model for the relationship between media, popular cultures, and communication trends" (2005, 60). The growing trend of individualized and personalized use of media in present digital societies has its roots in the time of Walkman in the 1980s and our hands on history analysis proves that personalized media has played a role in culture and society long before our digital age.

Notes

1 "This gadget, originally invented and marketed by Sony in the spring of 1980 in Japan, and soon exported, has become known throughout the West, however awkward its Japanese-made English may sound" (Hosokawa 1984, 165).

2 A starting point for my analysis are theories of the social construction of technologies – technological systems (Bijker, Hughes, and Pinch 2012), which see technologies as built in a process of social construction and negotiation, which are always driven by the social interests of its participants.

Bibliography

Bell, G. (2006) The Age of the Thumb: A Cultural Reading of Mobile Technologies from Asia. *Knowledge, Technology & Policy*, 19(2): 41–57.

Beniger, J. E. (1987) Personalization of Mass Media and the Growth of Pseudo-Community. *Communication Research*, 14(3): 352–371.

Bijker, W. E., Hughes, T. P. and Pinch, T. (2012) *The Social Construction of Technological Systems: New Directions in the Sociology and History of Technology*. Cambridge, MA: MIT Press.

Bovill, M. and Livingstone, S. M. (2001) *Bedroom Culture and the Privatization of Media Use* [online]. London: LSE Research Online. Available at: http://eprints.lse.ac.uk/archive/00000672 (Accessed 14 September 2017)

Boyd, D. (2014) *It's Complicated: The Social Lives of Networked Teens*. New Haven: Yale University Press.

Boym, S. (2001) *The Future of Nostalgia*. New York: Basic Books.

Burchell, K. (2015) Tasking the Everyday: Where Mobile and Online Communication Take Time. *Mobile Media & Communication*, 3(1): 36–52.

du Gay, P., Hall, S., Janes, L., Koed Madsen, A., Mackay, H. and Negus, K. (2013/1997) *Doing Cultural Studies: The Story of the Sony Walkman*. London: Sage.

Fang, I. (1997) *A History of Mass Communication: Six Information Revolutions*. Boston: Focal Press.

Geraghty, C. (2000) *British Cinema in the Fifties: Gender, Genre and the 'New Look'*. London: Routledge.

Goggin, G. (2011) *Global Mobile Media*. London: Routledge.

Hardt, H. (2004) *Myths for the Masses: An Essay on Mass Communication*. Malden and Oxford: Blackwell Publishing.

Hosokawa, S. (1984) The Walkman Effect. *Popular Music*, 4(1): 165–180.

Hjorth, L. and Lim, S. (2012) Mobile Intimacy in an Age of Affective Mobile Media. *Feminist Media Studies*, 12(4): 477–484.

Huhtamo, E. and Parikka, J. (2011) *Media Archaeology: Approaches, Applications and Implications*. Berkeley, CA: University of California Press.

Katz, J. E. (2008) *Handbook of Mobile Communication Studies*. Cambridge, MA: MIT Press.

Krajina, Z. (2014) *Negotiating the Mediated City: Everyday Encounters with Public Screens*. New York, London: Routledge.

Leung, L. and Wei, R. (1999) Who are the Mobile Phone Have-Nots? Influences and Consequences. *New Media & Society*, 1(2): 209–226.

Ling, R. (2008) *New Tech, New Ties: How Mobile Communication Is Reshaping Social Cohesion*. Cambridge, MA: MIT Press.

Ling, R. (2012) *Taken for Grantedness*. Cambridge, MA: MIT Press.

Ling, R. and Campbell, S. (2011) *Mobile Communication: Bringing Us Together and Tearing Us Apart*. New Brunswick, NJ: Transaction Publishers.

Livingstone, S. M. and Bovill, M. (2013) *Children and Their Changing Media Environment: A European Comparative Study*. New York: Routledge.

Luthar, B. (2006) Remembering Socialism: On Desire, Consumption and Surveillance. *Journal of Consumer Culture* 6(2): 229–259.

Luthar, B. (2010) Shame, Desire and Longing for the West: A Case Study of Consumption. In: B. Luthar and M. Pušnik, eds., *Remembering Utopia: The Culture of Everyday Life in Socialist Yugoslavia*. Washington: New Academia, 341–377.

Morley, D. (2007) *Media, Modernity and Technology: The Geography of the New*. London, New York: Routledge.

Nora, P. (1996) *Realms of Memory: The Construction of the French Past*. New York: Columbia University Press.

Okada, T. (2005) Youth Culture and the Shaping of Japanese Mobile Media: Personalization and the Keitai Internet as Multimedia. In: M. Ito, D. Okabe, M. Matsuda, eds., *Personal, Portable, Pedestrian: Mobile Phones in Japanese Life*. Cambridge, MA: MIT Press, 41–60.

Pajnik, M. (2015) Nano-Media and Connected Homeliness. *International Journal of Communication*, 19(9): 732–752.

Parikka, J. (2012) New Materialism as Media Theory: Media Natures and Dirty Matter. *Communication and Critical/Cultural Studies*, 9(1): 95–100.

Pušnik, M. (2010) Flirting with Television in Socialism: Proletarian Morality and the Lust for Abundance. In: B. Luthar, M. Pušnik, eds., *Remembering Utopia: The Culture of Everyday Life in Socialist Yugoslavia*. Washington: New Academia, 227–258.

Rando, D. P. (2017) *Hope and Wish Image in Music Technology*. London and New York: Palgrave Macmillan.

Rothenbuhler, E. W. (1998) *Ritual Communication: From Everyday Conversation to Mediated Ceremony*. Thousand Oaks: Sage.

Stock, P. V. (2010) Sociology and the Mixtape: A Metaphor of Creativity. *The American Sociologisti*, 41(3): 277–291.

Sutko, D. M. and de Souza e Silva, A. (2011) Location-aware Mobile Media and Urban Sociability. *New Media & Society*, 13(5): 807–823.

Wei, R. (2008) Motivations for Using the Mobile Phone for Mass Communications and Entertainment. *Telematics and Informatics*, 25 (1): 36–46.

Wellman, B. (2001) Physical Place and Cyberplace: The Rise of Personalized Networking. *International Journal of Urban and Regional Research*, 25(2): 227–252.

Westlund, O. (2013) Mobile News: A Review and Model of Journalism in an Age of Mobile Media. *Digital Journalism*, 1(1): 6–26.

Williams, R. (1974) *Television: Technology and Cultural Form*, London: Routledge and Kegan Paul.

Williams, R. (1998/1981). *Navadna kultura: izbrani spisi*. Ljubljana: ISH Fakulteta za podiplomski humanistični študij.

Wilska, T.-A. (2003) Mobile Phone Use as Part of Young People's Consumption Styles. *Journal of Consumer Policy*, 26(4): 441–463.

9

EXTENDED PLAY

Hands on with 40 years of English amusement arcades

Alex Wade

Amusement arcades are historically viewed as an unflattering venue where deviancy and dereliction run as free as the youth who populate them (see e.g. Fisher 1995; Huff and Collinson 1987). Popular books of the time reflect this, from the tongue-in-cheek narrative interpretation of Rubin's *Defending the Galaxy* (1982), to Amis's graphic – both visually and linguistically – *Invasion of the Space Invaders* (1982), to Sudnow's cold-war bad-trip of *Breakout* addiction *Pilgrim in the Microworld* (1983). Each documents and reinforces the popular notion of arcades as arenas where, as distinguished game designer Al Alcorn observes, "naughty things might happen" (Alcorn 2014, 25). The end result was a moral panic, which found its political manifestation in George Foulkes' infamous campaign to limit "the menace of video games" (Haddon 1988, 60), via the United Kingdom parliament in the *Control of Space Invaders (and other electronic games) Bill* (Foulkes 1981, cc287). This popular and political attention piqued the interest of sociologists, psychologists, and criminologists. The videogame amusement arcade became a favoured and fevered site of academic study, which, to the delight of writers and the panic of politicians and parents reinforced the notion that arcades were a locus of dubious, unethical, and perhaps even illegal behaviour. A large-scale study by the Centre for Leisure Research in the UK found that 80% of 2739 respondents disagreed that amusement arcades provided young people with a safe place to go, while 59% of the same cohort agreed that young people should be banned from amusement arcades (Centre for Leisure Research 1990). Another UK survey of 789 respondents showed that over 20% of those who frequented amusement arcades had been involved in a fight and nearly a fifth "had been approached by someone who makes them feel uncomfortable2 (Huxley and Carroll 1992). The common perception of amusement arcades being a site of moral panic reflects much of the contemporaneous work undertaken by Birmingham's Centre for Contemporary Cultural Studies. The social, economic and political *habitus* of amusement arcades places them geographically and culturally underground, or in what Young specifically terms the "subterranean world of play" (Young, 2005).

The perception of the underground space of the amusement arcade is predicated on their being at once open to the public, but requiring special and separate codes of operation and access, evidenced in the language (e.g. 'credit'; 'high score'; 'extra life'), cultural idiosyncrasies (e.g. placing money in full view on cabinets to have dibs on the next game) and bodily *habitus* (as Newman humorously recalls from an episode of *Seinfeld*, to succeed at *Pac-Man* requires the 'perfect combination of Mountain Dew and Mozzarella . . . just the right amount of grease on the joystick' (Newman 2016, 8)). These niceties are reflected in other shadowy, dark, and imperceptible places where subcultures abound, such as strip-clubs, snooker-halls, and strip-malls: spaces simultaneously symptomatic of the dangers of time-wasting, cash-sapping, leisure consumption, and traditionally linked to organized crime (see Trapunski 1979, 104).

As the literature outlined above demonstrates, videogames have a long, tiresome relationship with moral outrage. From the abhorrent story of a boy, who, while being sexually abused by a clergyman, spent the money that he was given on arcade games (Amis 1982, 29–30) through the shameful machinations of Gamergate and into the contemporary shill of lootboxes in top-tier releases, it can seem as if videogames achieve recognition only when fomenting moral panic. Now that videogames are a mature medium, moral panic is courted by some developers and utilized for its marketing advantages. The knowing satire of Rockstar's *Grand Theft Auto* franchise impels the mortal hand-wringing of politicians. Their kneejerk responses, including first amendment debates, class action lawsuits, and prohibition has the contradictory effect of adding gravitas to the 'trivial' position of games, while trivializing the grave business of politics. Yet most games do not achieve this level of notoriety in the wider public consciousness. Games continue to be viewed as a medium, which, in common with the subterranean world of play, are somehow positioned 'beneath' popular culture (Southern 2001, 2). As its starting point this chapter draws on historical literature from the dawn amusement arcades' in Victorian England. It is shown, from their inception, that while games were viewed by commentators as a subculture to be looked down upon, they were also an arena of innovation and a manifestation of changing working and leisure conditions seen at the time. These are features that extend into further discussion concerning the work and play that is required to maintain videogame machines' social and cultural status, particularly in their maintenance and curation. Rather than being machines of the past that occupy a separate space and time in a glass cabinet in a museum, it is shown that amusement arcades and particularly those who interact with them are living histories that can only be properly experienced and engaged by being fully hands on with them. To demonstrate this in practice, the second part of the chapter presents primary data gathered through interviews and participant observation of those who have been hands on in the construction of the histories of videogames in amusement arcades over the past 40 years. These are individuals who have played, worked, and owned amusement arcades during this time. The techniques, technologies, financial, and social capital are evidenced in a passion shown in their practice ensuring that the past lives on into the future through those who are hands on in the present.

Historical forces of amusement arcades

Videogames continue to occupy a position in the nether regions of popular culture that is as prevalent in the twenty-first century domestic realm of shiny consoles and consumer electronics as it was in the 1970s and 1980s fug of the neon-night of amusement arcades. This suggests that there are historical forces attached to videogames, and to games more generally, which mean that they are at best a waste of time and at worst corrupting the moral integrity of individuals within society. As with any study of the histories of videogames, this cannot be limited to the game itself, or the technology that gives rise to it, but is instead contingent on a confluence of factors, including social policy, human geography, and demographics. Bank holidays, inaugurated in the United Kingdom in 1872, were the first of many revisions of social policy that led to a "huge growth in demand, both for leisure time, and for activities to fill that leisure time" (Downs 2010, 56). Modest budgets and short holidays precluded long-distance travel, and so working class people from urban centres like Bolton and Manchester began to take holidays nearby, in places like Blackpool and Fleetwood. These trips offered holidaymakers the opportunity to 'experience a world set-apart from the everyday' (Downs 2010, 57) in nascent amusement arcades. This separateness has become an aspect central to the sociological investigation of games, which are seen invariably as a space separated from the everyday (see e.g. Caillois 2001; Huizinga 1970; Goffman 1961; Salen and Zimmerman 2005). Encouraged by the opportunities presented by the working class who finally had money to spend and the wherewithal to spend it, seaside entrepreneurs invested in new amusement attractions and increased the quality of existing ones. The result was a very early form of consumption operating as a function of production, certainly for those who previously were only economically valued due to their labour power. As Young notes, the values attached to subterranean activity meant that "hedonism [was] closely tied to productivity" (Young 2005, 150). The impression this left on the histories of record of the time shows how negatively this was viewed by the refined classes in Victorian Britain. From their perspective, the working classes debauched themselves to within an inch of their labour-intensive usefulness, all the while revelling in the revulsion of

> Crowded, noisy, vulgar, unbuttoned, uninhibited enjoyment, for better or worse. They epitomised carnival, saturnalia, the temporary triumph of the periphery over the core, the world turned upside down, the suspension of dignity and inhibitions, the temporary reversal of the civilising process, the reign of gluttony, extravagance and licentiousness.
>
> (Walton cited in Downs 2010, 56)

As seen in research on home coding and cracking in the 1980s (Wasiak 2013; Swalwell 2008) games shift traditional boundaries of work and play, through the introduction of new technologies, so that the "world of leisure and work are intimately related" (Young 2005, 151). Indeed, home coding drew on this extensively, becoming a cottage industry which briefly achieved the Marxist ideal of utopia between work and play. Yet for Young, originally writing in 1971, there was a tension, played out in the overlapping spheres of production and consumption which suggested that the 'subterranean values' of hedonism, autonomy and activities performed for their own sake were becoming more prevalent in subsections of society. These subsections generated subcultures, which had greater truck with the pleasure principle of play than the grind of the work ethic. A focus on immediate gratification, rather than delaying to an undefined future was the aim of the subjects of Young's study. These same ideals of subterranean values of play, of inverting norms in pursuit of hedonism, are as evident in the trips the working class took to the amusement arcade in the nineteenth century as to those in the late twentieth century. History suggests that the relationship between work and leisure is tightly entwined with the emergence and predominance of amusement arcades as a primary leisure activity.

Play as work

The symbiotic relationship between work and leisure is a phenomenon which is brought into sharp focus when considering the hands on work required to maintain amusement arcade machines. Whether fruit machines, pinball, shovellers (also known as penny drop) or videogames, the 'decay of gaming hardware [. . .] is a serious and potentially difficult to manage issue' (Newman 2012, 14). Some attempts have been made to preserve the past in a representation of working order by institutions such as museums, shifting the focus of videogames away from the incessant 'logic of the upgrade' (Newman 2012, 37), a defining feature of modern consumer electronics and specifically videogames. As part of the 'Game On' project, the Barbican museum in London collected, curated, and presented a host of videogames from the past, which then toured Europe, Asia, and America (Guins 2014, 281). The hands on nature of such exhibitions, where museum-goers are able to play the games on offer, is central to their success. Yet it removes the machines from their original context of the 'naughty place' of the amusement arcade and therefore inevitably cleanses the experience. By law and custom, smoking, eating, loud music, and neon are not promoted in the creaking halls of the Barbican. The sight and site of a *Ridge Racer* (1993) deluxe sit-down cabinet, in full working order with a notice next to it denoting its year of release and the reasons for its historical importance at once demonstrates how quickly past technologies age, while locating past videogames in a time and space when they were a new form of media (Newman 2012, 86–87). Meanwhile, as Guins observes, the placement of a *Space Invaders* (1978) cabinet on a pedestal behind glass in the Strong Museum of Play in New York detaches the videogame further from its original location and illuminates how the "historical conditions, context and experiences of coin-op arcade video games often go unremarked" (Guins 2014, 132).

In keeping with the historical literature around arcades, keeping the history of arcades rubs up against the same problems as any other curatorial activity. The original context is erased as the extinct dinosaurs move from the plains into the Great Halls. As Castells highlights, this is both a strength and a weakness of museums, which are "systems for the storage, processing and transmission of potentially interactive cultural messages, in and for a determined social context" (Castells 2001, 4). This social context is by economic and cultural necessity mostly – but not exclusively – the general public who consume cultural messages in the space and time of the museum. In the case of those seeking out games, these will be drawn from two main audiences. First, those who have not experienced this history first hand, but are acutely aware of the social context of museums that offer interactivity at every station from stone rubbing to touchscreens. The rapid pace of change involved in gaming and its technology amplifies this and all the while new media becomes old at an accelerated pace. The second audience, and those who are likely to attend specialist exhibitions at the Barbican or Strong Museums' *will* have had hands on experience with arcade games, either in their original incarnations in amusement arcades, as conversions to home microcomputers and consoles or as part of emulation (for discussion as to the legal complexity of this, see McFerran 2018). The net result is that museums attendees will have an acute awareness of the extensive hands on curatorial work, which, by default removes and places games from a specific historical context, into a specific social context and generates what Kocurek and Tobin (2014) have coined the 'undead arcade', an experience that in spite of not being able to be recaptured, continues to live, albeit in a distorted form.

This extended play as work of undead videogame amusement arcades outside of their specific historical context leads to the central consideration of this chapter. What has occurred and continues to occur in arenas where videogames remain within their historical context? Drawing on the position outlined through the literature that there are extensive historical forces evident in the work around protecting and playing arcade videogames, the discussion below is based on interviews and observations with individuals who are hands on throughout the history of these games. As shown below, individuals who have played and worked (and continue to do so) in amusement arcades which house videogames as living histories have first-hand, hands on experience of the videogame in the arcade. No matter how valiant the efforts of museums or emulation, this can never be attained by placing games into a specific social context., such as a museum.

Method

Interviews and participant observation were undertaken between March 2015 and August 2017. In keeping with themes in the historical literature by Downs, an English seaside town in Essex was chosen. This yielded one participant observation and three interviews with participants. This allows two separate, but overlapping arenas to be explored. First in the traditional 'seafront' amusement arcades where old videogames are arranged in a manner similar to those in the past where they would exist as part of a larger economy of gambling 'fruit' machines, pinball, change machines, and food vendors. These machines are unmodified to the point where the cabinets require old 10 pence pieces to be used to begin a game. The second arena, less than a kilometre away, is an 'inland' retro arcade, which includes both original games and emulated 'candy cabs' as well as a cordoned-off area for high-value payout (£200+) fruit machines, which can only be played by those over the age of 18. Finally, there is a separate floor for high-end PC and Local Area Network gaming.

The second location for participant observation and an interview is a large inland arcade located one of the Northern industrial towns that provided many of the patrons for Blackpool in the nineteenth century. Although its location is not traditional for arcades, it does draw on some of the more extreme historical idiosyncrasies of 'inland arcades'. A bar serves alcohol and patrons can play all night on videogames that are set to 'free play', meaning they do not require money to be deposited into them.

As veterans of arcades in 1970s and 1980s UK, all participants witnessed the introduction of videogames to amusement arcades. Similarly, as they all continue to have gainful employment in arcades either as gamblers, employees or owners of amusement arcades, they have witnessed the retrenchment of videogames within amusement arcades in the late 1990s and have seen a concurrent rise in interest around retro arcades, particularly the rise of inland arcades. The names of the participants have been anonymized and three-letter initials (e.g. PSD, FSH), which would traditionally have been input into high-score tables, have been used in their place.

The findings presented here are broadly separated into three sections that spotlight the different elements of hands on history as arcades have evolved in their historical context. The discussion first shows how amusement arcade subculture drew individuals in and how the playing of games and playing with norms worked on the players in a specific and appealing way. The next section demonstrates how, following this period of experimentation, amusement arcades became a source of work, income and sustenance during the 1980s, while maintaining subcultural and hedonistic elements. The final section explores how contemporary amusement arcades continue to exist and operate and the individuals' part in this. Throughout, the hands on notion of history is accentuated, which foregrounds the argument made here and in others' work that while the game can be taken out of the arcade, the arcade cannot be taken out of the game.

Getting into games

As discussed by Downs (2010), videogames are a relatively recent introduction to amusement arcades, broadly coinciding with the widespread commercial use of silicon technology in the last quarter of the twentieth century. Arcades were a popular leisure destination for the working class throughout the nineteenth and twentieth century and provided an induction into videogames via other coin-op games. This is observed very early on by PSD, the owner of an inland arcade in Essex who recalls the introduction of 'videos' to arcades in the mid-1970s

> The golden age in the US is talked about as '79 – '83, but mine was earlier, probably '72 – '76. We'd go on a week's holiday every year to Blackpool . . . and I'd be allowed to go into an arcade on my own. It felt like an hour, but you know it was probably only ten minutes . . . I was only seven as the coin-drop machines would take the pennies which went out of circulation in 1973.
>
> (PSD)

PSD's recollection follows in a rich tradition of relatively short holidays from the working class towns of Silloth to nearby Blackpool. This echoes a pattern of leisure consumption identified nearly a century before. PSD's memory is of parents who gave their son some change so that he could entertain himself while they did something else, possibly increasing the propensity for becoming inured to subcultures. The lack of extant surveillance from a moral guardian is in itself a method of attracting to young people visiting arcades (Tobin 2014), which somewhat contradictorily allows them to engage in "adult leisure which adolescents are impatient to experience" (Fisher 1995, 74), which would include, but not be limited to, gambling. This is especially salient here, because, as shown below, PSD would later become a professional gambler.

The continuum between young people, videogames, and deviant behaviour appears to be malleable and not wholly dependent on entering amusement arcades, as young people were "far more likely at an early age to encounter video games – widely spread throughout large stores, cafes, chip-shops etc." (Huff and Collinson 1987, 407). This is the extension of the subterranean values of play enshrined in the amusement arcade through the physical manifestation of the videogame: the cabinet and the game it contains. You can take the game out of the arcade, but not the arcade out of the game. As a result, the deviancy of amusement arcades proliferates, away from and beyond traditional underground sites and into supermarkets, takeaways, newsagents, and laundrettes (see Guins 2004). Indeed, anywhere that had a high volume of transitory, cash-rich passing trade, and required people to loiter or wait became an ideal locale for arcade games. This was another form of extended play: subterranean values that broadened into the formal, adult, social world. Yet, while many of these places appeared to be adult and mature, they were not even value-neutral proprietors of work and consumption. Instead, by selling fast, hot, cheap food, they offered some respite from the blancmange and semolina of school dinners and, in their own dubious practice, offered a reverse gateway

152 Alex Wade

to the subterranean experiences proffered by the arcade, their hot practices playing fast and loose with the law to maximize revenue, which even extended to illegal sales of cigarettes:

> I'd go into a Chinese and pay 50p for three goes on the videos. There was this chip-shop where you'd get a fag [cigarette] and a match for 5p, a portion of chips for 25p and the rest for the videos. I was 12. Totally illegal of course.
>
> (FSH)

The 'safe' spaces that were offered by games are very much in flux here. Clearly, FSH, now a staff member at one of the largest seafront arcades in Essex, was 'safe' from the moral guardians of parents and was able to smoke underage, safe in the knowledge that he wouldn't be caught. The risk to the proprietor is equally clear in selling cigarettes to minors: hiding the cigarettes surreptitiously from prying authority figures is a tactic employed by children as regards to evasion of the paternal gaze. The risk and reward that is key to success in arcade game play is extended here into the balance between restitution and destitution and arguably it is the formal, adult world of the fish and chip shop, which has the greatest amount to lose and the least amount to gain, while the risk to the schoolboy is minimal, the gains, via inducement into the adult world, are significant.

Perhaps it was the perceived success of amusement arcades and the increased revenue allied with the introduction of videos that encouraged individuals to welcome the arcade into everyday spaces. This is seen in recollections of amusement arcades from the 1970s and the difference that the shift from the chrome and gloam of electromechanicals to the smooth sheen of videos made to revenue and the environs of the amusement arcade:

> The charm of the arcades then was the noise of the electromechanicals [pinball, shovellers] dovetailing with the cutting edge of the videogames. Those games really made a difference. It was louder then [1970s] as there was no carpet in a lot of arcades, then by the 1980s arcades became better at making money and they had carpets. The videogames really made money.
>
> (PSD)

The psychology employed here has a genealogy that stretches back to Blackpool Pleasure Beach of the early twentieth century where machines were "bright and beautiful; coin chutes were designed to maximize the sounds of falling pennies to encourage the sensation of significant winnings" (Downs 2010, 58). The seductive gleam of arcades in the 1970s and 1980s is now augmented by the bleeping and winking of the screens of videogames. This potential for revenue extended play not only into everyday spaces, but, on a much larger scale, from the seafronts of holiday towns to the streets of factory towns, transferring the seaside to the urban and leisure to labour. This found its logical conclusion in an arcade in Workington, where, as was the dream for those who struggled with low-quality arcade conversions of their favourite games, the arcade experience quite literally 'came home':

> There were arcades everywhere back then [in 1981]. Silloth, Blackpool, Carlisle, Workington. Inland arcades too. One day I remember going a short cut into town [Workington] and in the middle of this street, in this terraced house there was an arcade. This wasn't a room, it was *every* room. These huge cabinets in a 100 square foot house, there wasn't enough room to breathe. Can you imagine being a neighbour to an arcade? It got shut down by the Council a fortnight later. It was just totally against the law.
>
> (HAM)

While arcade videogames were not ostensibly portable, they were able to be used in most locations. Generic 'woody' or 'candy cabs', which were uniform in size and used a standard 240v electrical outlet, made installing an arcade in a town house a relatively straightforward task. The domestic arcade described by HAM, who is now the owner of a large northern inland arcade, opened in 1981, appears as part of a wider trend towards the production of "events, spectacles that have an almost instantaneous turnover time" (Harvey 1989, 157) prefiguring the seasonal pop-up shops of contemporary high streets by over 30 years, characteristics that clearly appealed to young and impressionable, perhaps even bored young adults taking a quotidian shortcut through a residential area. In the contemporary realm the emphasis of sheen over situation has been taken to its logical conclusion. Recent arcade spectacles such as *SnoCross* or *Star Wars: Battlepod* continue to have an emphasis on quick turnover, of money and personnel, yet this is not contingent on *agon*, the skill of the player, but on arbitrary time-limits fixed by the developer or operator. Irrespective of the skill of the player, exposure to the game remains broadly the same: while practice and skill may improve social standing on the high-score table, it will never extend play either for the player, or into locations outside of the amusement arcade, where space is at a premium and other consumer electronics can be used as emulators or substitutions instead.

Working the game

If arcade games of the 1970s and 1980s were flexible in their location, they were equally flexible in the experiences they proffered, not only to the user, but to the arcade operator or proprietor. Printed circuit boards (PCBs) could be swapped in the same cabinet, often leading to humorous disjuncture between cabinet art and the actual game. Dipswitch changes permitted operators to alter the difficulty level of the game, new technological innovations impelled manufacturers to increase the price of cabinets and, in turn, increase the price charged to individuals playing the game, sometimes by as much as 100%.

While these changes to price and difficulty structures were expected, it did not mean that they were accepted and they had the greatest effect on how games were approached and played within arcades,

> I think it was *Galaxian* that came out and it was like 20p a play. Full colour, lovely backgrounds, but that was like twice the price of *Pac-Man* or *Space Invaders* or *Asteroids*. That's a big hike . . . for the faces [arcade regulars] they had to find ways to deal with this . . . you either got very good, found something else, or got good at playing the floor.
>
> (FSH)

The construction and maintenance of 'being a face' – a regular customer of social standing – was dependent on being proficient at a certain game, of 'getting good'. Proficiency required an investment of time matched only by the deposit of money. In distinction to Trapunski's idea that a coin offers *quid pro quo* and Kocurek's (2012) observation that play can be extended through practice and skill, there is a different type of play at work here, that of 'gaming' the wider arcade. FSH notes a clear delineation between being 'very good' at playing the game, and being 'good at playing the floor'. Playing the floor would be a hands on experience. It would normally mean gambling on fruit machines to increase funds, but sometimes involved practices that stretched or punctured the boundaries of legality, turning the mechanics, the *machinery* of the game inside out and back on itself

> I'd see it as a floorwalker [employee who looked after the machines and customers]. I'd go up to the change machine to get the money out and it'd just be water. People had put 50p pieces made of ice into the slot and it had given them 50p's worth of change in 10s. I guess they would go back into the videos. They were primitive then, you can't do it now of course.
>
> (FSH)

The tricks and 'systems' used to game the games show how, in the face of increased prices, hacks – novel solutions to complex problems and ways of manipulating regulatory technologies – can be explored and exploited. FSH also recalled that he never caught patrons stealing directly from change, fruit or video machines, but that infrequently, employees who had access to machines were caught stealing cash from pinball and arcade games. In this instance, it is not young people who were deviant or criminal, but the autonomy of workers in the amusement arcade that brings subterranean values to the surface, a by-product of unsupervised employment at the low-end of a cash-rich industry where dingy, dark corners, lit only by the screened-out faces of the vidkids would promote such behaviour. (Kent 2001, 50). Arcade operators attempted to reduce the widespread use of cash by using tokens, resulting in more sophisticated, 'grey' workarounds, involving collusion between staff and regular customers:

> You've got to work every angle. This is a minimum wage business, like a lot of entertainment industries, you end up spending your money where you've

earned it, on highscores on videos or pinballs . . . I would get the floorwalkers to tell me when they think a machine is going to pay [tokens]. I'd get the tokens and put them in a low-pay machine. Tokens in, cash out. They'd keep the cash and I'd keep half the tokens and put them in *Defender* or *Asteroids*.

(VIV)

This extension of play into manipulating machines and processes was sophisticated by its very nature: as techniques and technologies of control and command became more complex, so did the approaches required to circumnavigate them. There were simpler – and more elegant – ways of achieving desired outcomes. FSH recalled that removing the piezzo electric element from a cigarette lighter and arcing it across the coin slot of *Moon Cresta* could acquire "free plays, but sometimes it would just blow it up". Other players tried "changing the coin slot on shovellers so it took 2p instead of 10p, less money in, more money out" (VIV): because two pence pieces were larger than 10p pieces, they were also more likely to move the money at the front of the shoveller towards the chute. Both operators and players adapted within an arms race of institutional rules versus guerrilla tactics where the prize was cash and credit to play games. For many of the respondents, following their childhood initiation to arcades, their interest was maintained not by new games and graphics, but by learning about the challenges posed by new technology, how to overcome them and how to use their hands on knowledge of the arcade to their advantage. This expertise could be employed maliciously: the predilection for sexual assault noted by Amis (1982), Sudnow (1983) and Foulkes (1981) is emphasized by the observation of FSH

You remember *Donkey Kong*? There was this girl playing it and she was so into it that this guy just came up behind her and lifted her skirt up. She didn't even notice! He had it up all the time she was playing just because she was so into it [the game].

(FSH)

This advances the idea that the "nightclub-dark" of the arcade is closer to a casino or club, where "electronic jingles and pop music suppress normal conversation and keep the mind focused on the machines" (Needham 1982, 54; Fisher 1995, 75) to the point where the young woman in FSH's anecdote was so engrossed in a video game that she was unaware her skirt had been lifted. The proclivity of screens to captivate individuals – young and old – is a debate that continues from *Minecraft* to *Snapchat*. Knowledge gleaned from the arcades of the 1980s shows that these concerns are not new and with the ongoing problems associated with sexual bullying and violence in schools along with online predation among young people, neither are they trivial.

Reviving the game

In the amusement arcades of the 2010s, there is a revival of the 'naughty places', of the dim and dank corners of the past where moral panics and subcultures spawned side by side. For the seaside arcade, the experience can only be complete if the entire historical context is present. Reconfiguration of old *Track and Field* (1983) and *Pac-Man* (1980) cabinets to accept modern 10p pieces, or even to be switched to free play is not possible. Instead, old 10p pieces are exchanged at the counter, where the metallic stacks are piles of pounds. It requires a human to undertake the transaction from modern money to old iterations: modern change machines do not accept obsolete coins. The reliance on electromechanical technology, experienced in jammed coins in coin chutes, and screen-burn – where images remain on the screen even after the power supply is disconnected and ghosting, where images remain after they should have notionally disappeared – is part of the experience

> It's difficult to find that balance, but I don't know any other place in the country where you have to use old money for old games. Games in the past were about choice, if you wanted to put 10p in a machine to last all night you could if you were good enough. In an all you can play arcade, where you're paying a tenner [£10] for all night and you expect them all to work and I guess it's trying to get people in who haven't played [arcade] games before. When these machines go kaput, we can give the punter another go on another game. Because it is seen as free, people are often really happy.
>
> (VIV)

The assumption is that because the seafront arcade has a diversity in machines, that offering authenticity in both monetary exchange and the game experience, videogames remain in the spiritual homes of the seaside amusement arcade

> We can do that because it's not just what we do, if a machine goes kaput we can leave it off until the engineer fixes it, or we can have a go. Even though we have access to the coin box, the money isn't worth anything, not like the old days . . . I think the owner of this place, owned three scrapyards, not sure if he still does or not. Do you know how much it [the arcade] cost? Three million quid. That's the money he's holding in the place. When it was closed one day he lost £3000, not sure if that was revenue or profit, but it's not bad for a day's play.
>
> (FSH)

As VIV notes, for inland arcades, which rely on the proper functioning of old machines, and is central to what they do it is essential that they offer all of the games all of the time: maintenance of the social context is essential to its success. This is significant technical and logistical challenge, as HAM notes:

> We have two engineers on duty to look after all of these machines. They are in as close to perfect working order as any in the world. The screens are new

or refurbished, the boards the same. Often, this is not about over-use, but under-use: a game left on for 100 hours will continue to work, it's when you drop the power supply that the problems really start . . . The 100 or so games you see here are just part of our collection, we have a load more in storage and they can be a pig to get started when we bring them in here.

Furthermore, the maintenance of expectation in inland arcades incurs large economic costs, which must be offset by any means possible. Akin to the floorwalker in an arcade in the 1980s, the owner of a retro arcade in a city centre can only spend his money one way: by putting it back into arcade machines,

> I was a professional gambler until 2005. On the ferry between Portsmouth and Bilbao I could clear £2000–£3000 a trip . . . When I opened this place I put 250 thousand [pounds] of my own money into it, but it doesn't pay for itself, that's why we need adult fruits [fruit machines with high payouts] to support the retro gaming.
>
> (PSD)

More than in any other statement, PSD reveals here how hard individuals work at maintaining the amusement arcade. This is highly personal investment in an area where there is a relatively low demand, but the hands on work of the arcade proprietor, their investment in social and cultural capital is such that their financial capital is placed at risk. For FSH, gainful employment in a seaside arcade remains, but in one of the few places in the UK where a link to the past of arcade cabinets remains, not 'undead', but instead in the case of the Essex seafront, a place that has "done pretty well as arcades go as people know what they're getting, gambling, fairground, chip shops, fresh fish" (FSH).

Conclusion

This chapter posits that much of the literature written of the time and at the time reflects notions that amusement arcades, with their position geographically and culturally underground, gave rise to proliferating and, at times, nefarious subcultures. These grew out of these contradictorily safe places that allowed experimentation and innovation with subterranean values and extended into the formal, 'adult' social world. It is in how these social, financial and cultural notions, fermented in working class towns which hosted videogame amusement arcades in the 1970s and 1980s, influenced and even educated individuals into extending play into the realm of a postindustrial economy. While these subterranean values were initially located underground, through a lived, hands on history the amusement arcade continues to exist, inland, seaside, but always underground, not purely as hedonism and not only as work, but as a hands on way of life extending play through the present and into the future.

Bibliography

Alcorn, A. (2014) When Arcades Ruled the World: The Genesis of an Industry. *Retro Gamer*, Issue 127, April 2014.

Amis, M. (1982) *Invasion of the Space Invaders*. London: Hutchinson.

Caillois, R. (2001) *Man, Play and Games*. Urbana, IL: University of Illinois Press.

Castells, M. (2001) Museums in the information era: cultural connectors of time and space. Presentation given at *ICOM*, Barcelona, Spain 1–6 July 2001 available at http://icom.museum/fileadmin/user_upload/pdf/ICOM_2001/ICOM_ENG_10_2001_small.pdf, 4–8. Retrieved 28 March 2018.

Centre for Leisure Research (1990) *Playing the Machines: A Study of Leisure Behaviour*. Edinburgh: Citizens Advice Bureau.

DeLeon, C.L. (2014) Arcade-Style Game Design – Pinball's Connection to Coin-Op Videogames. *Kinephanos*, January 2014: 43–57.

Downs, C. (2010) Two Fat Ladies at the Seaside: the place of gambling in working class holidays. In Snape, R. and Smith, D. (eds). *Recording Leisure Lives: Holidays and Tourism in 20th Century Britain.*, Vol 112, Eastbourne: Leisure Studies Association, 51–73.

Fisher, S. (1995) The Amusement Arcade as a Social Space for Adolescents: An Empirical Study. *Journal of Adolescence*, 18: 71–86.

Foulkes, G. (1981) Control of Space Invaders and other Electronic Games. *HC Deb* 20 May 1981, 5: cc. 287–291.

Goffman, E. (1961) *The Presentation of Self in Everyday Life*. London: Penguin.

Guins, R. (2004) "Intruder Alert, Intruder Alert! Videogames in Space", *Journal of Visual Culture*, 3(2): 195–211.

Guins, R. (2014) *Game After: A Cultural Study of Videogame Afterlife*. Massachusetts, MA: MIT Press.

Haddon, L. (1988) "Electronic and Computer Games: The History of an Interactive Medium", *Screen*, 29(2): 52–73.

Harvey, D. (1989) *The Condition of Postmodernity*. Oxford: Blackwell.

Huizinga, J. (1970) *Homo Ludens: A Study of the Play Element in Culture*. London: Paladin.

Huff, G. and Collinson, F. (1987) Young Offenders, Gambling and Video Game Playing. *British Journal of Criminology*, 27(4): 401–410.

Huxley, J. and Carroll, D. (1992) A Survey of Fruit Machine Gambling in Adolescents, *Journal of Gambling Studies*, 8: 167–179.

Kent, S. L. (2001) *The Ultimate History of Videogames*. New York: Three Rivers Press.

Kocurek, C. A. (2012) Coin-drop Capitalism. In Mark J. P. (ed.). *Before the Crash*. Wolf, Detroit: Wayne State University Press, 189–208.

Kocurek, Carly A. and Tobin, Samuel. (2014) "Introduction to the Issue" *Reconstruction: Studies in Contemporary Culture* 14(1).

McFerran, D. (2018) The retro gaming industry could be killing video game preservation. Available at http://www.eurogamer.net/articles/2018-02-09-the-retro-gaming-industry-could-be-killing-video-game-preservation. Retrieved 8 March 2018.

Needham, N.R. (1982) Thirty Billion Quarters Can't be Wrong – Or Can They? *Today's Education*, 71: 53–55.

Newman, J. (2012) *Best Before: Videogames, supercession and obsolescence*. Abingdon: Routledge.

Newman, J. (2016) Mazes, Monsters and Multicursality: Mastering Pac-Man 1980–2016, *Cogent OA Arts and Humanities* 3(1) available at http://www.tandfonline.com/doi/full/10.1080/23311983.2016.1190439. Retrieved 13 March 2018.

Rubin, M. (1982) *Defending the Galaxy: The Complete Handbook of VideoGaming*, Gainesville: Triad Publishing Company.

Salen, K. and Zimmerman, E. (2005) Game Design and Meaningful Play. In Raessens, J. and Goldstein, J. (eds). *The Handbook of Computer Game Studies*, Massachusetts, MA: MIT Press.

Southern, M. (2001) The Cultural Study of Games: More Than Just Games. Paper presented at the 2001 Game Developers Conference Europe, London.

Sudnow, D. (1983) *Pilgrim in the Microworld: Eye, Mind and the Essence of Video Skill*. New York: Warner Books.

Swalwell, M. (2008) 1980s Home Coding: The Art of Amateur Programming. In Brennan, Stella and Ballard, Su (eds). *The Aotearoa Digital Arts Reader*, Auckland: Aotearoa Digital Arts and Clouds.

Tobin, S. (2014) Loitering in the Arcade of Game Studies, Paper presented at the conference of the Digital Games Research Association, Snowbird, Utah, 4 August, 2014.

Trapunski, E. (1979) *Special When Lit: A Visual and Anecdotal History of Pinball*. New York: Doubleday and Company.

Wasiak, P. (2013) Playing and Copying: Social Practices of Home Computer Users in Poland during the 1980s. In *Hacking Europe*, Gerard Alberts and Ruth Oldenzial (Eds) New York, NY: Springer, 129–150.

Young, J. (2005) The Subterranean World of Play. In *The Subcultures Reader*, Ken Ganlan (Ed.) Abingdon: Routledge, 148–156.

10

ENRICHING 'HANDS ON HISTORY' THROUGH COMMUNITY DISSEMINATION

A case study of the *Pebble Mill project*

Vanessa Jackson

Online platforms present us with opportunities to create and enrich hands on histories that complement and challenge traditional approaches. They support Andreas Fickers' assertion that "academic historiography has definitely lost its hegemonic power in the public sphere" (2012, 6). Fickers notes that the Internet offers abundant opportunities to share previously inaccessible sources with potentially unlimited users, but asks what kind of history this might produce. The *Pebble Mill project*, an online community archive focused on the history of BBC Pebble Mill in Birmingham, is one possible answer. It is not a history based on critical examination of documentary sources, within a culture of objectivity, with the aim of producing a synthesis of authenticated events in a scholarly, narrative form. Instead, the *Pebble Mill project* is a history of living people, written by the community whose past experience it is, and facilitated by me, as archivist, chronicler, interpreter, and citizen curator. Documentary sources, and particularly artefacts, are critically examined, albeit not necessarily in a scholarly manner, and particular events are retold in a narrative form, but there is no pretence of objectivity, because the writing concerns the community's lived experience. How the actors in these particular events felt and the position they took are germane to the narrative, and at the heart of *their* history. This is a qualitatively different kind of resource. It is an informal history, often written in the form of an online conversation, rather than academic prose. It is partial, subjective, and in places lacks accuracy, but it is the history that the community chooses to write, and to share, about itself. This imbues the resulting historical text with a different kind of authenticity, and a different kind of value. Though they may lack the academic rigour of a traditional history, such collections have a place in the archival world. They provide complementary collections to the institutional repositories, and to 'official' histories.

'Hands on history' is a concept open to diverse interpretation. Fickers and van den Oever's plea was for a practical approach to historical enquiry, where – through physically interacting with artefacts – we stimulate our sensory understanding of the past (2014, 273). However, the methods through which we get our hands on the history can be varied, and I will argue here that the physicality of the process is not as important as the grass roots interrogation of historical artefacts, which could, in fact, occur in a virtual space.

One of the challenges for hands on history is how to disseminate the experiential encounter with the historical materials to a broader audience, in a manner that does not revert to traditional written history. If the physicality of the encounter is at the crux of the method's success, then how can this be replicated beyond the experience of the individual participants? The necessity now is to explore diverse methods of engaging wider audiences with hands on history, particularly through online means. Experimentation using online media archaeology laboratory spaces can result in new historiographical practices.

This chapter explores one application of hands on history: the *Pebble Mill project*, which employs a hands on approach to the creation and dissemination of multimedia artefacts, in the process producing what Dougherty and Schneider (2011) term an 'idiosyncratic archive'. The project is a democratic community history endeavour to document the history of BBC Pebble Mill. This chapter focuses upon the enrichment of histories through engagement with the online community, and the rewards and difficulties that result from facilitating them. The project provides an example of social media functioning as a laboratory for a community of memory around the practices of television production. As the project unfolds, social media communities interact with the collaborative online oral history, with the platforms becoming the space and means to encourage, share, manage, and interpret 'hands on history'.

The context of the *Pebble Mill project*

I worked in television production at BBC Birmingham for 20 years, leaving in 2008, and this is the source of my interest in documenting its unofficial history. I began the *Pebble Mill project* in 2010 as a piece of academic research, and have seen it grow to a collection of over 1600 artefacts, as a result of community involvement. Through the project I have become a 'citizen curator', learning to navigate through the various challenges which have presented themselves at various points along the journey.

Pebble Mill was the first purpose-built broadcast centre in Europe to combine radio and television production (BBC 1962). It opened in Birmingham in 1971 and closed in 2004. At its height it produced around 10 per cent of BBC output (Wood 2005), boasting a renowned drama department, producing *Nuts in May* (1976, BBC Two) and *Boys from the Blackstuff* (1982, BBC Two) among many other programmes. The prolific factual unit produced the original series of *Top*

162 Vanessa Jackson

Gear (1977–2001, BBC Two), *Countryfile* (1988–present, BBC One) and *Gardeners' World* (1968–present, BBC Two), in addition to live studio programming such as *Pebble Mill at One* (1972–1986, BBC One). Much of Pebble Mill's output falls under Frances Bonner's definition of 'ordinary television', with an emphasis on factual formatted programming incorporating 'real people' (2003). These types of programme are often neglected in terms of scholarship and critical acclaim, and their history is not as well documented as those in the traditional canon.

The *Pebble Mill project* consists of a website and a Facebook page with over 1600 members, many of whom are former BBC employees. As a former colleague I have a personal connection to many members of the online community. Blogs are regularly posted on the website and copied to Facebook, where most of the community activity happens: comments and new artefacts are added by participants, facilitating lively online discussion. There is a symbiotic relationship between the website and Facebook page, with social media driving traffic to the website, and individuals commenting on Facebook, with the content then copied back to the website.

Towards a wider interpretation of hands on history

Fickers and van den Oever (2014) define 'hands on history' in a literal fashion, stressing the physical encounter in stimulating our sensorial understanding of the past. Whilst this proves very effective in the context of an individual or small group of investigators, it is challenging to expand its scale. This interpretation of hands on history appears quite narrow in its scope, and I suggest the adoption of a less literal definition, which could yield similarly valuable results, whilst having the benefits of scalability.

Through the operation of the *Pebble Mill project* I have developed a practice of 'citizen curation', which I consider to be hands on in a more figurative sense. The role of the 'citizen curator' will be explored in more depth later in this chapter. The majority of artefacts on the *Pebble Mill project* website (www.pebblemill. org) have been donated to me by members of the online community which has grown up around the project. These artefacts are frequently remediated digital versions of analogue texts, including photographs of productions, people and their workplaces. Members also contribute videos, audio, and written material including script pages. Sometimes I am given a physical artefact, but more usually I receive a digitized version. Other artefacts are produced specially as part of the project: these include career biographies written by members of the online community, video oral histories created by me to document staff's working lives, and contemporary photographs of staff and memorabilia. Some of the video oral histories include demonstrations of defunct production equipment, which would be encompassed in Fickers and van den Oever's literal hands on history. However, I consider the engagement with all these artefacts in the online laboratory of social media as hands on history. It is the online community's hands on their own history: many individual hands on many small pieces of history, which when combined create a "textual memory product" (Keightley and Pickering 2012). Collecting the pieces of this particular historical jigsaw puzzle is a worthwhile endeavour in its own right, but the really valuable part of the exercise comes when the remediated artefacts are shared and built-on by the very community that created them in the first place, and this is where the hands on history is enriched in a laboratory-like space by the layering of more hands upon it.

Creating and sharing hands on history

For the *Pebble Mill project,* the really hands on historiography happens on social media, and specifically on Facebook. This is where the online community interacts with the historical material, by including their own experiences and memories, and adding further artefacts. This activity echoes citizen science and public history projects. Much of my practice centres on facilitating and moderating the sharing of historical artefacts online with the community involved with their original production. In order to understand how the process of enrichment occurs, it is necessary to consider some particular examples.

In October 2017 I posted a photograph on the Pebble Mill Facebook page (see Figure 10.1). It dates from 1983 and shows a local radio engineer, Rod Fawcett, standing beside the Radio WM (West Midlands) radio car, parked behind the garage at Pebble Mill. The radio car would be driven to a location and enabled live broadcasting from the scene. I asked if anyone could add any information about the radio car and how it worked, and members of the online community responded to the request. The post reached over 3500 people, 39 individuals 'liked' it and 29 people took the trouble to comment on it. This was a relatively high level of engagement for the page.

I have selected some of the comments posted in reaction to the photograph, to illustrate how the original artefact is built upon by the online community.

> Keith Butler: I was attached as an engineer to Radio WM in 1983, and it was me who went down to Brookmans Park to collect this radio car and drive it back to Pebble Mill.
>
> Bob Chesworth: UHF transmitter to that aerial on top of the mast, VHF comms to and from base. Air compressor to drive mast up (with safety overrides!) . . . A lot of the vehicles had number plates reflecting the transmitter, Lincs was A219 SUL 'cos we were 219 on medium wave . . .
>
> Keith 'Scouse' Brook: Before I became a Pebble Mill cameraman, I worked at Radio Merseyside in the late 60s. Their radio car was a Ford Cortina and the whole of the cargo area filled with very heavy car batteries to power the transmitter. This made driving the thing great fun especially around corners when we were trying to stay close to a blue light police escort! Trying to get a signal back was problematic and the car had to be inched backwards or forwards until the signal strength was good enough. There was a switch at the base of the antenna to inhibit driving with it extended. To perform the 'inching' procedure, the switch was over-ridden with an old penny piece wedged between the contacts!

164 Vanessa Jackson

FIGURE 10.1   Former Radio WM engineer, Rod Fawcett, with the Radio WM radio car. (Photo by permission of Rod Fawcett)

These first-hand testimonies provide a historical context around the original artefact which would be difficult to replicate without social media. We learn, from the Radio WM engineer, how he collected this particular vehicle and drove it back to BBC Pebble Mill. We hear about the technical equipment in the car, and that the same cars were in use across all BBC local radio stations, which provides us with a useful national picture. The idiosyncrasies of the car's handling, because of the weight of the equipment, and the details about how to over-ride the safety cut-out switch, which prevented driving with the mast up, could only be added by someone who had used it professionally, and demonstrate the challenges of operating customized broadcast equipment. This kind of detail would be unlikely to be recorded in any institutional archive, because of the power dynamics around how archival documents are collected, with artefacts coming from 'official' – usually managerial – sources, rather than those reflecting the 'unofficial' experiences of the staff. Therefore, comments explaining the lived experience of using broadcast equipment become an extremely valuable resource in idiosyncratic archives, and prove the effectiveness of a social media laboratory approach. The contextual information that the comments provide add to the history being told. It is the result of motivated individuals remembering having their hands on a historical artefact. The photographic artefact rekindles the memory of physically interacting with the radio car, and the commenters take pleasure in sharing their memories with each other, and adding to the comments already posted.

The type of artefact used to stimulate the engagement of the online community can be varied, and the medium does not appear to dictate the value of the responses. Social media allows members of the online community not simply to add comments in response to posts, but to add their own artefacts as well. This phenomenon creates a virtuous circle, where one artefact leads to the digitization and display of another, which then leads the conversation, and therefore the history being written, in another direction. Considering a specific example will help explain the process.

Community dissemination 165

FIGURE 10.2 A BBC Radio links vehicle at Burghley Horse Trials. (Photo by permission of Steve Dellow)

FIGURE 10.3 Eagle Tower Dinky toy. (Photo by permission of Cyril Thompson)

In January 2017 I posted a 1985 photo of a radio links vehicle at the Burghley Horse Trials (see Figure 10.2). I copied the post onto Facebook, and asked the online community to explain how the radio links worked in relaying the signal from an outside broadcast to either a BBC centre or a main transmitter. A number of engineers explained how the process worked technically, and by way of illustration, posted up their own photographs. Telescopic towers were often necessary to relay the signal with a line of sight to a radio links vehicle. A member of the Pebble Mill online community, Cyril Thompson, added a photograph of the Dinky toy version of the Eagle Tower, a mobile tower used for transmitting outside broadcast signals. He had found the toy in the waiting room at his dentist's office. Another engineer, Stuart Gandy, added a 1980 photograph of BBC Pebble Mill's actual Eagle Tower, and Steve Dellow added a photograph of rigged Eagle Towers in operation at Silverstone, during the British Grand Prix.

FIGURE 10.4 Pebble Mill Eagle Tower. (Photo by permission of Stuart Gandy)

FIGURE 10.5 Rigged Eagle Towers at Silverstone. (Photo by permission of Steve Dellow)

Steve Dellow also scanned and posted the communications planning sheet from the Burghley Horse trials of 1985, which relate to the photograph I had originally posted. The radio links vehicle shown is number '356' on the planning sheet, and Steve was stationed at Tinwell Lodge (see the fourth column on the sheet). As part of his duties Steve needed to pay the landowner, a farmer, £25 for parking the vehicle on his land, plus £20 for the previous year, which had not been paid. The planning sheet gives an insight into the intricate preparations that accompanied each outside broadcast, and provides a fascinating contextualization to the photographs.

The artefacts that were added by the Pebble Mill online community in response to the original radio links vehicle photograph, sparked several related posts on the website, as I re-purposed the material from the Facebook page. This supports the notion of the community carrying out its own hands on historical investigation, determining what it chooses to include and share in a laboratory-like setting.

Community dissemination   **167**

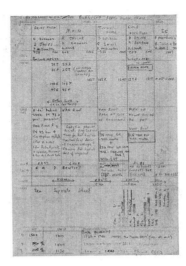

FIGURE 10.6 Outside broadcast communications sheet. (Photography by permission of Steve Dellow)

The role of the citizen curator

I consider my role in the *Pebble Mill project* as that of a 'citizen curator'; I select, organize, look after, and present the history of the community that has grown around the project. Without someone carrying out this complex role and facilitating the online interaction the project would lose momentum. To curate is to care: a curator is the keeper or custodian of a collection, derived from the Latin 'curare', to take care of. 'Taking care' is a crucial aspect of the role, and extends to the care of the artefacts which are entrusted to me, the care of the history being told, and having a duty of care towards the project's participants. It is an ethical position involving a sensibility of care and a responsibility to the community. Caring for the materials and also the contributors, and their memories, suggests a shift from museum curation around the care for artefacts, to the wider care for the participants as well, as part of a 'living heritage', involved in the production of a living history. When projects involve oral histories, and continued interaction with an active community, extending a duty of care to include the contributors is entirely appropriate. This indicates a development in the curation role, and the necessity of a flexible approach which can respond to the demands of the project, rather than following traditional curatorial practice.

Citizen curation is a manifestation of engaged citizenry, and shares similarities with the better documented examples of citizen science, as well as community or alternative media and public history. It is part of what James Curran describes as "a new culture, that is critical, selective and participatory" (2003, 227). Jonathan Silvertown defines the citizen–scientist as a volunteer who collects and sometimes even processes data as part of a scientific study (2009, 467). In a similar vein Clemencia Rodriguez coined the term 'citizens' media' to encompass community,

168 Vanessa Jackson

radical, participatory and alternative media, highlighting the transformative effects from participants to active citizens (2003, 190). Such citizens provide labour, skills and enthusiasm at no monetary cost. However, the scale of activity differs hugely between projects. A citizen–science project may simply involve an hour's garden birdwatching as part of the Royal Society for the Protection of Birds' annual 'Big Garden Birdwatch'. Running a hyperlocal news site, or curating a community history project like that of the *Pebble Mill project*, requires sustained commitment on a daily basis. It is akin to a job, with (self-imposed) responsibilities and deadlines.

The citizen curator is in a position of power. They are taking care of a collection, deciding what belongs in that collection, how it is preserved and importantly they are the gate-keeper of it, making judgements on who has access and in what circumstances. Bailey et al. note that the Internet can be "ab(used) by those who hold the power, to give participants the illusion of participation" (2008, 106). I am conscious of the privileged and powerful position I hold, and feel a responsibility to use this power wisely, with the best interests of the community and the project at heart. The position of power distinguishes the curator from the community, even if they are embedded within it.

I want to care for the collection as best I can, but I have a very different approach to gate-keeping to most professional curators, because disseminating the archive openly and publicly is at the heart of the project. This does not mean, however, that there are no controls in place. There is moderation, although the operation is light-touch. In terms of the website, the first time a person comments, I as administrator have to approve it, thereafter that commenter is approved. This prevents the posting of spam or abusive comments. On the Facebook page, as administrator I can delete any inappropriate posts, but I have found that it is generally more effective for the online community to police itself. In the past contributors have realized when a comment they have written is inappropriate and have edited it themselves, or other members of the community have made it clear through the use of an emoticon when a comment makes them angry or upset. There are challenges that can occur, such as conflict becoming apparent within a project. In running the *Pebble Mill project* I have observed occasional hostility between different groupings within the community, or tension between staff who worked at Pebble Mill and outsiders, and negativity or abuse towards individuals featured on the site, due to incidents in the past. Deciding how to manage conflict can require careful thought on a case by case basis, particularly if an intervention is necessary.

Curation requires the selection of material, meaning that some material is discarded or unexplored; this process circumscribes the history being told. There are some unsavoury aspects to Pebble Mill's past that the community chooses not to remember publicly, for example, allegations of inappropriate sexual behaviour, or the dismissal of staff. The online community has never discussed these subjects, and I do not feel that it is appropriate for me to push them to confront them, although individuals have on occasion mentioned them to me privately. I feel that I would be stepping outside my role if I behaved more proactively here, and

I would risk alienating members of the online community. This does raise questions concerning the nature of the history being told, which risks presenting a sanitized version, reflecting nostalgically on the past, rather than addressing difficult issues. I would argue that I am led by the community on what is included in the history, and would not describe the *Pebble Mill project* as an objective history. Rather it is a subjective account written by and for the community who has created it. If the history was an academic account of BBC Pebble Mill then these issues should be included, but when it is a community-driven endeavour, then it should include what the community chooses to share. There is a tension between the desire to articulate all aspects of Pebble Mill's history, and the sensitivities towards unsavoury aspects of it.

It is tempting to concentrate on the positives of efforts like the *Pebble Mill project*, but it is important to consider the ethical role of the citizen curator at the centre of such collaborations, and to caution against overzealous sharing. The citizen curator moderates content and decides what should, and what should not, be included in the 'idiosyncratic archive'. It is his or her hands on the community's memories. Some decisions are very easy to make: if a personal comment is made about someone's private life, it is straightforward to see that a line has been crossed, however, there is an area of semi-public/private comments, where the issue is more nuanced, and where it is easy to make a poor decision. Nick Couldry describes areas of the Internet as a "private subzone of public space", and this is where ambiguities arise over what participants perceive as public or private (2003, 51). I have found funerals to be particularly sensitive subjects regarding the public/ private divide, and here I have learnt by my mistakes. I am frequently alerted to the deaths of former colleagues, and funeral details are shared with me. I often post the details on the Pebble Mill website and Facebook page, as people may wish to attend a former colleague's funeral. However, it is easy to intrude on a family's grief, as I discovered when a widow contacted me, after being offended that I had posted details of her husband's funeral. She felt I was encouraging people to take advantage of her hospitality, which was not my intention. I apologized and removed the post. Since then I have adjusted my practice, and now only post funeral details on the Facebook page, keeping posts about the deaths of BBC staff on the website very neutral, concentrating on their BBC history, and avoiding details about their deaths. This incident illustrates the need to adapt one's practice in the light of experience, and to be aware of the duty of care towards individuals. There are ethical boundaries that require careful consideration, especially in balancing the tensions between privacy and reputation, against community interest and historical record. New historiographical methods require new ethical frameworks and guidance, which are only now beginning to emerge.

The era of collaborative online oral history

The examples in this chapter have illustrated how the Pebble Mill virtual community, facilitated by me as its citizen curator, builds the online archive that documents the history of the broadcast centre, through a hands on interaction with historical media artefacts. Shared visuals and text evoke memories in others, who are prompted to contribute their own individual responses, which then builds the history further, with each person adding their piece of the collective jigsaw puzzle. The new digital media ecology created by social media for contemporary short-term memory work enables us to write history in new ways. The *Pebble Mill project* uses these platforms for historical remembering, and harvests the articulated memories from the online community.

The use of interactive online platforms to create hands on histories, through initiatives like the *Pebble Mill project*, constitute a paradigm shift in the writing of oral histories. We are now entering the era of collective, online, oral history. The interrelationship of the process of historiography and the creation of a collective textual memory product is crucial here, and both have interactive online platforms at their core. This form of online oral history projects presents us with new ethical challenges, with a duty of care needing to be extended to participants.

Flinn et. al. draw attention to the role of archives in stimulating memory (2009, 76), and this is what we see in practice with the *Pebble Mill project*: the posting of a media artefact online evokes memories, which are captured, curated, and then fed back to enhance the archive itself. The examples seen earlier in this chapter, concerning how artefacts are posted and commented upon, are testament to this new departure in oral history writing. The examples illustrate how, why, and what individuals contribute to the project, and demonstrate how this creates an idiosyncratic archive, telling a history using an experimental method that would be impossible through other means. This process demonstrates social media's ability to transform non-fictional narrative, by effectively crowd-sourcing it in a non-linear fashion, a concept which questions Cobley's assertion that "social media have not wrought a transformation of narrative any more than email or telephone did" (2014, 186). Social media does have the ability to transform non-fictional narrative, and to collectively build a multi-authored, non-linear, multi-media oral history. The artefacts and stories to be included in the Pebble Mill history are pre-dominantly chosen and donated by members of the online community. They are then remediated by me on the website and Facebook page, with some additional information, followed by the online community building on the original post with their comments, anecdotes and further photographs or additional artefacts. This is a circular creative process by which the community collectively produces their own history. Through this process a multiplicity of views is gathered, which provide a context far more nuanced than would be possible in an institutional archive, with personal first-hand testimony being key, rather than an institutional perspective. How individuals react to a particular multi-media blog post is not necessarily pre-dictable, with some seemingly innocuous posts eliciting high response levels, and online conversations frequently taking an unexpected direction, but this adds to the democratic empowerment of the community, leading and authoring the collection down particular paths.

What is not yet clear is the extent to which other community projects will exploit the possibilities of collective, online, oral history making. In time the opportunities afforded by interactive technologies are likely to become more visible to community and oral history projects, and the historians involved will hopefully capitalize on them, facilitating many communities in getting their hands on their own histories, interpreting and enriching them in the process.

Bibliography

Bailey, O.G., B. Cammaerts, and Carpentier, N. (2008) *Understanding Alternative Media.* London: Open University Press/McGraw Hill.

BBC (1962) Press release dated 12 November 1962, accessed at BBC Archives, Caversham, folder M10/23/10

Bonner, F. (2003) *Ordinary Television.* London: Sage Publications.

Cobley, P. (2014) *Narrative* (2nd edition). Abingdon, Oxon, New York: Routledge.

Couldry, N. (2003) Beyond the Hall of Mirrors? Some Theoretical Reflections on the Global Contestation of Media Power. In Couldry, N. and Curran, J. (eds). *Contesting Media Power: Alternative Media in a Networked World.* Maryland: Rowman & Littlefield Publishers.

Curran, J. (2003) Global Journalism: A Case Study of the Internet. In Couldry, N. and Curran, J. (eds). *Contesting Media Power: Alternative Media in a Networked World.* Maryland: Rowman & Littlefield Publishers.

Dougherty, M. & Schneider, S. M. (2011) Web Historiography and the Emergence of New Archival Forms. In Park, D. W., Jankowski, N. W. and Jones, S. (eds). *The Long History of New Media, Technology, Historiography, and Contextualising Newness,* New York: Peter Laing Publishing Inc.

Fickers, A. (2012) Towards a New Digital Historicism? Doing History in the Age of Abundance. *Journal of European History and Culture,* 1: 1–9.

Fickers, A. and Van Den Oever, A. (2014) Experimental Media Archaeology: A Plea for New Directions. In Annie van den Oever (ed.). *Techne/Technology: Researching Cinema and Media Technologies – Their Development, Use and Impact,* Amsterdam University Press, 272–278.

Flinn, A., Stevens, M., and Shepherd, E. (2009) Whose Memories, Whose Archives? Independent Community Archives, Autonomy and the Mainstream, *Archival Science,* 9(1–2): 71–86, Springer Science+Business Media.

Keightley, E. and Pickering, M. (2012) *The Mnemonic Imagination: Remembering as Creative Practice.* Basingstoke, New York: Palgrave Macmillan.

Rodriguez, C. (2003) The Bishop and His Star: Citizens' Communication in Southern Chile. In Couldry, N. and Curran, J. (eds) *Contesting Media Power: Alternative Media in a Networked World.* Maryland: Rowman & Littlefield Publishers.

Silvertown, J., (2009) A New Dawn for Citizen Science. *Trends in Ecology & Evolution,* 24(9): 467–471.

Wake, W. (accessed 10 Nov 2017) Live TV Drama. *BFI Screenonline* http://www.screenon line.org.uk/tv/id/1351821/index.html

Wood, J. (2005) *Prospero* (BBC retirees magazine). See article at http://www.pebblemill. org/blog/2005-prospero-article-john-wood/

PART III

Labs, archives and museums

11

THE MEDIA ARCHAEOLOGY LAB AS PLATFORM FOR UNDOING AND REIMAGINING MEDIA HISTORY

Lori Emerson

It is hard not to notice the rapid proliferation of *labs* in the arts and humanities over the last ten years or so – labs that now number in the thousands in North America alone and that are anything from physical spaces for hands on learning and research to nothing more than a name for an idea or a group of people with similar research interests, or perhaps a group of people who share only a reading list and have no need for physical space and no interest in taking on infrastructural thinking through shared physical space. Regardless of their administrative organization, focus, funding, equipment or outputs (or lack thereof), the proliferation of these labs reflects a sea-change in how the humanities are trying to move away from the nineteenth-century model of academic work typified by the single scholar who works in the boundaries of a self-contained office and within the confines of their discipline to produce a single-authored book that promotes a clearly defined set of ideas.

Instead, humanities scholars seem to be rallying around the term 'lab' (along with 'innovation' and 'interdisciplinary' and 'collaborative' – terms that are all invoked whenever the topic of labs come up), likely because this particular term and structure helps scholars put into better focus their desires for a mode of knowledge production appropriate to the twenty-first century – what one might call 'posthumanities' after Rosi Braidotti's articulation of it in *The Posthuman* as a humanities practice focused on human-non-human relationships, "heteronomy and multi-faceted relationality" and one that also openly admits, in Braidotti's words once more, that "things are never clear-cut when it comes to developing a consistent posthuman stance, and linear thinking may not be the best way to go about it". For me, in more concrete terms, this version of posthumanities work means pursuing modes of knowledge production that are quick on their feet, responsive, conversational or dialogical, emergent, collaborative, transparent, and self-conscious. They are interested in recording their knowledge production

176 Lori Emerson

processes, and experimental about what constitutes a rigorous knowledge production and distribution process. These are perhaps by now tired clichés of the kind of work many would like to do, many believe they do, and that many administrators would like to see humanists do; but it is still worth noting that – more because of a longstanding lack of access to both material and immaterial resources than a lack of imagination – very few are actually able do this kind of work. This trend to create labs, even if only in name, is also a response to pressures humanists are feeling to both legitimize and even 'pre-legitimize' what they do as increasingly they are expected not just to 'perform' but, more importantly, to prove they're performing. The proof of performance is possibly now more important than the performance itself. And where else do we get our ideas about 'proof' but from some notion of how the sciences are in the business of proving the rightness or wrongness of theories about reality by way of the 'discovery' of facts that takes place in a laboratory environment?

As popular figures in Science and Technology Studies such as Bruno Latour (particularly in his classic *Laboratory Life* from 1979, co-written with Steve Woolgar) and Donna Haraway (in her essay "Situated Knowledges: The Science Question in Feminism and the Privilege of Partial Perspective", 1988) have been teaching us for several decades: these notions about proof and the scientific method do not need to have any grounding in how scientific truth is actually produced or manufactured – it is more about trying to figure out why the continual circulation of a particular cultural belief is *necessary*. I have come to see that the staying power of this belief about the nature of proof and scientific practice is derived not so much from scholars' obliviousness or ignorance about these convention-bound processes of legitimation but instead from the importance of maintaining belief in *humanism*, even though it appears we are just talking about science. A belief about how scientists 'discover' truth depends on the related belief that scientists are not affected by the agency of their tools, machines, the outside world, other people (Latour and Woolgar 1986). This is a belief that is a cornerstone of humanism and thus it is just as much a part of the humanities as it is a part of the sciences, for the prevailing belief in the humanities seems to be that humanists are also not affected by their tools, machines, the outside world, other people. Microsoft Word is simply a tool I use to produce articles and books. Google is simply a search engine I use to discover relevant information. The Graphical User Interface just happens to be the easiest way for me to interact with my computer. Regardless of the constant admonition from administrators to innovate, collaborate, incubate and whatever other entrepreneurial terminology you can think of, at the end of the day our raises, appointments, ability to get jobs, and much else besides, depends on continually manufacturing the illusion of a clear separation between ourselves, others, and the rest of the material world.

It is true that some humanities labs appropriate a traditional notion of labs from the sciences as a way to continue humanism but they do so under the auspices of innovation – the Stanford Literary Lab, when it was under the directorship of Franco Moretti, is the most well-known example of this as Moretti described the lab's main project of 'distant reading' as one driven by the desire for "a more rational literary history" because "[q]uantitative research provides a type of data which is ideally independent of interpretations" (Moretti 2003, 72). But, these instances aside, what does a uniquely humanities lab look like – or what could such a lab look like if it did not feel compelled to respond to the aforementioned pressures to perform and 'objectively' measure such performance? How could such a lab even creatively make the most of its more limited access to the kinds of resources large science labs depend on and instead embrace what I called above the posthumanities?

The Lab Book: Situated Practices in Media Studies (forthcoming from the University of Minnesota Press and co-written by me along with Jussi Parikka and Darren Wershler) investigates the history as well as the contemporary landscape of humanities-based media labs – including, of course, labs that openly identify as being engaged – in terms of situated practices – with the digital humanities. Part of the book's documentation of the explosion of labs or lab-like entities around the world over the last decade or so includes a body of over 60 interviews with lab directors and denizens. The interviews not only reveal profound variability in terms of these labs' driving philosophy, funding structures, infrastructures, administration, and outputs. They also clearly demonstrate how many of these labs do not explicitly either embody or refute scientificity so much as they pursue twenty-first-century humanities objectives (which could include anything from research into processes of subjectivation, agency, and materiality in computational culture to the production of narratives, performances, games, and/or music) in a mode that openly both acknowledges and carefully situates research process as well as research products, the role of collaboration, and the influence of physical and virtual infrastructure. While, outside of higher education, 'lab' can now refer to anything from a line of men's grooming products to a department store display or even a company dedicated to psychometric tracking, across the arts and humanities 'lab' still has tremendous, untapped potential to capture a remarkable array of methodically delineated and self-consciously documented entities for experimentation and collaboration that may or may not include an attention to history – though they almost always include an emphasis on 'doing' or hands on work of some kind.

I also view *The Lab Book* as an opportunity to position the Media Archaeology Lab (MAL) in the contemporary landscape of these aforementioned humanities/media labs. Since 2009, when I founded the MAL, the lab has become known as one that undoes many assumptions about what labs should be or do. Unlike labs that are structured hierarchically and driven by a single person with a single vision, the MAL takes many shapes: it is an archive for original works of early digital art/literature along with their original platforms; it is an apparatus through which we come to understand a complex history of media and the consequences of that history; it is a site for artistic interventions, experiments, and projects; it is a flexible, fluid space for students and faculty from a range of disciplines to undertake practice-based research; it is a means by which graduate students come for hands on training in fields ranging from digital humanities, literary studies, media studies, and curatorial studies to community outreach and education. In other words, the MAL is an intervention in 'labness' insofar as it is a place where, depending on your approach, you will find opportunities for research and teaching in myriad configurations as well as a host of other, less clearly defined activities made possible by a collection that is both object and tool. My hope is that the MAL can stand as a unique humanities lab that is not interested in scientificity but that is instead interested in experiments with temporality, with a see-saw and even disruptive relationship between past, present, and future, and in experiments with lab infrastructure in general.

From Archaeological Media Lab to Media Archaeology Lab

The MAL is now a place for hands on, experimental teaching, research, artistic practice, and training using one of the largest collections in North America of still functioning media spanning roughly a 130 year period – from a camera from 1880, a collection of early twentieth century magic lanterns and an Edison diamond disc phonograph player to hardware, software and game consoles from the mid-1970s through the early 2000s. However, the MAL initially came to life in 2008–2009 as the Archaeological Media Lab. At that time, the field of media archaeology had not yet become well known in North America and the lab was nothing more than a small room on the campus of the University of Colorado at Boulder containing 15 Apple IIe computers, floppy drives, and copies on 5.25" floppy disks of a work I had come to admire very much: *First Screening*, one of the first (if not the first) digital kinetic poems created by the Canadian experimental poet bpNichol.

I began the lab partly because I wanted to start experimenting with stockpiling hardware and software as a complementary preservationist strategy to creating emulations such as the one of *First Screening* that had recently been made available. Without being aware of the very nascent debates in archivist communities that

FIGURE 11.1 Apple Platinum IIe computer, from 1987, housed in the Media Archaeology Lab.

The Media Archaeology Lab **179**

FIGURE 11.2 5.25" floppies of 'manuscript' versions of bpNichol's digital poem "First Screening" from 1982–1983, housed in the Media Archaeology Lab.

were then pitting emulation against original hardware/software, I wanted to augment students' and scholars' access to early works of digital literature and art while also collecting other works and their original platforms in order to eventually make available emulations of these works.

However, I also created the lab because I wanted to bring in small undergraduate and graduate classes to work directly on the machines, with the original work by bpNichol, rather than only study the emulated version. In other words, the lab allowed me to think through with my students the difference the original material, tactile environment makes to our understanding of *First Screening*. It was a straightforward enough experiment, but even now in 2017, the implications of this kind of literary/historical work are far reaching and unsettling to the discipline. The foregoing first involves turning away from close reading and from studying literary products (as surface effects), to studying instead the literary production process – looking at how a literary work was made and how the author pushed up against the limits and possibilities of particular writing media. From there, the ramifications of such an approach start to become more obvious as soon as one realizes that learning and teaching 'the how' of literary production cannot take place without access to the tools themselves in a hands on lab environment. That said, while using hands on work not just as an added feature but as the driving force behind teaching and research is quite new to the humanities, the production-oriented approach to interpreting literature has been around in one form or another since the early twentieth century. As many are fond of pointing out, nearly all foundational media studies scholars (from Walter Benjamin to Marshall McLuhan and Friedrich Kittler) were first literary scholars; moreover, one can read the long history of experimental writers, especially poets, as one that is inherently about experimenting with writing media – whether pens, pencils, paper, or typewriters and personal computers.

Since my academic background is in twentieth-century experimental poetry and poetics, the move to exploring the materiality of early digital poetry was a logical next step. Furthermore, once my attention turned to the intertwinement of *First Screening* with the Apple IIe, it likewise made sense to add to the lab's collection other, comparable personal computers from the early 1980s such as the Commodore 64 – at least partly to get a sense of why bpNichol might have chosen to spend $1395 on the IIe rather than $595 on the C64. (The answer likely lies in the fact that the IIe was one of the first affordable computers to include uppercase and lowercase along with an 80-column screen, rather than the C64's 40-column display for uppercase letters only.)

In these early years, I tried to sell the lab to the larger public by saying that it was an entity for supporting a locavore approach to sustaining digital literature – a pitch I also hoped justified our very modest online presence while also underscoring the necessity of working directly with the machines in the lab rather than accessing, say, an Apple IIe or Commodore 64 emulator online. Thus, from 2009 until 2012, the 'Archaeological Media Lab' maintained its modest collection of early digital literature and hardware/software from the early 1980s and gradually increased its network of supporters – from eBay sellers who had become ardent supporters of the lab, to students and faculty from disciplines ranging from Computer Science, Art, Film Studies, and English literature, to digital archivists. However, 2012 was a turning point for the lab for a number of reasons: first, and most importantly, the lab was given a 1000 square foot space in the basement of an older home on the edge of campus, making it possible for the lab to become the open-ended, experimental space it is today with the largest collections of still-functioning media in North America; second, I renamed the lab the 'Media Archaeology Lab' to better align it with the field of media archaeology I was then immersed in; and third, the MAL became a community enterprise no longer synonymous just with me – now the lab has an international advisory board of scholars, archivists, and entrepreneurs, which I consult every six months, faculty fellows from CU Boulder, a regularly rotating cohort of

FIGURE 11.3 Commodore 64 computer, from 1982, housed in the Media Archaeology Lab.

undergraduate interns, graduate research assistants, post-graduate affiliates, and volunteers from the general public.

The lab, called the Media Archaeology Lab since 2012, is also now a kind of anti-museum museum in that all of its hundreds of devices, analogue and digital, are meant to be turned on and actively played with, opened up, tinkered with, experimented with, created with, and moved around and juxtaposed next to any other device. Again, everything that is on display is functional, though we also have a decent stockpile of spare parts and extra devices. The MAL is particularly strong in its collection of personal computers and gaming devices from the 1970s through the 1990s ranging from the Altair 8800b (1976), the complete line of Apple desktop computers from an Apple I replica (1976/2012) to models from the early 2000s, desktops from Sweden (1981) and East Germany (1986), a Canon Cat computer (1987 – I discuss this machine in detail in the following section), and game consoles such as Magnavox Odyssey (1972), Video Sports (1977), Intellivision (1979), Atari 2600 (1982), Vectrex (1982), NES (1983) and other Nintendo

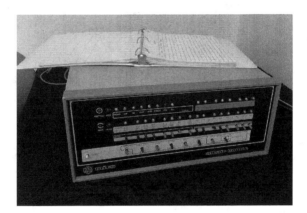

FIGURE 11.4   Altair 8800b computer, from 1976, housed in the Media Archaeology Lab.

FIGURE 11.5   Vectrex game console, from 1983, housed in the Media Archaeology Lab.

FIGURE 11.6 Xerox typewriter, likely from around 1987, housed in the Media Archaeology Lab.

FIGURE 11.7 Magic Lantern, likely from around 1910, housed in the Media Archaeology Lab.

devices. These are just a handful of examples of hundreds of machines in the MAL collection in addition to thousands of pieces of software, magazines, books, and manuals on computing from the 1950s to the present as well as the aforementioned analogue media we house from the nineteenth and twentieth centuries.

A case study in undoing and reimagining computer history: the Canon Cat

While I am attempting to illustrate the remarkable scope of the MAL's collection, I am also trying to show how anomalies in the collection quietly show how media history, especially the history of computing, is anything but a neat progression of devices simply improving upon and building upon what came before; instead, we can understand the waxing and waning of devices more in terms of a phylogenetic tree whereby devices change over time, split into separate branches, hybridize, or are terminated. Importantly, none of these actions (altering, splitting, hybridizing, or terminating) implies a process of technological improvement and thus, rather than stand as a paean to a notion of linear technological history and progress, the MAL acts as a platform for undoing and then reimagining what media history is or could be by way of these anomalies.

The Canon Cat is one of the best examples I've come up with of a machine that disrupts any attempt to narrativize a linear arc of past/present/future that supports notions of progress or even notions of regression. This machine was designed by Jef Raskin after he left Apple in the early 1980s and it was introduced to the public by Canon in 1987 for $1495 – roughly $3316 in 2017, the year of this writing. Although the Cat was discontinued after only six months, around 20,000 units were sold during this time. The Canon Cat is a particularly unusual device as it was neither behind the times nor ahead of its time – it was actually very much *of* its time, albeit a time that does not fit into our usual narrative of the history of personal computing.

First, this machine was marketed as an 'Advanced *Work* Processor'. Although it looks like a word processor, the Cat was meant to be a step beyond both the IBM Selectric Typewriter and conventional word processors. It came with standard office suite programs, a built-in communications device, a 90,000 word dictionary, and the ability to program in Forth and assembly language. While the Cat was explicitly not a word processor, it was also not supposed to be called a 'personal computer' because its interface was distinctly different from both the command-line interface and the Graphical User Interface (GUI) that, by 1987, had already become inseparable from the idea of a personal computer. Try to imagine a computer that had no concept of files and no concept of menus. Instead, all data was seen as a long 'stream' of text broken into several pages. And so even though the interface was text based (it does not make use of mouse, icons or graphics), its functions were built right into the keyboard. Whereas with a machine that uses a GUI

FIGURE 11.8 Canon Cat computer, from 1987, housed in the Media Archaeology Lab.

184   Lori Emerson

you might use the mouse to navigate to a menu and select the command 'FIND', with the Cat you use the 'LEAP' keys.

But before I can explain how LEAP works, I need to explain the remarkable way Raskin designed the cursor, because the cursor is part-and-parcel of the LEAP function. The Cat's cursor has several states: narrow, wide, and extended. In addition to the variable cursor states, the cursor blink rate also indicates the state of the text. The cursor blink rate has two states: clean (whereby the cursor blinks at a rate of roughly 3 Hz to indicate that all changes to the text have been saved to a disk) and dirty (whereby the cursor blinks at a rate of about 1 Hz to indicate that changes have been made to the text and they have not been saved to a disk). Leaping, then, is the Cat's method of cursor movement; you can leap forward and backward using the LEAP FORWARD and LEAP BACKWARD keys. While the LEAP FORWARD key is held, a pattern may be typed. While the pattern is being typed, the cursor immediately moves forward and lands on the first character of the first occurrence of the pattern in the text. LEAP BACKWARD behaves the same as LEAP FORWARD except that the cursor moves in the opposite direction through the text. Note that LEAP was, at that time, roughly 50 times faster than the same function on the Apple Macintosh and possibly just as fast as 'FIND' is on our contemporary machines.

I have only discussed two features of the Cat – the cursor functionality and LEAP, both of which make it possible to do many more things than we can do today with FIND or control-F or with our generally single-purpose cursor. My point is that, just on the face of it, the Canon Cat disrupts even the most nuanced genealogical accounts of computers and digital devices. Where does a Work Processor fit in the history of computing – a history that nearly always glides seamlessly from IBM Selectric, to kit computers, mini computers, microcomputers, word processors and personal computers? More, this disruption only becomes evident when you look not at the Cat's outward appearance, its style and design, but at its functionality.

It is also important to note the bundle of contradictions and inaccuracies the Cat's functionality brings to light as they show us the mismatch between what we believe is the history of computing versus the disruptions to this story represented by machines such as the Cat. For example, while, beginning with the Macintosh, Apple may have had an uncanny knack for weaving design into marketing, that certainly wasn't the case across the board. The design and marketing of computers in the 1980s were not necessarily one and the same as Raskin's vision for the machine was consistently contradicted by Canon. For example, Canon sold the Cat as a secretarial workstation and therefore represented it in promotional materials as a closed system. While, in fact, the Cat was designed not only to integrate with third-party software but it also had a connector and software hooks for a pointing device that could be added on later. Moreover, despite Canon's efforts to market the machine as closed, somehow Raskin was able to make sure the Cat came with a repair manual and very detailed schematics for how to dis-assemble and re-assemble every single part of the machine. The Apple Macintosh, by contrast, never came with anything like schematics; in fact, Apple openly discouraged people from opening up the Macintosh and repairing it themselves, in the same way that our Apple devices nowadays are similarly hermetically sealed (Emerson 2014). Furthermore, while the Cat was consistently marketed by Canon in terms of its speed and efficiency, reinforcing our belief that these are the two markers of progress when it comes to digital technology, Raskin himself seemed to take pride in making heretical statements about how his designs were based on an "implementation philosophy which demanded generality and human usability over execution speed and efficiency" (quoted in Feinstein 2006). By contrast, every single bit of Canon's promotional material for the Cat – from videos to magazine ads to the manuals themselves – emphasized the machine's incredible speed.

A variantology of hands on practices

The MAL, then, is essential for exploring the functionality of historically important media objects – functionality that cannot be understood in any depth if one only has access to promotional material or archival documents and that fundamentally shapes one's understanding of the media object's place in the history of technology. Otherwise put, the lab invites one to reread media history in terms of non-linear and non-teleological series of media phenomena – or ruptures – as a way to avoid reinstating a model of media history that tends toward narratives of progress and generally ignores neglected, failed, or dead media.

I have also come to understand the MAL as a sort of 'variantological' space in its own right, a place where, depending on your approach, you will find opportunities for research and teaching in myriad configurations as well as a host of other, less clearly defined activities made possible by a collection of functioning items that are both object and tool. In other words, the lab is both an archive of hardware and software that are themselves objects of research at the same time as the hardware and software generate new research and teaching opportunities.

For example, in terms of the latter, in the last three years the lab's vitality has grown substantially because of the role of three PhD students who are developing their own unique career trajectories in and through the lab. The results have already been extraordinary. One student, who wishes to obtain an academic position after graduation, has created a hands on archive of scanners in conjunction with a dissertation chapter, soon to be published as an article, on the connections between the technical affordances of scanners and online digital archives. Another student, who wishes to obtain a curatorship after graduation, founded an event series called MALfunctions, which pairs nationally and internationally recognized artists with critics on topics related to the MAL collection; this student also arranges residencies at the lab for these visiting artists/critics who, in turn, generate technical reports on their time spent in the MAL; furthermore, as a result of her work with this event series, this student has been invited to be a curator for annual media arts festivals and local museums and galleries. Yet another student, who wishes to pursue a career in alternative modes of teaching and learning, has started a monthly retro games night targeted specifically for members of the LGBTQ community at CU; she also is running monthly workshops teaching students and members of the public how to fix vintage computers and game consoles as well as the basics of surveillance and privacy; as a result of her work, this student was invited to run a workshop at the Red Hat Summit in Boston, MA in Spring 2017.

In sum, the MAL is unique for a number of reasons. Rather than being hierarchical and classificatory both in its display of objects as well as its administrative organization of people, the MAL is porous, flat, and branching; objects are organized in any way participants want; everything is functional and made to be turned on. Rather than setting out to adhere to specific outcomes and five year plans, we change from semester to semester and year to year depending on who's spending time in the lab. Rather than being an entity you need to apply to be a part of or something you can only participate in as a researcher, librarian, PhD student, anyone may participate in the lab and have a say about what projects we take on, what kinds of work we do. Rather than being about the display of precious objects whereby you only ever get a sense of the external appearance or even external functionality of the objects, we encourage people to tinker, play, open things up, disassemble. Rather than the perpetuation of neat, historical narratives about how things came to be, we encourage an experimental approach to time – put Edison disks beside contemporary proprietary software or put the Vectrex and its lightpen up next to a contemporary tablet and stylus to see what we can learn through the juxtapositions. And finally, rather than participating in the process of erasing the knowledge production process or perpetuating the illusion of a separation between those who work in the lab and the machines they work on and hiding the agency of the machines themselves as well as the agency of the larger infrastructure of the lab, we are interested in constantly situating anything and everything we do in the lab and being self-conscious, descriptive about the minute particularities of the production process for any projects we undertake.

In short, it's my hope that the MAL can be a tool for moving away from humanism and traditional humanities work and instead tentatively, provisionally model what posthumanities work might look like.

Bibliography

Braidotti, Rosi. (2013) *The Posthuman*. Oxford, UK: Polity, 143.

Emerson, Lori. (2014) *Reading Writing Interfaces: From the Digital to the Bookbound*. Minneapolis, MN: University of Minnesota Press, 47–85.

Feinstein, Jonathan S. (2006) *The Nature of Creative Development*. Stanford, CA: Stanford University Press, 148.

Haraway, Donna. (1988) Situated Knowledges: The Science Question in Feminism and the Privilege of Partial Perspective. *Feminist Studies*, 14(3) (Autumn): 575–599.

Latour, Bruno and Steve Woolgar. (1986) *Laboratory Life: The Construction of Scientific Facts*. 2nd edition. Princeton, NJ: Princeton University Press, 240.

Moretti, Franco. (2003) Graphs, Maps, and Trees: Abstract Models for Literary History. *New Left Review* 24 (November–December): 67–93.

12

REFLECTIONS AND REMINISCENCES

Tactile encounters and participatory research
with vintage media technology in the museum

Christian Hviid Mortensen and Lise Kapper

Introduction

Museums dedicated to aspects of media and communication heritage have been
in existence since 1872. The earliest examples include the Postal Museum (now
the Museum of Communication) in Berlin and the Telegraph Museum (now
A.S. Popov Central Museum of Communications) in Saint Petersburg. It was not
until a hundred years later, however, that this museum trend took off in earnest.
Towards the end of the twentieth century the rapid development of new media
technologies, rendering old media technologies obsolete, reached a point where
it became pertinent to conserve these obsolete technologies for posterity and put
them on display in museums (Mortensen 2017). Thereby, media technologies now
constitute part of our cultural memory both in the potential state of the archive and
in the actual state of exhibitions (Assmann 1995).

However, as interactive objects, media technologies proved to be an unsuit-
able match for the conventional modes of museum representation: static objects
displayed behind glass beyond the reach of visitors. As the media archaeologist
Wolfgang Ernst remarked:

> [. . .] a medium that is not performing in its medium state is just a piece of
> furniture. A television on display in a museum which does not show the
> screen working is not shown as a medium; it's just a piece of hardware, a
> design object.
>
> (Henning and Ernst 2015, 6)

In an attempt to overcome the inherent blackboxing (Hertz and Parikka 2012;
Latour 2000) of media technology in many museum displays Ernst established the
Media Archaeological Fundus – a collection of old media technology in Berlin – that

is also a 'tinkering space', where scholars and students can gain insight into the old media by operating them (Parikka 2012, 131). Such a hands on approach to media history tallies with the novel approach of Haptic Media Studies that addresses the "practices of touching and being touched by mediation technologies" (Parisi et al. 2017, 1517). This kind of object handling was not always anathema to museums. In the early museums of the seventeenth and eighteenth centuries visitors, the privileged few members of the social elite, were allowed to handle artefacts. Hands on experiences were seen as central to the knowledge production within the museum. The ocular-centric conventions of museum display are a product of the nineteenth century, when museums became public spaces for the mass audience (Candlin 2008). However, towards the end of the twentieth century there has been a revalorization of touch in the museum and object handling has again become a common offering (Howes 2014).

A hands on approach to history is part of our DNA at The Media Museum in Odense, Denmark.[1] Since the beginning in 1984 open workshops manned by retired craftsmen have been part of our exhibitions. The workshops demonstrated diverse printing technologies, bookbinding techniques, and fundamental paper manufacture, but lacked a participatory aspect as visitors rarely engaged directly in the activities. We have experimented with visitor object handling in temporary exhibitions on gaming culture, where interactivity is essential to understanding (Mortensen and Kapper 2015). Taking further inspiration from the Media Archaeological Fundus, and similar initiatives, we decided to establish our own Media Archaeological Laboratory (MAL) and make the hands on approach to media history a permanent feature for visitors at our museum.[2] This chapter will present the ideas underlying our concept of a media archaeological laboratory within a museological context and in the concrete setting of the MAL. Then we will show the kind of knowledge production that the lab enables by accounting for our first round of data collection. We rely primarily on self-administered questionnaires

FIGURE 12.1 Detail from the open workshops at the Media Museum. Printer Hans Hansen operating a Heidelberg printing press.

in our gathering of data. Secondarily, we have used observation and interview. We expect the MAL to produce two kinds of knowledge from participants' tactile encounters with vintage media technology: first, reminiscences or memories concerning media use (Neiger et al. 2011); second, reflections triggered from this encounter. Either fresh insights, encountering this media technology for the first time or reflections stemming from the juxtaposition of reminiscence with new experiences. The chapter ends with a discussion of the future perspectives for this endeavour.

Concept: media – archaeology – laboratory

The concept of a *Media Archaeological Laboratory* juxtaposes two metaphors, archaeology and laboratory, that have attained prominence recently within the cultural sciences. Foucault (2000) famously adopted archaeology as a conceptual metaphor for his historical analytical method in *The Archaeology of Knowledge* designating a completely different form of 'digging' than archaeology proper in his excavation of the conditions of existence for cultural phenomena. The heterogeneous notion of media archaeology is promoted as a turn away from human-centred approaches within media studies focusing on discourse and interpretation towards a materialist technology-centred and object-oriented approach (Parikka 2012; Strauven 2012). Further, Fickers and van den Oever have proposed that media archaeology should take inspiration from experimental archaeology utilizing reenactments and other experimental methods in order to reflect on the tacit knowledge that informs our encounters with media technologies (Fickers and van der Oever 2013, 273).

Similarly, the laboratory as a site for knowledge production has migrated from the natural sciences to the humanities where it is presented as a central feature of the Digital Humanities paradigm (Burdick et al. 2012). These media labs, established in connection with universities and colleges, are mostly oriented towards the future with a focus on design and new technologies, but some also have a historical focus and address other temporalities. The combination of old and contemporary technologies enables new forms of knowledge. In this way, the value of technological artefacts is displaced from being the objects of knowledge a priori to being a precondition for the production of new knowledge (Parikka 2016).

Often access to these laboratories, such as the Media Archaeological Fundus, are restricted. You need to be a faculty member or enrolled as a student to gain access or you will need to seek permission to visit the laboratory collection in advance. In contrast, we intend our MAL to be a public space open to all walk-in visitors. Museum galleries are, of course, open to everyone (often only after having paid the price of admission). However, ordinary visitors are conventionally restricted from hands on object handling, and participate only as spectators. Recently, the scope has widened for more involved forms of participation for visitors within museums (Carpentier 2011; Simon 2010). This development also includes sensory approaches that address not only our sense of sight, but also hearing, touch, smell, and taste (Howes 2014). Early museum collections came in two forms: the royal cabinet, that had a representative function showcasing the wealth, sophistication, and (implied) knowledge of the owner, and collections with a more practical and scientific purpose (Imprey and MacGregor 1985). We envision the MAL to be a return to the hands on approach and scientific purpose of the museum collection. It will be open not just to experts but to the general public, thus enabling new forms of knowledge production within the museum, what has been called citizen science and maybe even, depending on scale, crowd science as a collaborative enterprise (Franzoni and Sauermann 2014). Similar open initiatives are currently developed at other museums: the Museum of Copenhagen's Makerspace and Archaeological Workshop are one example. Also, Makerspaces are becoming a popular feature at libraries across Denmark.

The founding idea of the MAL is that encountering the otherness of media technologies on display, and experimenting with them, will give visitors new insights that further provoke reflections on their contemporary media environment. Elsaesser calls this attention to otherness a "hermeneutics of astonishment" (Elsaesser 2004, 113). Essentially, we wish to revitalize 'dead' media, providing them with an afterlife beyond obsolescence by displaying them in their working state within the museum, thereby turning them into "zombie media" (Hertz and Parikka 2012). It is our hope that the insights of ordinary museum visitors, non-experts with little or no prior knowledge of the displayed artefacts, will provide fresh perspectives that can challenge the tacit knowledge of expert users such as media scholars and curators. We aim to foster encounters like the one seen in a popular YouTube video in which children interpret the two sockets in a cassette tape as intended for watching movies (Crane 2017). Clearly the affordances of the cassette tape design are not that obvious.

On the other hand, for many the reaction to an encounter with media artefacts from the recent past will not be one of otherness but of familiarity with objects from one's own past. Rather than astonishment, such an encounter will likely elicit reminiscence and even nostalgia. Among historians' nostalgia is often disregarded as providing just an emotionally distorted view of the past. However, elsewhere we have argued for the potential for reflection inherent in nostalgic relations with the past (Mortensen and Kapper 2015; Mortensen and Madsen 2015). Here we find useful the three-tier framework of nostalgia into simple, reflexive, and interpretative forms, developed by Davis (1979), for understanding nostalgic reactions and enabling further reflections. Simple, first-order nostalgia is the belief that things were better before than now; in second-order, reflexive nostalgia, the feeling is accompanied by empirical reflections concerning the truth and accuracy of the nostalgic memory; in third-order interpretative nostalgia reflections move beyond issues of historical accuracy and address the nostalgic experience itself. Regarding the older generations of visitors, the activities of MAL will contribute to the field of Memory Studies as the memories concerning media are another form of data we wish to collect and study.

Whether as new insights or as reflections on media memories these experiences constitute reflections on different temporalities. According to Strauven, such a rethinking of temporalities is at the core of media archaeology, either seeking the new in the old or the old within the new as "history is the study not only of the past, but also of the (potential) present and the possible futures" (Strauven 2012, 68). Each generation of visitors have been surrounded by different objective and symbolic media environments (Bolin 2016), and will thus create a meeting of different temporalities that we hope will result in intergenerational sharing of knowledge and experiences.

Setting: The museum exhibition vs. the laboratory

The first generation of our MAL contains three workstations each with a different experimental set-up all based on magnetic tape technology: cassette tape players (and Walkmans), VCR and VHS tapes, and a Commodore 64 computer with a datasette. These popular forms of media consumption (listening to music, watching films, and playing games) are all now enabled by the smartphone, and are displayed in juxtaposition with their different technological platforms. Each workstation is supplied with a worksheet with written instructions for using the technology on display, which the participant can refer to, if they are stuck with the unfamiliar user interface. In time, we intend to replace or supplement these media technologies with others in later generations of the MAL.

In support of the lab metaphor, the furniture in the room is utilitarian and the decorations sparse. We intend to focus the attention of the participants primarily on the media technologies on display, thus keeping other environmental variables at a minimum. Therefore, we decided against adopting an interior design approach to exhibitions creating tableaus of different settings for media use e.g. the family living room or the teenager's dorm as seen, for example, in the Finnish Museum of Games in Tampere or the Museum of Computer Games in Berlin.

The laboratory experience is framed by the following introduction:

> A media archaeologist examines media of the past by experimenting with the technologies of the past. The Media Museum has excavated outdated media technologies and made them available for your experiments in the MediaArch Lab. [. . .] We hope these experiments will provide you with new perspectives on today's media. [. . .] We'd like to know the results of your experiments, so please share your thoughts, memories and observations with us by filling out the questionnaire located at each experimental setup. The results will be included in our collection of data focusing on media use in the past and present.

The laboratory atmosphere is underscored by the way that the users are explicitly invited to experiment with the objects on display and to record their observances and experiences on a questionnaire. Further, the knowledge production and data collection that takes place in the MAL are visualized when the users leave their filled-out questionnaires in a box on the wall, where they can also

FIGURE 12.2 The authors 'excavating' at two of the three workstations in the MAL. From the right VHS, Commodore 64 and cassette tapes.

FIGURE 12.3 Example of interior approach to the display of media technologies at the *Finnish Museum of Games*. (Credit: Saana Säilynoja, Tampere Museums, Vapriikki Photo Archives)

browse the questionnaires from other users. In time, this display of "raw" data will be supplemented with findings from our analysis of the aggregated data. Informed by our initial round of data collection, we intend to extend this passive form of collecting data with a more active approach by facilitating focus groups with different compositions depending on what areas we want to explore further.

The Media Museum exhibitions span approximately 1500 square metres on the third floor of a former industrial textile mill. While the museum also contains traditional exhibitions on Danish media history the MAL is the latest in a series of activities involving visitors in experimenting with different aspects of media which the museum has engaged in. From 2006 to 2016 we had a fully functional television studio facility where school groups could make their own productions under

FIGURE 12.4 Detail of the MAL VHS workstation. Fresh questionnaires are available on the left and the user can leave their filled-out questionnaire in the box when they leave the workstation.

the tuition of our TV producer. In 2010 we established the MediaMixer with three simulated production facilities were visitors can experiment with the craft of the foley artist, live reportage, and take "the hot seat" in front of a virtual TV journalist (Mortensen and Vestergaard 2011).

The Media Museum has evolved from being a primarily technology-oriented museum focusing on the printing industry to becoming a museum with a broader scope and holistic approach to media history, including also electronic and digital media, and involving aspects of both media production, consumption, and content. A heightened focus on visitors and adoption of experimental approaches has been a priority area in Danish cultural policy administered by the Danish Agency for Culture for a number of years (Lundgaard and Jensen 2013). Therefore, as a public funded museum, the obligation to experiment with and evolve our visitor-engaging activities is now embedded in our mission statement.

Knowledge: reflections and reminiscences

In the following we will account for the findings of the first round of data collection in the MAL.[3] As stated above we envision the open MAL to enable a kind of citizen science via participatory research (Cornwall and Jewkes 1995), where the visitors become participants by engaging in a form of collaborative media ethnography by experimenting with the technology at the work stations and recording their reflections and experiences on a questionnaire. The questionnaire consists of two parts: one with closed questions, designed to present an overview of the participants and a part with open questions inviting the participants to elaborate on their experiences. In the first part of the questionnaire we want to

TABLE 12.1 Aggregate of data collected from the first section of the questionnaires

N=68	Visitor Age	No	Yes
0–14 years	8		
15–24 years	34		
25–44 years	21		
45–65 years	5		
66+ years	0		
Group visit		13	55
Familiar with tech		14	54
Have used tech before		30	38

know the age of the visitors, whether they visit alone or in a group, if they are familiar with the technologies on display and finally if they have used the technology before. Table 12.1 shows the quantitative findings from the first part of the questionnaire.

Almost all the visitors that have engaged with the displayed technology and filled out a questionnaire are under 44 years old with half being in the 15–24 age group. The latter group were not even born when these technologies were in vogue. Still, a vast majority are familiar with the technologies and just over half of them have used one or more of these technologies before. Apparently, media technologies linger and hands on experience with them are not restricted to the generation that grew up with them. Meanwhile, the older age groups, who are traditionally the most frequent museum visitors, seem not to be attracted to the technologies and hands on approach of the MAL. Observations confirm that older couples in their fifties will enter the MAL but not engage with the workstations. Our findings also confirm the common finding within visitor studies that visiting a museum is primarily a social activity as most visitors to the MAL are part of a group such as a family (Falk and Dierking 2013). This social embeddedness profoundly influences the museum experience creating the potential for learning within the family unit: parents who want to show their children technology from their youth are drawn to the MAL.

In the second part of the questionnaire, we first ask participants to record any immediate thoughts and memories from their encounter with the media technologies. Then we ask them to reflect on any similarities or dissimilarities between contemporary media technologies and the technologies on display. The formulation of Q2 was intended to assist the participant in moving beyond simple reminiscence and engage in reflection and interpretation. Finally, we invited them to provide any further comments. Table 12.2 provides an overview of our findings from the second part of the questionnaire. The answers to the three questions have been coded on two levels. First, we distinguished between answers containing reminiscence and/or reflection – the two forms of knowledge we were aiming for. Second, we identified the different associations connected with reminiscence and the different themes connected with reflections (only a selection is shown in Table 12.2).

The ratio between reminiscences and reflections changes significantly between Q1 and Q2 from 28/15 to 3/33. This shift indicates that designing the question

TABLE 12.2 Overview of data from the second section of the questionnaires

N=39		Q1: What are your immediate thoughts about this media technology? Does it evoke any memories?				
Reminiscences	28	**Reflections**		15	**Both**	8
					Neither	4
Nostalgia	5					
Associations:		**Themes:**				
Practices		Tech speed		5		
Sleep over Video rental Long car journeys First love-tape		Tech development		3		
		Functionality		2		
		Low quality		2		
		Simple, yet complex		1		
Media content Disney: Winnie the Poo Teletubbies		Poor, Eastern Europe		1		
Other vintage techs Sodastream						
N=36		Q2: What similarities and differences do you notice between this technology and the media tehcnologies of today?				
Reminiscences	4	**Reflections**		33	**Both**	4
					Neither	3
		Similarities		9	Both	7
		Differences		27	Neither	3
Low quality		Similarities Similar content Symbols (e.g. play icon) Qwerty keyboard Screen required Similar layout Functions (e.g. copy, record) Entertainment Extending ourselves	Differences No graphic user interface Quality Speed Usability Size Options Hurts the eyes Manual controls (joystick) Less buttons Simple/advanced			
Miss Snake and Monty						
A smaller World						
It was magical: more realistic/real						

(*Continued*)

196 Christian Hviid Mortensen and Lise Kapper

TABLE 12.2 (Continued)

N=24		Q3: Do you have any further comments?			
Reminiscences	3	**Reflections**	7	**Both**	1
				Neither	15
VHS is not the past		**Themes:**			
		Patience/lack of speed			
Imagination compensated for low quality		Quality			
		Function			
Bee Gees		Magnetic tape technology			
		Felt old			

towards eliciting reflection, here juxtaposing historic and contemporary media technologies, shifts participants from a mode of reminiscence towards a mode of reflection. This is promising regarding targeting future explorations of specific themes in the MAL. Most of the answers to Q3 contain neither reminiscence nor reflection. Instead, the participants have used the open invitation to provide value judgments on their experience in the MAL such as "Boring" or "I love it". Almost all value judgments are of a positive disposition.

Based on previous findings (Mortensen and Kapper 2015) we expected the immediate reminiscences following the tactile encounter to be dominated by nostalgia. However, only few participants explicitly express nostalgia or the normative belief that things were better before, for example: "Absolutely, it is beautiful. It reminds me of the good old days". Rather, the reminiscences are value-neutral and descriptive such as: "Yes. It evokes memories of a youth spent in video rental shops, sleep overs and popcorn, soda and pizza". Naturally, the vintage media technologies remind participants of their childhood and youth. Following Mannheim in that experiences in youth are especially formative, Bolin argues for the concept of media generations, based on common experiences with media technologies. Further, he argues for the impossibility of intergenerational sharing of this experience (Bolin 2016, 110). But participants also associate the media technology with other related practices (sleep over; video rental; car journeys and making a 'love-tape'[4]) that they previously engaged in, specific media content (*Winnie the Pooh*; *Teletubbies*) or other vintage technologies (Sodastream). This shows that using media technology is often embedded in other social practices and identified with the specific content that is accessed via the technology. Collecting such media memories enables us to better understand this social embeddedness and further identify 'memorable' media content for different media generations.

For some participants reminiscence is followed by reflection. For example: "It evokes memories of childhood and a time before laptops and smartphones became so important in everyday life". Another participant follows reflection with further interpretation of his experience: "It evokes memories of my childhood. I think this technology seems simultaneously both simple and complex. It's like stepping back in a time capsule from my youth". In this way the forms of reminiscence, with or without nostalgia, enabled in the MAL mirrors the three-tiered distinction between simple, reflexive and interpretative nostalgia (Davis 1979). Overall the immediate reflections of participants gravitate towards different themes. The most common theme is the low speed of the technology on display or the amount of patience it requires; next, visitors reflect on technological development from then until now. Participants also reflect on the inferior quality of the media content accessed via the technology such as low resolution graphics and low-fidelity sounds as well as the basic operation of the technology. However, there are also more inspired reflections such as the one quoted above wondering about the simple, yet complex technology. The effect of blackboxing is less prominent with vintage technologies than modern digital technologies, because their separate storage media, output and input devices require manual actions. Thus, they can appear more complex because the functionality becomes visible. As one participant states: "You see/hear how it works, many buttons to press, not only one screen to touch". Finally, for another participant the encounter elicited socio-economic reflections associating the vintage technology with being poor and with Eastern Europe. Presumably, new media technologies became available to consumers more slowly in Eastern Europe and therefore vintage technology lingered for longer.

In the second section of the questionnaire, where we explicitly ask the participants to reflect on the differences and similarities between the technologies on display and the media technologies of today, the same reflections concerning quality, speed, size and usability resurface. A majority of participants (27) have recorded differences, while a minority have recorded similarities (9). Participants notice the lack of graphic user interface, and manual controls; for one participant the vintage technology makes "the eyes hurt". Rather than eliciting astonishment the otherness of the vintage technology manifests itself in a primarily negative way for a majority of users as lacking quality and usability with unfamiliar technical obstacles. The tactile aspect of the hands on encounter manifests itself in reflections regarding the disappearance of buttons and external input devices such as joysticks.

The similarities recorded include similar content (films, games, music), as the overall purpose of entertainment is the same, and the technology still feels like an extension of ourselves despite being more cumbersome. But participants also recognize symbols, that are still in use on "virtual buttons", the QWERTY keyboard, and that most contemporary media technologies still require a screen. For some participants, their reflections are accompanied by reminiscences: one recalls a smaller world, without the new cultures we encounter today. Another feels nostalgic: "It was more difficult to use, but it was magic – it seemed more realistic/real". Despite the hyperrealism of much media content today, this participant still feels that it seemed more real then. Apparently, the material aspects of both media technology and content with pixelated, grainy pictures and scratchy sound underscore the experience of the real. Another participant elaborates on a similar point in the free comment section:

> The sound and video quality are so low fidelity that I wonder how I missed it in its heyday. I wonder how much I relied upon my own imagination to make the images more vivid. I see this in the continuum of the moving image becoming so 'hi def' as to become unattractive to me in its pursuit of perfection.

In this way, digitalization is addressed in the MAL by its absence, which participants notice immediately.

In the final section for further comments most participants take the opportunity to make value judgements on the vintage technology and the MAL experience. A few record reflections, most of whom address the familiar issues of speed, quality and usability. One participant, who had never used a C64 herself before, was amazed that it was possible to play videogames from a cassette tape she knew well from listening to music. For another participant, the vintage technology made him feel old. This feeling could be both a function of the rapid development of media technology and of the experience of discovering familiar objects from one's youth on display in a museum.

A few participants also expressed reminiscence in this section. Apart from the articulate reflection on the dynamic between lo-fi and imagination quoted above, one participant states that "VHS does not belong to the past!" This statement might follow from current retro sensibilities that are giving VHS a revival as a collector's object, especially with regard to vintage horror B-movies (Joy 2015). Further, the aesthetics of VHS has also gained new interest with a popular retro camcorder app recreating the look of the 1980s (Pierce 2015).

Even though the sample is small, the data material shows a potential for producing knowledge in the MAL and collecting two kinds of knowledge: reminiscences and reflections. While there are some profound responses, answers typically lack detail. But the questionnaires can still generate a selection of issues and themes which could be explored in more in-depth data collection activities such as a focus group. Also, we can support the hermeneutics of astonishment with the participants further by foreclosing some of the common reflections on quality, speed and usability in the way we ask. Reformulating question 2 as: "Apart from issues regarding quality, speed and usability. Which differences and similarities do you notice between this technology and the media technology of today?" might push participants beyond the obvious reflections. Another possibility is to provide more structure to the experiments of the participants. For example, by asking them to undertake specific tasks that require them to engage more creatively with the vintage technology. Participants could be prompted to "create a mix tape using multiple sources", highlighting the role of users as early 'produsers'. This activity might not only elicit more profound reflections, but also strong reminiscences as mix tapes, because they are labour intensive, are strong triggers of memories (Bolin 2016; Jansen 2009).

However, does this process constitute participatory research as we intended? Participation has become a 'floating signifier' and it is often regarded as inherently beneficial without considering the concrete participatory practices and their impact on participants (Carpentier 2011). Any normative claims for participation requires a framework for description and comparative analysis of participatory processes. Elsewhere, we have used the framework developed by Kelty et al. (2015) based on an extensive literature review of participation across different domains, to evaluate participatory activities in the museum (Mortensen and Kapper 2015). Kelty et al. suggest a framework consisting of seven dimensions that encompass the complexity of participation:

1. Educative dividend. The degree to which participants learn something valuable.
2. Goals and tasks. The degree to which participants not only undertake tasks but also help set goals.
3. Resource control. The degree to which participants get control of resources, not merely produce them.
4. Exit. The degree to which participants have the capacity to leave without penalty.
5. Voice. The degree to which participants have opportunity to 'speak back' to influence outcomes.
6. Visible metrics. The degree to which there are empirical demonstrations of the connection between participation and outcomes.
7. Affective/communicative capacity. The degree to which participants experience collective effervescence and the experience of being part of an audience.

These dimensions posit different continuums and we can now estimate the degree of participation in the activities of MAL using a five-point Likert scale ranging from none, low, some, high and very high as shown in table 3.

The amount of reflection following the tactile encounters in MAL show a clear educative dividend, however, as discussed above, it can appear shallow judging from the detail of the answers on the questionnaire. But it is entirely plausible that the reflections continue to have an effect beyond the museum visit in future

TABLE 12.3 Estimate of the degree of participation in the activities of MAL

Dimension of participation	Degree in MAL
Educative dividend	Some
Goals and tasks	None
Resource control	Low
Exit	Very high
Voice	Very high
Visible metrics	Some
Affective/communicative capacity	Some

engagements with different media technologies. This lingering learning effect of museum visits have also been demonstrated by Falk and Dierking (2013). The participants have no influence on the goals and tasks of the MAL activities, namely collecting reminiscences and reflections via tactile encounters with vintage media technologies, as they have been predefined in the concept of MAL. Visitors can, of course, refuse to participate by not engaging with the technology on display or by not filling out a questionnaire afterwards. Presently, participants also have little control of the resources of MAL. They can only engage with three media technologies and the form of engagement is limited to simple consumer behaviour, as participants are not allowed to disassemble or modify the technologies on display.

On the other hand, participants are free to leave the MAL at any moment and with the open comment section on the questionnaire they have ample opportunity to talk back and voice any concerns, for example request written instructions in English. The MAL also contains some degree of visible metrics with the filled-out questionnaires displayed in the open. However, here is room for improvements as a visualization of aggregate data would be more illustrative of the connection between participation and outcome. We intend to strengthen this aspect in the future, for example with a word cloud showing the relative commonalities of the different associations resulting from the tactile experiments. Finally, there are some affective/communicative capacity as most participants are part of a group. Again, there is scope for improvement and we expect that further visualizations of data aggregates would help convey the feeling to participants that they are part of and contributing to a larger endeavour – an ongoing research project in which their input is highly valued.

Concluding remarks

The MAL as a knowledge-producing facility is clearly a work-in-progress. Initially, the concept of utilizing technological museum artefacts to generate knowledge, thereby displacing the value of the artefacts from being objects of knowledge a priori to acting as a precondition for new knowledge, seems promising. The tactile hands on encounters elicited two kinds of knowledge: reminiscences and reflections. Judging from the reports on the questionnaires collected in MAL the generated knowledge appears rather superficial. Most of the immediate responses of participants are reminiscences and only a few of them move beyond simple reminiscence to the reflexive and interpretative forms. When we explicitly ask the participants to compare contemporary technology with vintage technology the amount of reflections increases significantly. This makes the case for experimenting further with other means of scaffolding reflection. Both in the way we collect data, but also in the experimental setup where participants could be given specific tasks to perform, for example. We also expected more intergenerational dialogue following from the tactile encounters, than what appears on the questionnaires, as most participants visits as a group often including different generations. However, the questionnaire form is rather labour-intensive, and thus is detrimental to recording nuanced observations comprising different generational perspectives. Another form of recording observations, such as video, might be better suited for these kinds of interactions.

While the 'hermeneutics of astonishment' following from the encounter with the otherness of vintage technologies in the MAL for most participants resulted in negative reflections regarding their lack of quality and usability, in a few instances it elicited a profound rethinking of temporalities questioning the linear continued progress of media history. Thus, practising hands on media archaeology can challenge the established narratives of technological progress even if performed by ordinary media users as non-experts. Therefore, we see a potential for increasing the educative dividend of participants by further developing the media archaeological experiments as participatory research within the MAL. In particular, we are curious to see what effect a better visualization of their contributions and the outcomes of the data collection within the MAL might have.

Notes

1 The Media Museum was established as a printing museum. The museum merged with The Danish Press Museum and Archive in 1989 and in 2000 the remit of the museum was extended to also include the heritage of electronic and digital media as The Media Museum of Denmark. In 2010 the museum changed its name to The Media Museum in recognition of the transnational nature of media. See http://museum.odense.dk/en/museums/media-museum

2 Due to a relocation of the Media Museum the MAL closed on 30 December 2018. We intend to reopen the MAL activities at our new location, when possible.

3 The data consist of 42 completed questionnaires from 68 visitors collected from 31 March to 31 May 2017. In addition, we draw on two observations of visitor behavior in the MAL and an semi-structured interview with a family of four on 23 April 2017.

4 Presumably, the practice of compiling a mixtape for a loved one.

Bibliography

Assmann, J. (1995) Collective Memory and Cultural Identity. *New German Critique*, 65: 125–133.

Bolin, G. (2016) *Media Generations: Experience, Identity and Mediatised Social Change.* London: Routledge.

Burdick, A., Drucker, J., Lunenfeld, P., Presner, T., and Schnapp, J. (2012) *Digital_Humanities.* Cambridge, MA and London: The MIT Press.

Candlin, F. (2008) Museums, Modernity and the Class Politics of Touching Objects. In Chatterjee, H.J. (ed.). *Touch in Museums. Policy and Practice in Object Handling.* Oxford and New York: Berg.

Carpentier, N. (2011) *Media and Participation. A Site of Ideological-democratic Struggle.* Bristol, UK and Chicago, USA: Intellect.

Cornwall, A. and Jewkes, R. (1995) What is Participatory Research?. *Social Science & Medicine*, 41(12): 1667–1676.

Crane, C. (2017) *Kids Have No Idea What a Cassette Tape Is!* [Online]. Available at: https://www.youtube.com/watch?v=Z27sDA5Lz8A (Accessed 11 March 2017)

Davis, F. (1979) *Yearning for Yesterday: A Sociology of Nostalgia.* New York: The Free Press.

Elsaesser, T. (2005) Early Film History and Multi-Media. An Archaeology of Possible Futures?. In Chun, W.H., Keenan, T. (eds). *New Media, Old Media*. New York: Routledge, 13–25.

Elsaesser, T. (2004) The New Film History as Media Archaeology. *CiNéMAS*, 14(2): 75–117.

Falk, J.H. and Dierking, L.D. (2013) *The Museum Experience Revisited*. Walnut Creek, CA: Left Coast Press.

Fickers, A. and van der Oever, A. (2013) Experimental Media Archaeology. A Plea for New Directions. In *Téchne /Technology. Researching Cinema and Media Technologies, Their Development, Use and Impact*. Amsterdam: Amsterdam University Press, 272–278.

Foucault, M. (2000) *The Archaeology of Knowledge*. Reprinted ed. A library of theory and research in the human sciences. London: Routledge.

Franzoni, C. and Sauermann, H. (2014) Crowd Science: The Organization of Scientific Research in Open Collaborative Projects. *Research Policy*, 43: 1–20.

Henning, M. and Ernst, W. (2015) Museums and Media Archaeology. An Interview with Wolfgang Ernst. In Henning, M. (ed.). *Museum Media, The International Handbooks of Museum Studies* [online]. John Wiley and Sons, Ltd, 3–22.

Hertz, G. and Parikka, J. (2012) Zombie Media: Circuit Bending Media Archaeology into an Art Method. *Leonardo*, 45(5): 424–430.

Howes, D. (2014) Introduction to Sensory Museology. *The Senses and Society*, 9(3): 259–267.

Imprey, O. and MacGregor, A. (eds.) (1985) *The Origins of Museums, the Cabinet of Curiosities in Sixteenth- and Seventeenth-century Europe* (1st ed.). Oxford: Clarendon.

Jansen, B. (2009) Tape Cassettes and Former Selves: How Mix Tapes Mediate Memories. In Bijsterveld, K., van Dijck, J. (eds). *Sound Souvenirs. Audio Technologies, Memory and Cultural Practices*. Amsterdam: Amsterdam University Press, 43–54.

Joy, K. (2015) VHS Recordings Are Enjoying Retro Revival. *The Colombus Dispatch* [online]. Available at: http://www.dispatch.com/content/stories/life_and_entertainment/2015/04/21/1-tape-replay.html (accessed 15 November 2017)

Kelty, C., Panofsky, A., Currie, M., Crooks, R., Erikson, S., Garcia, P., Wartenbe, M., and Wood, S. (2015) Seven Dimensions of Contemporary Participation Disentangled. *Journal of the Association of Information Science and Technology*, 66(3): 474–488.

Latour, B. (2000) *Pandora's Hope. Essays' on the Reality of Science Studies*. Cambridge, MA: Harvard University Press.

Lundgaard, I. Brændholt and Jensen, J. T. (2013) *Museums – Social Learning Spaces and Knowledge Producing Processes*. Copenhagen: Kulturstyrelsen – Danish Agency for Culture.

Mortensen, C.H. (2017) The Legacy of Mediatization. When Media Became Cultural Heritage. In Hjarvard, S., Hepp, A., Bolin, G. and Driessens, O. (eds). *Dynamics of Mediatization: Institutional Change and Everyday Transformations in a Digital Age*. Cham: Palgrave Macmillan.

Mortensen, C.H. and Kapper, L. (2015) Beyond Simple Nostalgia: Transforming Visitors' View of Retro-gaming and Vintage Computing in the Museum. *Aktuel Forskning. Litteratur, kultur og medier*, Special Issue on Cultural Participation [online]. Available at: https://www.sdu.dk/-/media/files/om_sdu/institutter/ikv/videnskabelige+tidskrifter/deltagelse+som+transformation+i+kunst+og+kultur/7+christian+og+lise.pdf, pp. 63–74.

Mortensen, C.H. and Madsen, J.W. (2015) The Sound of Yesteryear on Display. A Rethinking of Nostalgia as a Strategy for Exhibiting Pop/Rock Heritage. *International Journal of Heritage Studies*, 21(3): 250–263.

Mortensen, C.H. and Vestergaard, V. (2011) The Media Mixer. User Creativity through Production, Deconstruction and Reconstruction of Digital Media Content. *Nordisk Museologi*, 1: 15–34.

Neiger, M., Meyers, O. and Zandberg, E. (2011) *On Media Memory. Collective Memory in a New Media Age*, Palgrave Macmillan Memory Studies. Basingstoke: Palgrave Macmillan.

Parikka, J. (2012) *What is Media Archaeology?*. Cambridge, UK: Polity Press.

Parikka, J. (2016) The Lab Imaginary: Speculative Practices in Situ. In Bishop, R., Gansing, K., Parikka, J., Wilk, E. (eds). *Across and Beyond: A Transmediale Reader on Post-Digital Practices, Concepts, and Institutions*. Berlin: Sternberg Press.

Parisi, D., Paterson, M. and Archer, J.E. (2017) Haptic Media Studies. *New Media & Society*, 19(10): 1513–1522.

Pierce, D. (2015) How a Retro Camcorder App Became a Huge Iphone Hit. *Wired* [online]. Available at: https://www.wired.com/2015/08/vhs-camcorder/ (Accessed 16 November 2017)

Simon, N. (2010) *The Participatory Museum*. Santa Cruz: Museum 2.0.

Strauven, W. (2012) Media Archaeology: Where Film History, Media Art and New Media (Can) Meet. In Nordegraaf, J., Saba, C.G., Maïtre, B. le, and Hediger, V. (eds). *Preserving and Exhibiting: Challenges and Perspectives*. Amsterdam: Amsterdam University Press.

13
A VISION IN BAKELITE

Exploring the aesthetic, material and operational potential of the Bush TV22

Elinor Groom

FIGURE 13.1 The Bush TV22, part of the Science Museum Group collection, inventory number 1979–624/721, Science Museum Group.

The museum, traditionally, brings the general public into contact with objects of historic value. This is particularly the presumption surrounding national museums: that these historic buildings contain historic collections through which our national history can be told. Their fundamental civic duty is to collect and steward such objects, and to provide unimpeded access to them. The evidence for this presupposition of historic value and duty is in structures of governance and regulation: one of the pillars of the government's sponsorship of national museums is to facilitate 'free public access to the national collections' (DCMS 2015). Whatever the details of care and access, the overarching aim remains the same. Object engagement is entirely determined by the museum's curatorially motivated decisions over what, when, how, and why objects are collected or displayed. Such curatorial gatekeeping is the pinnacle of hands-off history: a one-directional knowledge exchange wherein all the museumgoer brings is their eyes. However, as this chapter argues, within current museum discourse there is the will to shift the rules of engagement. The spirit of hands on history is incrementally shifting how museumgoers engage with objects, and that shift is evident in the changing ways in which individual museum objects are utilised.

This chapter comprises a case study of how a common 1950s television receiver, the Bush TV22, has been documented, interpreted, and displayed by the Science Museum Group (SMG). A survey of the times when the Science Museum in London and the National Science and Media Museum in Bradford have exhibited the Bush TV22 in various galleries since the late 1980s reveals certain commonalities in how this familiar domestic appliance is understood and explained to museumgoers. It also demonstrates that the primary mode of encounter has remained largely unchanged since the first Bush TV22 went on display in 1971: the visitor can see the set but they cannot touch it. While this case study considers a single model of television receiver, there are five separate Bush TV22 television sets in the SMG collection, which will be looked at in turn. The descriptions of the television receivers are taken from the SMG catalogue, and other documentation from the corporate archives of the Science Museum provide evidence of when and how each of the TV22s has been publicly displayed in the museum. I argue that there is potential for televisual encounters beyond just looking at an object, and that the hands on history approach developed by the ADAPT project (Ellis 2016) and media archaeologists could be adapted and applied to museum collections.

However, I also argue that there are a number of critical considerations and pragmatic decisions that come to bear when assessing how a museumgoer can or should encounter an object like a television set. I also caution against the assumption that simply looking at a television set is an encounter lacking in value, or that a hands on encounter has greater inherent value. The ADAPT project used innovative methods to elicit tacit knowledge from veterans of television production to inform a better understanding of the operational history of television practice. The project was designed to nurture an empowering co-production of knowledge between the academy and industry, considered to be peer repositories of subject specialist knowledge. By contrast, the museum is a space where, traditionally, subject specialists bestow knowledge on visitors through inanimate displays and informational, largely text-based interpretation. Using the hands on history approach could radically upend this tradition, actively involving the museumgoer in the object encounter and allowing their physical experience of the object to become their main source for understanding or appreciating it. However, in order to do so, the hands on history approach must be adapted to suit the needs of the museumgoer who does not necessarily have any tacit experience to bring to the knowledge exchange. In plain English: not everyone knows how to turn the set on.

Watching the box: looking at the Bush TV22

In 2016, the BBC celebrated the 80th anniversary of the inaugural British Television Service broadcast. A specially commissioned documentary, *Television's Opening Night: How the Box was Born*, traced the history of that first broadcast in 1936, and culminated in an ambitious restaging of the opening night programme. That restaging was achieved with historically accurate technology based on the convoluted and dangerous electro-mechanical equipment of the Baird Company. The technology had to be recreated from scratch as so few objects from this period survive. Presenter Dallas Campbell gamely donned suit and heavy stage makeup and recited the words of original BBC announcer, Leslie Mitchell, from a black box on the studio floor, while a large spinning disc scanned his face. The experiment was broadcast live to a television receiver in an adjacent room, where it was watched by 91-year-old tap dancer Lily Fry, who had herself appeared on television as a child in the 1930s. The whole recreation, from the content to the programme format to the technology, was executed with as much historical accuracy possible within the parameters of the resources available. The only exception was the television set used to broadcast it. As the voiceover admits, the small, square, table top box dates from the 1950s but was being used to display a system 20 years older than that (Figure 13.2).

The television receiver used was a Bush TV22. It is a recognizable television set, particularly among collectors of vintage broadcast technology. Online forums feature many threads that recount efforts to purchase, store, restore and adapt TV22s.[1] It is a model that is indicative of mid-twentieth century domestic design, particularly in its thermo-set Bakelite outer shell, designed to mimic veneered walnut wood. At the same time, it is recognizable by its own unique features: the lighter colour surrounding the nine inch cathode ray tube, the rounded ends of the screen, the two simple knobs on the front, two further screw dials, the Art Deco curvature of the sides and the speaker grilles. It evokes a specific period of time and has the

FIGURE 13.2 Screen grab from *Television's Opening Night: How the Box was Born*, showing the Bush TV22 alongside the historic reenactment studio.

potential to provoke explicit memories of usage in the home. Restorer Stephen Ostler, who once created his own modern replica of the set dubbed 'The Retrovisor', calls the Bush TV22 "the quintessential 'vintage television'" (Ostler no date). Perhaps the timeless quality of its aesthetics is why the set stood in for a much older receiver. However, its wide availability – even today – and the number of working models may also have played a part.

The Bush TV22: a brief history

In 1948 the British radio and television manufacturer Bush brought the Bush TV12 to market. At this point the fledgling BBC Television Service was only available in and around London, so when the Sutton Coldfield transmitter began broadcasting the service to the Birmingham area in 1949, Bush sold an updated set – the Bush TV12-BM – for viewers in the Midlands. By 1950, yet another highly similar set was manufactured: the Bush TV22, capable of tuning into the two existing transmitters carrying the BBC Television Service alongside three channels earmarked for future use. The dimensions, materials, components and finish of these sets were almost identical – the screen surround of the TV12 was squarer and some of the internal components changed – but the flexibility of the Bush TV22 meant that it quickly outnumbered the TV12 and remained on the market for many years.

There is keen awareness of the working potential of the Bush TV22 among the enthusiast community. Roger Grant, a member of the British Vintage Wireless Society, wrote about 'Fixing my Bush TV22' in the Society's magazine, and expressed a nuanced understanding of the exact interventions he was making to his set:

> This project is not a restoration – as the title of this article suggests, it's a repair to get the set working, keeping it in its original state with [*sic*] only replacing what's necessary to get it working.
>
> (Grant 2016)

The subtle distinction between 'repair' and 'restoration' underlines the difference between a working receiver and a receiver restored to its original condition. It demonstrates a pragmatic approach to the care of an old television: operational functionality is valued more highly than adherence to original, historical condition. Grant referred to the original instructions to retailers for the set to guide his repair work, detailing the components and electrics that had to be replaced or adjusted. In describing his methods he also demonstrates the particular knowledge and skills of enthusiasts and other people familiar with the mechanics of old domestic appliances. In theory, so long as the receivers and the information contained in historic ephemera such as trade sheets survive, these skills and knowledges can be learned and put to use.

Beyond enthusiast communities, the example of the Bush TV22 in the BBC's documentary demonstrates that the aesthetics of the set make it immediately recognizable as a vintage television even by non-specialists. The remediation of the television as an object or set dressing solidifies its recognition. Moreover, that remediation solidifies the image of the television receiver in the context of the home, which Deborah Chambers argues links the object to the rituals of domestic life:

> Production, design and advertising comprise powerful media imaginaries that attempt to "pre-domesticate" technologies to conform to domestic values and meanings.
>
> (Chambers 2016, 44)

More than any other technology, the television receiver triggers immediate and specific visions of domesticity: the living room, the corner tabled-set, angled toward the sofa or armchair (see Chambers 2011; Spigel 2001; Morley 1986). The constant remediation of this vision of home life in the twentieth century has led to two consequences relevant to museums that display televisions. One is that, no matter the positioning or the surrounding context of the museum display containing the television, the visitor can populate the rest of the image of home around the object, regardless of whether the object played a part in their lived experience. The second is that it reinforces only a partial image of television viewing: the passive end, television either on or off. The operation of the television – warming up the CRT, adjusting the aerial, tuning to channels, sweeping dust from the statically charged speakers and screen, the weight of the receiver as it is shuffled into its corner unit; all of these tactile prompts are denied to the hands-off museumgoer. In many respects, the post-domesticated television set is tough to understand in isolation from visions of domesticity, but visions alone cannot communicate the tacit experience of using a television set.

Tacit televisions: materiality and the museum

In 2016, the Science Museum Group convened its first research conference. Head of Research Tim Boon summarized one of the strands of discussion at the conference, when curators and researchers brainstormed ways to promote histories of use and tacit histories of collection objects in museum environments:

> In these enthusiastic encounters, the potential of re-enactment, reconstruction, replication, restoration of behaviour and object-guided oral history to enrich understanding of practice and objects had become clear.
>
> (Boon 2017)

The word 'potential' is tricky. It implies a critique of current practice but stops short of enacting change. Yet Boon's perspective as a museum professional offers a diverse range of methods to engage visitors in the historic operation of objects that are usually displayed, inanimate, behind glass. Boon and other museum professionals working with historic technology built these conversations on recent curatorial work with operating objects and/or participatory projects (see Boon, van der Art and Price 2004). Already there is the will to progress beyond inanimate technology displays, and an increase in case studies of objects being used to actively engage and involve museumgoers in the practice and historic usage of museum collection objects.

While the museum world looks to active approaches to engaging museum visitors with the objects they have travelled to see, academic projects are also adopting more participatory research methods. The ADAPT project's compound method is engineered around usage of historic objects:

> ADAPT uses the method of 'hands-on history' by reuniting retired television equipment with the professionals who once used these machines on a daily basis.
>
> (Murphy et al. 2015)

The approach utilizes the original material kit of broadcast production as a prompt for the embodied tacit knowledge of the project's veteran broadcaster collaborators. While the objects are genuine examples of historic technology, they are not framed as historic objects, but rather as 'kit', 'equipment' or 'machines' – language drawn from the everyday working world the participants operated within. This perspective takes its cues from the work of media archaeologists who have argued for opportunities for haptic, tacit and operational encounters with historic technology (see Huhtamo and Parikka 2011). The call to action was succinctly expressed by Andreas Fickers and Annie van den Oever: 'the materiality of media technologies and the practices of use need more attention' (Fickers and van den Oever 2013, 12).

Media archaeologists have developed laboratories stocked with machines and components for students and researchers to tinker with – at least one, the Media Archaeology Fundus founded by Wolfgang Ernst at the Humboldt University of Berlin, has a Bush TV22 available for hacking (see Parikka 2016; Emerson, 2016). The ADAPT approach is participatory in a different way, collaborating with professionals with embodied memories of operating technology that are linked to the rituals of their working lives:

> The participants are asked to demonstrate what they used to do regularly: how their machines worked, how they worked together, what their routines once were.
>
> (Murphy et al. 2015)

The twinned approach of tinkering with historic objects and user-led participation stands in opposition to typical object encounters in a museum. Jean-Francois

210 Elinor Groom

Gauvin, following on from Jean Baudrillard, argues that the function of an historic object is lost once the object has been decommissioned and retired behind glass:

> The performing object then becomes a 'pure object', an object pushed onto an aesthetic plane that no longer belongs to the practical and tangible space of functionality.
>
> (Gauvin 2016)

Sandra Dudley explains that the tradition of glass cabinet display comes, at least in part, from the public expectation that museums are "authoritative temples of enlightenment and culture", and so long as the objects are displayed in stasis museums remain "places of edification available to the ordinary visitor" (2010, 5–6). As is the tradition of museums as repositories of material culture, there are rules: look, but don't touch (see Dudley 2010 and Pearce 1992). Inclusion in museum collections and displays can enhance the status of an object, but this power and esteem accrues to the object alone. Handling historic objects gives the handler a share in that power, and acknowledges that they have the skills and knowledge to produce their own meaningful conclusions from their encounter (see Graham 2016).

However, the question remains whether tacit methods can be used to engage people with no direct experience of the object at hand. Some – indeed many – museumgoers do not have knowledge, understanding or experience with analogue television receivers. There are complicated consequences in allowing tacit experiences only for those with tacit memories to refer to. What defines a tacit experience or participatory experience in a museum? Joshua P. Gutwill, Nina Hido and Lisa Sindorf asked similar questions of a similar phenomenon: the proliferation of 'tinkering/making' spaces in museums: 'What, if anything, constitutes learning for museumgoers participating in tinkering' (2015)? Acknowledgment or foregrounding of the material properties of an object is not the same as experiencing that materiality through handling. Equally, handling an object is not a fully realized method for understanding tacit histories of that object. The productive outputs of tacit engagements may also be limited in scope, and as with any targeted activity the outputs may be difficult to disseminate to more casual visitors to museums. When it comes to objects donated to museum collections, there are also legal, ethical and practical considerations. Acquiring an object to the SMG collection is a curatorially motivated act, done in accordance with the museum's Collection Policy and subject to the Collections Trust's Spectrum standard for collection care and management (SMG 2017; Collections Trust 2017). That means that considerations such as protecting museumgoers from hazardous substances cannot be ignored. Collection objects are not for tinkering with.

One further consideration is that an object used for user-led handling is often experienced away from the usual trappings of the museum, including textual information or visually stimulating displays. For example, at the National Science and Media Museum handling activities usually take place in the reading room of the museum's research centre, Insight. Moreover, it is also separated from its provenance prior to its life in the museum, which is often relayed through text on gallery or in the museum catalogue, and is difficult to conjure through handling or even operating an object. However, as Samuel Alberti articulates, the biography of the object does not end with its accession into a museum collection:

> We can trace the careers of museum things from acquisition to arrangement to viewing, through the different contexts and the many changes of value incurred by these shifts.
>
> (Alberti 2005, 560)

In basic terms, that is what this chapter will now do: trace the journeys of every Bush TV22 accessioned by the Science Museum Group (SMG) that is still within the museum, within the limits of institutional knowledge available. Most of the information has been gleaned from the SMG object catalogue. The catalogue data includes names, materials, dimensions, descriptions, and some of these fields are accessible to the public through the Collections Online website. There are also a number of linked records charting the usage of each object under discussion, which detail any changes in location, in valuation, or in the condition of the object. Such records are dated, providing a reasonably accurate timeline of activity and handling of each example of the Bush TV22, give or take human error or documentation gaps. However, when the core object information is changed or updated it supplants the information before it, and therefore the descriptions cited are as they stood in 2018, and we cannot know how descriptive information has been edited over time.

Making the modern world and the Bush TV22 1971–76

According to the catalogue, the first Bush TV 22 in the Science Museum Group collection was accessioned in 1971, as a gift from a private individual. Since 2000 it has been on display in the Science Museum's permanent gallery *Making the Modern World*. The gallery occupies the ground floor of a large central atrium, which most visitors cross as they make their way through the museum. The TV22 is placed in large case alongside several other domestic objects, and rows of similar cases flank the long sides of the gallery, forming a timeline of technology (see Figure 13.4). As Science Museum curator David Rooney reflected in 2005, 'the main exhibits were embedded in a background of 2000 items from everyday life' (Rooney 2005, 26). So the TV22 sits within a narrative of the industrial revolution and the technological progression that followed. Yet despite residing behind glass, in a mass display, as part of a roughly chronologically themed 'background' display, the sheer amount of technology on display gives the *Making the Modern World* gallery an added frisson of excitement:

> These artefacts have awesome power. It is a thrilling, humbling, life-changing experience simply to be in their presence.
>
> (Rooney 2005, 26)

Here the phenomenological aspect of the television receiver that is emphasized. The 'power' is considered to be intrinsic to the object, and the power is experienced simply by occupying the same space as the object – though it is worth noting that Rooney's perspective is curatorial, and does not presume prospective visitors would be awed in the same manner.

Compared to the large and imposing nature of the *Making the Modern World* gallery, the catalogue description of the Bush TV22 on display in it is relatively muted:

> One of the most popular television sets in the early 1950s, this Bush television set has a 'walnut' Bakelite cabinet and an innovatory [sic] nine-inch screen.

The 'walnut' is in inverted commas because the Bakelite shell mimics the colour and grain of walnut wood. The description also notes that Bakelite was 'a cheaper alternative to the standard wooden case', one of the reasons cited for the popularity of the set. The innovation of the screen most likely refers to the fact that the cathode ray tubes inside many Bush receivers manufactured in this time were made exclusively for Bush by British manufacturer Mullard, making the Bush television set "one of the first to use an aluminised cathode ray tube [. . .] giving a brighter image" (Mullard, year unknown). This information is confirmed by Mullard's own marketing materials from the time, which boast of the light emitting properties of the CRTs manufactured for Bush (Figure 13.3).

Overall, engagement with this particular TV22, either through viewing it on display or reading about it in SMG documentation, would result in an overall understanding of the television set in relation to technological progress of the twentieth century writ large. It 'earns' its place in the object-rich gallery due to its popularity and the features that are emblematic to the period in time, particularly

FIGURE 13.3 Mullard leaflet advertising its aluminized cathode ray tubes, from the Kodak Collection held at the National Science and Media Museum, 1990–5036/TI51, Science Museum Group.

FIGURE 13.4 The Pilot ACE computer is moved from its case in the *Making the Modern World* gallery; the Bush TV22 1971–76 is visible in its case in the background, 2014, Science Museum Group.

its material properties. While it is positioned in a mass display of consumer appliances, it is up to the visitor to connect the object to social history. The specificity and provenance of that particular set is not highlighted or explored, nor is the growth of television as an entertainment medium and cultural phenomenon.

Experience TV and the Bush TV22, 1979–624/721

While the *Making the Modern World* gallery is about objects, manufacturing and engineering, the *Experience TV* gallery in Bradford was all about television as a medium. The gallery's opening in 2006 coincided with the renaming of National Museum of Photography, Film and Television as the National Media Museum. The gallery was closed and decanted in 2016 to make way for the fully interactive *Wonderlab* gallery, which heralded the site's further renaming as the National Science and Media Museum in 2017. The Bradford museum has a tighter subject remit than the Science Museum, so while a television receiver in the Science Museum might be displayed close to objects from the realms of aeronautics or computing, in Bradford the same model of receiver was displayed in a gallery solely dedicated to television. Thus the mission statement of the museum has a meaningful impact on how the museumgoer encounters object displays, and on what they get out of that engagement.

According to catalogue data, the receiver 1979–624/721 was purchased by the Science Museum alongside 292 other plastic objects mostly from the 1920s and 1930s (making the Bush TV22 one of the exceptions) for its Plastics and Modern Materials collection. Whether these items were purchased from a single source or several acquisitions consolidated into a thematic collection is unknown. Either way, the exact provenance of this television set is unrecorded. From the late 1990s it featured in a display case of plastic goods in the *Challenge of Materials* gallery, before it was removed and transported to Bradford for *Experience TV*. There, the receiver was on open display on a rotating plinth at the bottom of the 'Wall of Televisions', a section of the gallery described by Amy Holdsworth as 'a point of memory for older visitors, who remember living with the various sets, and a point of history for younger ones' (2011, 139; see Figure 13.5).

Caroline Worthington reviewed the gallery for the *Museums Journal* following its launch, noting that the gallery contained both collection objects and a popular array of large scale interactive exhibits including a news studio, chromakey screen, vision editing desk and a television studio (see Worthington 2006). These interactives used real, fully operational production equipment including Ikegami camera heads on Vinten pedestals, and a teleprompter fed with a mocked-up television news script. Even in 2006 Worthington considered the interactives somewhat old hat, expressing that a 'Big Brother set with a diary room would have been more fun and topical' than repeating a local news story after a pre-recorded lead in from Huw Edwards (Worthington 2006, 47). Nevertheless, the 'Production Zone' had a high degree of verisimilitude to real-life television studio environments, and as the original curatorial team relayed to Amy Holdsworth, it was developed 'in consultation with practitioners' (2011, 136). Visitors had first-hand interaction with real kit, and though the experiences were carefully scripted and developed to be a contained interaction, the materiality and basic function of the production kit was maintained.

Meanwhile, the televisions mounted on the double height wall were not operational. The Bush TV22 display was at least more kinetic than most. There was also a small degree of interactivity in the interpretation, as the object descriptions were accessible through a touch screen where the visitor would tap a picture of the television they wanted to know more about. Yet, while the wall of televisions was only moderately more animated than standard museum display, the space and the open display of multiple historic receivers 'ranging from ones

FIGURE 13.5 Photograph of the Wall of Televisions in the *Experience TV* gallery of the National Media Museum, 2006, Science Museum Group.

A vision in Bakelite **215**

disguised as Chippendale cabinets to space-age bubbles' was also arresting and impactful (Worthington 2006, 46).

The interpretation available to the visitors relayed the same information about the Bush TV22 as the catalogue description of the set in the Science Museum, albeit in different words and with subtly different emphasis. This particular receiver is described as being 'made of brown phenolic plastic', but the longer web and touch screen description embellished the information: '[t]he Bush TV22 is an icon of early 1950s Bakelite sets and highly desirable today, although in its day it was one of the cheapest sets available'. Then there is further more editorialising, as the description argues that the 'TV22's main claim to fame is that it was the first British television that could be tuned by the owner to any one of the two then current BBC transmitters'. The tuning capability of the set is verified information, but the assertion that the Bush TV22 is 'an icon' and 'highly desirable' with famous features is mildly contentious. Like the other TV22s in the SMG collection, the provenance of the set has not been recorded and does not feature in the interpretation. Equally, while the set is highlighted on its plinth, it was still one of a wide range of televisions, and for the majority of visitors the display would have been experienced en masse, and the specificity of the object (including details of its cost, materials, manufacture) was available only to the visitors engaged enough to pursue it. The display is also comprised entirely of television receivers, set within a larger narrative of television production and reception. The image of the television receiver in the home, the way most casual visitors would have encountered television receivers in their own lives, was absent from the *Experience TV* gallery.

The Secret Life of the Home, Information Age and the Bush TV22 1983–692

Essentially, museumgoers look to gallery interpretation to tell them more about the objects on display. This is knowledge that they do not have that curators do, and is at the crux of the asymmetrical curator-museumgoer knowledge exchange. This knowledge exchange is complicated when objects enter the museum with little documentation, and particularly difficult when they remain undocumented. The Bush TV22 with the object identifier 1983–692 (part of the Radio Communication collection of the Science Museum) is one such object, currently on display in *Information Age*, a permanent gallery opened in 2014. It was originally purchased by the museum from a private collector of British vintage radio equipment in 1983. It is difficult to trace exactly how and where it was used prior to 2014, but it appears that it was on display in *The Secret Life of the Home* gallery from the mid-1990s until its redisplay in *Information Age*. *The Secret Life of the Home* is still a feature of the Science Museum: it is a permanent gallery in the lower ground floor of the museum, which the museum website describes as taking 'a closer look at household appliances'. Here again we see the Bush TV22 as emblematic of domestic life in the twentieth century.

The Secret Life of the Home has several televisions and associated paraphernalia, so it was evidently not the specific qualities of the Bush TV22 that would have led to its inclusion, nor was it spotlighted as any kind of key object. In the set's more recent installation in *Information Age*, however, its interpretation is more specific to that model of television, spotlighting the set in new ways. The Bush TV22 was signposted as an exhibit in the new gallery in advance of gallery installation, when the project was under its working title of *Making Modern Communications*. A picture of the Bush TV22 (albeit a different example to the one eventually on display) was used on the front cover of a pamphlet promoting the proposed galleries to potential sponsors and donors. Inside the pamphlet, the same Bush TV22 features alongside a brief rundown of where radio and television fitted in the gallery plans:

> Through this Network [i.e. thematic zone of the gallery] we will look in detail at the impact that broadcasting has had on audience and users.
> (*Making Modern Communications*, c. 2010)

Here, again, we see the vision of a Bush TV22 without the context of its surroundings or content on its screen, in close quarters with 'the impact of broadcasting' – the aggregated significance of the entire technological advancement and cultural sea change that resulted from the growth of the television industry. However, the document also alluded to the eventual event that the Bush TV22 was used to illustrate:

> The coronation of Queen Elizabeth II in 1953, when millions watched television in Britain and across the world.

The television set sits in *Information Age* alongside other objects representing the broadcast of the coronation of Queen Elizabeth II. As a television receiver

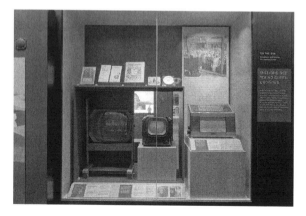

FIGURE 13.6 Display, including the Bush TV22, in the *Information Age* gallery of the Science Museum, 2014, Science Museum Group.

widely available at the time of the coronation, its choice is a sound one. Many of the 20 million purported viewers of the coronation would have watched the event on a Bush TV22. The 1986–692 television resides in a conservation-grade glass case along with the other collection objects relating to the coronation broadcast (Figure 13.6). However, that case adjoins an experience best described as something between an interactive exhibit and a piece of audio-visual interpretation. The gallery's building contractors, Beck Interiors, commissioned 3D modelmakers Berry Place to manufacture a replica of the Bush TV22. The replica is easily and purposefully identifiable: the shell is bright white plastic, rather than imitation-wood Bakelite, and the screen is a curved LED screen rather than a cathode ray tube.[2] There is an armchair facing the replica, where visitors can watch the BBC's archive recording of the original broadcast of the coronation on loop. At the opening of the gallery, Queen Elizabeth and Prince Phillip were photographed with this exhibit, the Queen watching her own coronation more than 50 years later on a screen designed to mimic the original experience of 1953 (Figure 13.7).

The description of the television is comprehensive, in part because its installation in the *Information Age* gallery in 2014 was accompanied by a strategy for digital engagement with the gallery, including full photography of each object and quality-controlled descriptions. The descriptive paragraph encompasses most of the facets highlighted in the other Bush TV22s in the SMG collection: Bakelite plastic, mass production, multi-transmitter reception, and adaptation for ITV signals. Moreover, inside the fairly straightforward and informative text are a few value statements that hint to the motivation behind its selection as part of the *Information Age* gallery: the set is 'now seen as iconic' and at the time was an 'inexpensive and popular television set'. It is the reconstruction of the historic moment, using the Bush TV22, that feels innovative, particularly the chance to sit and watch the television. Even if the seat is a hard bench and the audio is

FIGURE 13.7 Queen Elizabeth II and Prince Phillip are shown the coronation on a replica Bush TV22, 2014, Science Museum Group.

218 Elinor Groom

played through headphones, it still gives a facsimile of the time, place and practice of watching television.

Experience TV again and the Bush TV22 1986–5005

Of the five Bush TV22s in the Science Museum Group, the National Science and Media Museum acquired only two. 1986–5005 was purchased by the National Museum of Photography, Film and Television from an individual donor in 1986. It was also on display in *Experience TV*, but it was not part of the Wall of Televisions. Instead, it was on open display on a plinth next to a Pye television set from the same era. The Pye set sat with a small Bakelite Band III converter box. Together these objects formed a display designed to tell the story of when the ITV network launched in the 1950s. In particular, these three objects shifted the focus of the historical moment away from changes on screen to changes in viewers' homes, as they adapted or bought television sets capable of receiving the new channel.[3] However, this interpretation is relayed once again through only two mechanisms: text and placement in relation to other. Both require the museumgoer to participate, but only with their eyes.

The web description is identical to that of the other Bush TV22 that was on display in *Experience TV*. The interpretive focus of both receivers situated the historical context of the Bush TV22 in relation to ITV, as reflected in the catalogue:

> [The Bush TV22] remained in production (with circuit improvements) for several years, and in 1955 a Band III converter was produced which could be fitted to existing sets to enable them to receive the new ITV programmes.

Like the receiver in *Information Age*, the Bush TV22 in *Experience TV* was tethered to a cultural moment in the history of television viewership. However, unlike in *Information Age* that cultural moment is not articulated through archive broadcasts. As with the Wall of Televisions, it was largely up to the visitor to make that connection between the object and its historical context and interpretation (in the case of this receiver, the interpretation was made available through text panels and laminated object information sheets). The interpretation and documentation that was available to visitors did not highlight the content of the ITV network, but rather the growth in sales and rentals of television sets, and the adaptions to receivers to allow them to tune in to Britain's first commercial television broadcaster. This interpretive viewpoint kept the visitor's attention on the object, but the object remained inoperable, understood only by looking and reading.

The handling collection and the Bush TV22A, E2015.0479.1

The final Bush TV22 held by the Science Museum Group is not, strictly speaking, a collection object, and its exact provenance is undocumented. The object – actually a later version of the same model, a Bush TV22A – was classified as 'found in museum' at the National Media Museum in 2015, which is when it was assigned the entry number E2015.0479.1, but it had been used by the museum for an unspecified amount of time before then. The only catalogue information beyond the model, maker and date of the set (c. 1955) is that it was 'adapted for contemporary use as working display model'.

The receiver was added to the collection only to be formally deaccessioned soon after and absorbed into the museum's handling collection (though the location records show that the process of moving it out was protracted, as the receiver had to be surveyed for potential asbestos). The handling collection is an informal group of original, historical objects that can be used by the learning department – such as the gallery 'Explainers' who lead workshops for family, community and school groups – as well as collections staff. It is not formally catalogued, nor is it subject to the same rigorous standards of conservation, display, storage or access as objects in the national collections are. It is therefore the only Bush TV22A within the Science Museum Group currently available to operate, and available to be handled by members of the public. However, there are a few critical downsides and parameters to the utilization of this particular set. The receiver works, but since the digital switchover completed in 2012 there is no broadcast television to watch on it. Any television content would need to be pre-selected and digitized like the coronation in *Information Age* (albeit through an original CRT, rather than a modern LED replica).

That is not to say that this Bush TV22A does not have operational potential, but rather that its potential in terms of the restoration of its original operation is limited. However, that is not the barometer of a working object's value when put to use with hands on history or media archaeological methods. Those methods emphasize tinkering and repairing historic objects to understand them and how they worked. Having a historic analogue broadcast stream is not necessary to gain that insight. However, the museological ideal for such an encounter would arguably be for visitors to gain an understanding of how and why viewers switched on their sets.

Switching on the Bush TV22?

This overview of one common model of historic television receiver and its multiple stagings in the galleries of the Science Museum and the National Science and Media Museum demonstrates that an object holds the potential for multiple modes of engagement as well multiple narratives. However, it also demonstrates that there are recurring elements in the way that this model and its significance has been understood and articulated in museum environments. A lack of recorded provenance means the set is interpreted in relation to its wider historical context, but it also means that the individual receivers are largely interchangeable, inserted into displays because they are generally recognizable and of the period. When information specific to the model of television is relayed, it is through a prosaic highlighting of aesthetic or material features such as its Bakelite shell and CRT, alongside general information such as its price or its receiving capabilities. The histories of users and usage of the Bush TV22 has been lost in the mix. The object-centred interpretation described in this chapter, while diverse, belies a dearth of the histories of practice and of provenance that could encourage empathic connection between the museumgoer, the object, and the people who owned it in the first place.

Media archaeologists, historians, museum curators, visitors, veterans and technology enthusiasts have all identified the lack of and need for hands on engagement with collection objects in museums. However, for the hands on history method to be applied effectively in museums, both the object and the method need to be adapted. This note is particularly relevant when considering applying the hands on history methods to domestic technology. While the acquisition of television sets to the national collection affords the sets a certain status, one that ensures its survival and keeps its material integrity intact, it also brings literal barriers to access. That is why the de-accessioned television receiver holds the greatest potential for user-led, hands on interaction. The archive footage encased in a replica of a Bush TV22 in the *Information Age* gallery is testament to the will of curators to replicate the experience of watching television on a historic set, but it is still not a truly hands on experience. The television in the museum is now switched on, the next step is to enable users to switch it on themselves.

Notes

1 See the search results for 'Bush TV22' on the 'UK Vintage Radio Repair and Restoration Discussion Forum': https://www.vintage-radio.net/forum/index.php?s=40c74f1b33b04 d25c24d30fff535041f

2 For more information, see the Berry Place website: http://www.berryplace.co.uk/exhi bition-display/

3 Other gallery objects represented the change to television content heralded by ITV, including the Associated Rediffusion in-vision clock – the first visual to be seen on the commercial network.

Bibliography

Alberti, S. (2005) Objects and the Museum. *Isis*, 96(4): 559–571.

Boon, T. (2017) A Symposium on Histories of Use and Tacit Skills. *Science Museum Group Journal*, 8. doi: 10.15180/170808/001

Boon, T., van der Vaart, M. and Price, K. (2014) Oramics to Electronica: Investigating Lay Understandings of the History of Technology through a Participatory Project. *Science Museum Group Journal*, 2. doi: 10.15180/140206

Chambers, D. (2011) The Material Form of the Television Set. *Media History*, 17(4): 359–375.

Chambers, D. (2016) *Changing Media, Homes and Households: Cultures, Technologies and Meanings*. London: Routledge.

Collections Trust (2017) *Introduction to Spectrum 5.0*. https://collectionstrust.org.uk/spec trum/spectrum-5/ (Accessed: 3 December 2017)

Dudley, S. (2010) Museum Materialities: Objects, Sense and Feeling. In Dudley, S. (ed.). *Museum Materialities: Objects, Engagements, Interpretations*. London: Routledge.

Department for Culture, Media and Sport (DCMS) (2015) *2010 to 2015 Government Policy: Museums and Galleries*.

Ellis, J. (2016) Between Human and Machine: The Operating System. *Journal of Contemporary Archaeology*, Extended Forum, 2(1): S24–S27.

Emerson, L. (2016) Sister labs // Signal Lab & Media Archaeological Fundus. https://loriemerson.net/2016/02/16/sister-labs-the-signal-lab-media-archaeological-fundus/ (Accessed: 5 December 2017)

Fickers, A. and van der Oever, A. (2013) Experimental Media Archaeology: A Plea for New Directions. In van der Oeven, A. (ed.), *Techné/Technology. Researching Cinema and Media Technologies – Their Development, Use, and Impact*. Amsterdam: Amsterdam University Press.

Gauvin, J. (2016) Functionless: Science Museums and the Display of "Pure Objects". *Science Museum Group Journal*, 6. doi: 10.15180/160506

Graham, H. (2016) The "Co" in Co-production: Museums, Community Participation and Science and Technology Studies. *Science Museum Group Journal*, 5. doi: 10.15180/160502

Grant, R. (2016) Fixing My Bush TV22. *BVWS Bulletin*, 41(3): 4–11.

Gutwill, J., Hido, N. and Sindorf, L. (2015) Research to Practice: Observing Learning in Tinkering Activities. *Curator: The Museum Journal*, 58(2): 151–168.

Holdsworth, A. (2011) *Television, Memory and Nostalgia*. Basingstoke: Palgrave Macmillan.

Huhtamo, E. and Parikka, J. (eds) (2011) *Media Archaeology: Approaches, Applications, and Implications*. Berkeley, CA: University of California Press.

Morley, D. (1986) *Family Television: Cultural Power and Domestic Leisure*. London: Routledge.

Mullard. (year unknown) Advertising leaflet. Kodak Collection, National Science and Media Museum. Object number 1990–5036/TI51, Science Museum Group.

Murphy, A., Aust, R., Jackson, V. and Ellis, J. (2015) 16mm Film Editing: Using Filmed Simulation as a Hands-on Approach to TV history. *VIEW: Journal of European Television History and Culture*, 4(7). doi:10.18146/2213-0969.2015.JETHC077

Ostler, S. (no date) Restoration of a 1951 Bush TV22. http://www.radiocraft.co.uk/902.htm (Accessed: 3 December 2017)

Parikka, J. (2016) On Media Labs and the University. *What is a Media Lab? Situated Practices in Media Studies*. https://whatisamedialab.com/2016/01/22/on-media-labs-and-the-university/ (Accessed: 3 December 2017)

Pearce, S. (1992) *Objects, Museums and Collections: A Cultural Study*. Leicester: Leicester University Press.

Rooney, D. (2005) Making the Modern World: The Shock of the Real at the Science Museum. *Primary History*, 39: 26–27.

Science Museum Group (2010) *Making Modern Communications*.

Science Museum Group (2017) *SMG Collection Policy*. https://group.sciencemuseum.org.uk/wp-content/uploads/2018/01/SMG-collecting-policy-2016.pdf (Accessed: 6 December 2017)

Spigel, L. (2001) *Welcome to the Dreamhouse: Popular Media and Postwar Suburbs*. Durham, NC: Duke University Press.

Staubermann, K. (2017) Museums, Tools and the Tacit. *Science Museum Group Journal*, 8. doi:10.15180/170808/002

Worthington, C. (2006) Broadcasting Encounters: *Experience TV*, National Museum of Photography, Film and Television. *Museums Journal*, 106(11): 46–47.

14

HANDS ON CIRCUITS

Preserving the semantic surplus of circuit-level functionality with programmable logic devices

Fabian Offert

When museums started to exhibit culturally significant computational objects in the late 1970s, two major problems became immediately apparent: the problem of preservation and the problem of display. How can we preserve computational objects, so their cultural significance can be experienced by future generations? And how can we structure this experience visually and spatially?

While both the problem of preservation and the problem of display are first and foremost pragmatic, technical problems, they have latent philosophical implications. In this chapter I focus on the latent philosophical implications of the problem of preservation. I propose that an investigation of these implications can not only enrich the philosophical discourse but can also inform a critical technical practice (Agre 1995), which manifests itself here as a critical conservation practice.

As part of this critical conservation practice, I propose a new preservation strategy for culturally significant computational objects. This new strategy exploits one of the latent philosophical implications of the problem of preservation: the fact that software and hardware can be 'translated' into each other. Concretely, I propose to investigate hardware description languages (formal languages that describe discrete electronic circuits) and programmable logic devices (discrete electronic circuits that can be physically altered through software to assume the role of any other discrete electronic circuit) as possible preservation media. Based on an analysis of successful experiments with such programmable logic devices and hardware description languages in the retrocomputing scene I propose this strategy as a way to preserve culturally significant computational objects that exhibit a semantic surplus of circuit-level functionality – computational objects that derive meaning from specific idiosyncrasies in their hardware.

Pragmatic strategies of preservation subscribe to specific notions of authenticity

With the preservation of culturally significant computational objects like computer-based digital artworks and historic computing machines, museums and collections face the double challenge of caring not only for an object itself, but also for its context (Rinehart, 2000). The boundaries between object and context, however, are often blurry, and depend on the individual preservation case, the focus of the academic disciplines involved, and the computational object itself. Such objects might include components which are hidden (circuit boards), only accessible remotely (web servers), or entirely inaccessible (external binaries).[1] Even if we consider a narrow definition of context, the very notion of a computational object itself inevitably suggests an assemblage of both material and immaterial components, of software and hardware (DeLanda 2011). This links the problem of preservation back to the problem of display: the very possibility of exhibiting computational objects necessarily acknowledges their 'mixed' ontological status. Thus, there is also no 'pure' approach to the preservation of computational objects, no approach that avoids the philosophical quicksand that emerges from the double constitution of computational objects as material and symbolic. To borrow Philip Agre's words: preservation of computational objects is "philosophy underneath" (Agre 1995).

Computational objects mirror the discreteness of digital logic on the macroscopic level: they either run or don't. A single malfunctioning component, software or hardware, can break a complex computational object consisting of millions of parts. Furthermore, while some computational objects break in a literal sense, others break epistemically: they remain perfectly functional, but nobody knows how to use them. At least since Richard Rinehart first described the preservation of computational objects as "the straw that broke the museum's back" (Rinehart 2000), these issues have also been acknowledged academically.[2] The subject has also spawned a multitude of publications, conferences and research projects.[3] Furthermore, in the mid-2000s, media archaeology emerged as an academic field, adding the media-philosophical considerations of Kittler, Zielinski, Parikka, Huhtamo, Ernst, Kirschenbaum, and others to the pragmatic reasons for preservation brought forward by museums and collections. Media archaeology labs, such as the one run by Lori Emerson at the University of Colorado at Boulder, add a practical component to these media-philosophical considerations as well.

Today, a succession of three basic strategies is used in the majority of preservation cases: substitution – the simple repair or replacement of broken hardware; emulation – the simulation of hardware in software; and portation/migration – the adaption of a computational object to an entirely new hardware and software context. The peculiarity of this succession becomes apparent if we place it into one-to-one correspondence with the strategies employed in the preservation of more traditional media. To preserve an oil painting, for instance, the simple repair or replacement of its 'hardware' (canvas, paint, frame etc.) is a viable strategy. But would a conservator really consider re-painting a Rembrandt ('portation') if the repair fails? What constitutes a successful preservation effort differs widely for the digital and non-digital domains. In other words: different pragmatic strategies of preservation subscribe to widely different philosophical notions of authenticity.

We could call the notion of authenticity that underlies more traditional strategies, like the preservation of the oil painting described above, a material notion of authenticity. A material notion of authenticity puts the artefact first and is concerned primarily with the preservation of this artefact, all the way down to its chemical composition. In comparison, the preservation of digital art is often aimed at what has been called functional authenticity – a notion of authenticity that focuses on the interplay of interfaces and users, rather than the material substrate that these interfaces rely upon. For only if such a notion of authenticity is assumed, preservation strategies like emulation and portation become feasible in the first place, as they require significant material interventions, concretely changing parts of the artefact (substitution), or even getting rid of them completely (emulation). While preservation is traditionally the domain of the institution, many digital artists share this functional notion of authenticity. Jeffrey Shaw, for instance, even offered to re-sign – re-authenticate – his work The Legible City after it was ported from a Silicon Graphics Indigo 2 workstation to an off-the-shelf PC running Linux (Serexhe 2013).

Many culturally significant computational objects, however, employ both software and hardware in complex and highly idiosyncratic ways that make them literally irreplaceable, and thus render a purely functional notion of authenticity unfeasible. Particularly with computer-based digital artworks, the aesthetic investigation of the notion of context itself is often a dedicated focus of a work. These computational objects are worth preserving exactly because of how they handle or even exploit glitches and bugs, design quirks, and exotic components. They contain a semantic surplus of circuit-level functionality, an additional level of meaning that exclusively rests on a number of low-level peculiarities. Such objects call for a consolidation of the material and the functional aspects of authenticity, or at least for a pragmatic approach that takes this semantic surplus of circuit-level functionality into account. The strategy presented in this chapter is one possible manifestation of such a pragmatic approach. It is based on the observation that we can understand the preservation of culturally significant computational objects as a form of translation.

Preservation as a problem of translation

What would it mean to understand preservation as translation? First of all, we would need to adopt an extended notion of language. 'Language' would not be confined to the realm of the symbolic anymore, it would extend into the realm of the material, into the world of objects. We would arrive at a "language of technology that is not the specialized language of technicians", as Walter Benjamin has put it (2002a).[4] 'Translating' objects would thus imply the possibility of material transformations.

More specifically, it would imply the possibility of transformations from the material to the symbolic – and vice versa. Formally, between two 'extended' languages, we could define the operation 'translation' as the application of a set of material or symbolic transformations to a set of material or symbolic objects structured by the rules of the first language, resulting in a different set of objects structured by the rules of the second language. It is important to note, however, that these transformations necessarily 'fix' the transformed set of material or symbolic objects to the historical moment of the translation. A split is introduced between the two 'extended' languages, where any further development of the original language will stop to affect the translation, which, in turn, is affected by the further development of the target language. Original and translation thus drift apart. It is again Walter Benjamin who has developed this argument in "Die Aufgabe des Übersetzers". It should be noted that the title of Benjamin's essay itself exemplifies the problems discussed in the essay: 'Aufgabe', in German, can either mean 'task' or can be a nominalization of 'aufgeben', 'to give up', rendering the title either 'The Translator's Task' – which is the actual title of the official translation – or 'The Relinquishment of Translation', a meaning that is lost in the translation. Benjamin writes:

> For any translation of a work originating in a specific stage of linguistic history represents, in regard to a specific aspect of its content, translation into all other languages. Thus, ironically, translation transplants the original into a more definite linguistic realm, since it can no longer be displaced by a secondary rendering. The original can only be raised there anew and at other points of time.
>
> (Benjamin 2002b, 258)[5]

We can easily see that this assumption also holds for computational objects. Generally, any translation of a computational object from one context to another will introduce such a split in the manner that Benjamin describes. The preservation of a piece of software by means of portation from one operating system to another, for instance, will detach the software from any possible future changes in the original operating system, and subject it to all possible future changes in the target operating system. This is, of course, by design: we want the software to become independent of the – presumably outdated and unmaintained – original operating system, to subject it to a – presumably current and maintained – target operating system. Such a process, however, also implies that all 'ties' of the computational object to the original context will be cut, and with them all meaning exclusively derived from the original context. One of the core questions of the preservation of culturally significant computational objects is thus how to minimize this loss of information that the translation introduces.

Translation as a problem of engineering

In the quest for such a 'best possible' translation between contexts, it is important to remember that the distinction between software and hardware could be regarded as somewhat artificial, up to the point where we could say, with Kittler, that it is completely ideological (Kittler 2013a; Kittler 2013b). Computers are symbolic machines, materialized Boolean logic (Shannon 1938). Hardware and software essentially speak the same language. This means: hardware can be translated 'back' into software. More precisely, hardware can be translated 'back' into a text in a formal language – a program – that necessarily and sufficiently describes it.

In fact, we can show, with Andrei Kolmogorov's notion of algorithmic complexity, that, if there is a difference between the source and the target of such a technical translation, it is negligible in the precise mathematical sense. Kolmogorov, in "Three Approaches to the Quantitative Definition of Information" (Kolmogorov 1965), posits that a reliable measure for the complexity of a string of symbols is the length of the shortest program in any Turing-complete programming language necessary to reproduce this string. This becomes apparent if we imagine two different strings of symbols: 'AAAAAAAAA' and 'ATCCEXGHI'. While the first string could be programmed in the general form "print 'A' 9 times", the second string has to be programmed as "print 'ATCCEXGHI'", which seems to be no big difference in effort. However, if we imagine two much bigger strings of symbols, one with a thousand times 'A', and a second one with a thousand random characters, things change. The programming effort to print the first string is still relatively small; to be exact, the difference is only three bytes, because the number '1000' instead of the number '9' is included in the source code. For the second string, however, the difference is 991 bytes, because, as there is no 'pattern' in this string, it has a higher complexity and therefore it must be literally included in the reproducing program.

In other words, the hypothetical program consists of two parts: the part used for the actual information, the string-pattern, and the part used for the commands and structures to reproduce this string pattern algorithmically. While the size of the 'information' part changes with the complexity of the string-pattern, the size of the 'commands' part stays more or less the same. Mathematically, its size is a constant that does not change in relation to the complexity of the information. Kolmogorov proves that the maximum difference between the same program in two different Turing-complete programming languages is the size of the bigger one of two hypothetical translation programs for these languages (A into B or B into A) and therefore a constant.

On a theoretical level, the translation of hardware into software is a perfect translation because both can be expressed by formal languages that do not allow for ambiguity in the first place. As Sibylle Krämer has pointed out, the very idea of formalization can be traced back historically to the quest for a method that separates thinking from meaning. This separation usually comes at the price of a loss of ambiguity.

> The basic principle of formalization is to detach the manipulation of chains of symbols from their interpretation. This is a trick [Kunstgriff], a 'technē' to relieve the mind from the labor of interpretation. However, such a relief

comes at a price, as we now have to account for the preconditions of rendering actions of the mind into formal operations.[6]

In the case of the preservation of computational objects, however, this formalization 'debt' has already been paid. The object of preservation is already, on a technical level, free of any ambiguity. What makes its preservation a challenge nonetheless is simply the fact that it is distributed between hardware and software.

Taking all this into account, the 'translation' of culturally significant computational objects thus becomes a matter of finding a good approximation of the theoretically possible perfect translation from hardware into software, and from software into hardware. In other words, it becomes a problem of engineering.

Programmable logic devices as media of preservation

Recent technological advances allow the development of a promising strategy for such an approximation: the translation of hardware into standardized hardware description languages and the 'resurrection' of hardware preserved this way by means of programmable logic devices. Hardware description languages are Turing-complete formal languages that can be used to describe discrete electronic circuits as 'programs'. Such descriptions can be cast back into hardware with the help of programmable logic devices, discrete electronic circuits that can be physically altered through software to assume the role of any other discrete electronic circuit, within the limit of their storage capacity. One of the most popular programmable logic devices is the field programmable gate array (FPGA). FPGAs, in simple terms, are variable arrays of logic gates. Unlike in a regular integrated circuit, the specific functions of these logic gates are programmable: they can be defined in software by a 'program' written in a hardware description language like VHDL or Verilog. This makes it possible not to emulate, but to *clone* nearly every piece of computing hardware imaginable: the FPGA *becomes* the hardware it is programmed to be. FPGAs, in a sense, are the stem cells of the hardware world. This analogy should be taken somewhat literally: experimental uses of FPGAs include the development of evolvable hardware, hardware that is able to adapt to changes in its environment, inspired by biological evolution (Higuchi et al. 1996). While evolvable hardware is still in its infancy, more recent use cases of FPGAs often include the creation of highly specialized and adaptable circuits. Microsoft reportedly uses FPGAs to power the Bing search engine, and FPGAs have been used extensively for the so called 'mining' of cryptocurrencies. Other applications include the distribution of hardware upgrades over the Internet.

With the help of hardware description languages and FPGAs, it becomes possible to operationalize the translation between hardware and software. The hardware of the object of preservation is translated into a program in a hardware description language and 'resurrected' with the help of an FPGA. As software is

228 Fabian Offert

always already symbolic, and as the preserved hardware will behave exactly like the original hardware, the original software can be supplied 'as is' to the preserved hardware to form a fully functional computational object. While the result will still be an approximation of the theoretically perfect translation, as the number of possible incompatibilities between the object of preservation and the capabilities of a specific model of FPGA increases rapidly with the complexity of the object of preservation, this strategy can be successful in preserving the semantic surplus of circuit-level functionality.

In the next section of this chapter I present a non-exhaustive list of retrocomputing projects that already employ variations of the proposed strategy, examining one of these projects – a reconstruction of Pong on an FPGA – more closely to exemplify the concept of a semantic surplus of circuit-level functionality.

Retrocomputing with FPGAs

Pong, the famous tennis-like game that has been implemented on generations of computing devices, is often regarded as one of the first computer games ever made. In 2012, Stephan A. Edwards, a professor of computer science at Columbia University, reconstructed an early version of Pong on an FPGA. His choice of an FPGA is specifically tied to the goal of a 'cycle accurate' reproduction that "exhibits many idiosyncrasies of the original" (Edwards 2012). Cycle-accuracy, in this case refers to the fact that all computers are discrete state machines. The operation of any discrete state machine is synchronized by an internal 'clock' component which advances the state of the machine according to a given frequency. A 'cycle accurate' reconstruction thus implies that it is possible to synchronize the state-change of the reconstruction with the state-change of the original. In any given discrete moment, the states of both machines will be similar. Among the original idiosyncrasies Edwards discovered in the process, next to "some sloppy timing", is "a previously unidentified bug that subtly affected gameplay" (ibid.). Because of some incorrect wiring (which, as Edwards points out, can even be found in some unauthorized hardware clones of Pong), the area in the centre of the paddle that reflects the ball exactly perpendicular to the paddle is larger than the 'physics' that the circuitry implements would suggest. This changes the gameplay: it is easier to rebound the ball in a horizontal fashion.

We see that the steps of our proposed strategy of preservation are clearly outlined here for this specific project. Edwards identifies programmable logic devices as the appropriate medium of preservation for a culturally significant computational object due to its semantic surplus of circuit-level functionality, here a specific faulty wiring that affects gameplay in a subtle way. He then 'translates' the object from hardware to software (Edwards uses a custom hardware description language) and back to hardware (FPGA), arriving at a 'cycle accurate' reconstruction.

Many other projects like this have been attempted. Edwards, next to his translation of Pong, has also realized an FPGA implementation of a 1977 Apple II

FIGURE 14.1 'Die shot' (close-up photography of an integrated circuit treated with acid to reveal its circuit layout) of the Soviet KR580VM80A microprocessor. High-resolution photos like this one serve as guidelines for the reverse-engineering of computational objects, and their re-implementation by means of programmable logic devices. The pictured processor has been successfully translated to Verilog, and re-implemented on an FPGA by a group of Russian enthusiasts.

(Edwards 2009). An electrical engineer named Chris Fenton has implemented a Cray 'supercomputer', the famous 1975 model 1A installed in Los Alamos on a Xilinx Spartan-3E 1600 FPGA (Fenton 2015), making the 'translation' publicly available under the New BSD open source licence. Dan Strother has provided an FPGA version of a Nintendo Entertainment System (1983) (Strother 2010). Jamie Iles has recently released an Intel 80186 (1982) FPGA implementation, although without focusing on cycle-accuracy (Iles 2017). Other classic systems that have been implemented include the 1984 Amstrad CPC 6128 (FPGAmstrad 2018), the 1982 Sinclair ZX Spectrum (ZX-UNO 2018), the 1981 BBC Micro (BBC Model B 2017), with the most recent version utilizing a myStorm development board, the Acorn Atom (Acorn Atom 2017), and even a 1980 Soviet Mikro-80 (Mikro-80 2018). Many more idiosyncratic interpretations, or complete re-inventions of classic systems or specific components of classic systems can be found on the Internet. Finally, as examples of particularly complex efforts of hardware analysis, we should mention the complete transcription of the seminal Intel 4004 processor in the framework of the Intel 4004 45th Anniversary Project (2016) and the complete transcription of the Soviet Intel 8080 compatible KR580VM80A (2015).

Irrespective of their sometimes just partial success, all these projects demonstrate that even highly complex, exotic hardware can be reconstructed with a succession of hardware analysis and re-implementation on an FPGA, given enough time has passed for a community of enthusiasts to appear. They also demonstrate, however, that nothing can be reconstructed from a void: even with redundant

230 Fabian Offert

storage possibilities, material is lost if it is assessed as obsolete. As Chris Fenton writes in regard to his Cray-1A reconstruction:

> When I started building this, I thought "Oh, I'll just swing by the ol' Internet and find some groovy 70's-era software to run on it." It turns out I was wrong. One of the sad things about pre-Internet machines (especially ones that were primarily purchased by 3-letter government agencies) is that practically no software exists for them.
>
> (Fenton 2015)

Pragmatic considerations

The conservator's task is never fully described by any strategy of preservation, nor any notion of authenticity. It is a holistic approach that first and foremost identifies what aspect of a computational object is worth preserving, and only in a second step identifies which concepts and strategies are the right tools for a specific task, finding a good balance, or compromise, between material and functional authenticity.

The proposed strategy, as a strategy for the preservation of culturally significant computational objects in the context of institutions like museums and collections, is speculative insofar as, at the time of writing and to the knowledge of the author, it has not been employed within these contexts yet. Instead, at the present moment, most institutions implement a variation of the succession of substitution, emulation, and portation. For highly complex or exotic computational objects, video ethnography has also come to play an important role in the process of preservation,[7] replacing text-based documentation with footage of experts using the computational objects in question (of course, this is only a viable strategy if the object has already been kept functional by means of other strategies of preservation). If it is adopted, the proposed strategy will certainly not replace either of these existing strategies. Where there is no semantic surplus of circuit-level functionality, i.e. where circuit-level peculiarities are irrelevant, there is no need to preserve them. A high-level work of digital art that is based on an off-the-shelf PC running the Microsoft Windows operating system will certainly not benefit from a cycle-accurate reconstruction, as any semantic surplus of circuit-level functionality will be abstracted away by the operating system.

A final important caveat has to be mentioned: in comparison to the tools and strategies available for the preservation of software, the world of FPGAs is largely a closed-source affair. Two major manufacturers, Xilinx and now Intel (formerly Altera) have consistently dominated the market for FPGAs, with market shares around 90% combined. And while open-hardware development boards like the Papilio FPGA platform (2018) exist, and platforms like OpenCores (2018) have been providing open-source hardware description language implementations of various hardware components for a long time, the closed-source software from either of the two manufacturers is a necessary prerequisite to using both to their full capacity. Concretely, while anybody can translate any circuit into a hardware description language like VHDL or Verilog, it is the process of 'compiling' such a 'program' for a specific FPGA chip or development board that is heavily policed by the two manufacturers mentioned, by keeping the respective compilers closed-source. In short: "The FPGA manufacturers are not only unhelpful, they do not want there to be open tools" (Exxum 2015). Recently, small initiatives like IceStorm (2018), and the related myStorm development board have begun to open up the FPGA toolchain, albeit not without going through a long and complex process of reverse engineering existing FPGAs (like the Lattice iCE40). One could speculate that the demand for custom hardware solutions propelled by the rise of neural network technologies will also increase the demand for open FPGA toolchains.

Considering the philosophical implications of the preservation of computational objects has led us to consider their ontological constitution, their double existence as material and symbolic objects. This, in turn, has allowed us to understand the preservation of computational objects as a process of translation. Finally, we have considered hardware description languages and programmable logic devices as the medium to realize this process of translation as a concrete strategy of preservation.

A general critical conservation practice, I argue, would entail this kind of material thinking that uses the philosophical to devise the pragmatic, and the pragmatic as a lens into the philosophical. A kind of thinking that devises concrete, material strategies of preservation to make it possible to think about a computational object in terms of the object itself. A critical conservation practice would thus answer the plea for an experimental media archaeology (Fickers and van den Oever 2013) with the specificity of circuit-level, hands on work. The conservator's task, much like the translator's task for Benjamin, first and foremost would thus be to realize – to both understand and put to use – the fact that preservation is indeed philosophy underneath.

Notes

1 Outside the open-source movement, programs are often transformed into binary machine code (compiled) before distribution. It is hard to impossible to infer the functional logic of a program from such a binary file.

2 Of course, libraries and other institutions were struggling with digital preservation way before it became an issue for museums. See, for instance, Rothenberg (1998). Digital preservation has even become a matter of military security, as indicated by a recent call for proposals put out by DARPA (Defense Advanced Research Projects Agency 2015).

3 In 2015 alone, three international conferences examined the preservation of digital art: "TechFocus III: Caring for Software-based Art" at the Guggenheim, New York, "Media in Transition" at the Tate Modern, London, and "Preservation and Access to Born-digital Culture" at iMAL, Brussels. Major research projects include the Software Preservation Group at the Computer History Museum in Mountain View, California, "Matters

in Media Art" (Tate Modern, MoMA, SFMoMA), "Digital Art Conservation" (ZKM Karlsruhe, Haus für Elektronische Künste Basel, Espace Multimedia Gantner), and the "Variable Media Network" (Guggenheim, Fondation Langlois).

4 "Jede Äußerung menschlichen Geisteslebens kann als eine Art der Sprache aufgefaßt werden, und diese Auffassung erschließt nach einer Art wahrhaften Methode überall neue Fragestellungen. Man kann von einer Sprache der Musik und der Plastik reden, von einer Sprache der Justiz, die nichts mit denjenigen, in denen deutsche oder englische Rechtssprüche abgefaßt sind, unmittelbar zu tun hat, von einer Sprache der Technik, die nicht die Fachsprache der Techniker ist" (Benjamin 1974a).

5 "Denn jede Übersetzung eines Werkes aus einem bestimmten Zeitpunkt der Sprachgeschichte repräsentiert hinsichtlich einer bestimmten Seite seines Gehaltes diejenigen in allen übrigen Sprachen. Übersetzung verpflanzt also das Original in einen wenigstens insofern – ironisch – endgültigeren Sprachbereich, als es aus diesem durch keinerlei Übertragung mehr zu versetzen ist, sondern in ihn nur immer von neuem und an andern Teilen erhoben zu werden vermag" (Benjamin 1974b).

6 "Die Grundidee der Formalisierung besteht darin, das Manipulieren von Symbolreihen von ihrer Interpretation abzutrennen. Solches Vorgehen ist ein Kunstgriff, eine 'technē', die zum Ziel hat, den Verstand zu entlasten von den Mühen der Interpretation. Doch solche Entlastung hat ihren Preis, welcher zutage tritt, sobald wir uns Rechenschaft ablegen über jene Bedingungen, die erfüllt sein müssen, damit Handlungen des Verstandes als formale Operationen durchführbar werden" (Krämer 1988) [Author's translation].

7 See, for instance, the Computer History Museum's recent documentation of the ICARUS (Integrated Circuit ARtwork Utility System) graphical integrated circuit layout design tool on the Xerox Alto (ICARUS 2017).

Bibliography

Acorn Atom. (2017) Acorn Atom Implementation for myStorm BlackIce. Available at: https://forum.mystorm.uk/t/acorn-atom-implementation-for-mystorm-blackice/228 (Accessed 12 May 2018)

Agre, P.E. (1995) The Soul Gained and Lost. Artificial Intelligence as a Philosophical Project. *Stanford Humanities Review* 4, 1–19.

Agre, P.E. (1997) *Computation and Human Experience*. Cambridge, Cambridge University Press.

BBC Model B. (2017) BBC Model B Implementatation [sic] for myStorm BlackIce. Available at: https://forum.mystorm.uk/t/bbc-model-b-implementatation-for-mystorm-blackice/258 (Accessed 12 May 2018)

Benjamin, W. (2002a) On Language as Such and on the Language of Man. In Bullock, M. and Jennings, M.W. (Eds.), *Selected Writings*. Cambridge, MA, Harvard University Press.

Benjamin, W. (2002b) The Task of the Translator. In Bullock, M. and Jennings, M.W. (eds.), *Selected Writings*. Cambridge, MA, Harvard University Press.

Benjamin, W. (1974a) Über die Sprache überhaupt und über die Sprache des Menschen. In: Tiedemann, R., Schweppenhäuser, H. (Eds.). *Gesammelte Schriften II-1*. Frankfurt am Main, Suhrkamp.

Benjamin, W. (1974b) Die Aufgabe des Übersetzers. In: Tiedemann, R., Schweppenhäuser, H. (Eds.). *Gesammelte Schriften IV-1*. Frankfurt am Main, Suhrkamp.

Defense Advanced Research Projects Agency, I.I.O. (2015) *Building Resource Adaptive Software Systems* (BRASS), DARPA-BAA-15-36.

DeLanda, M. (2016) *Assemblage Theory*. Edinburgh, Edinburgh University Press.

Edwards, S.A. (2012) *Reconstructing Pong on an FPGA*. Columbia University, Department of Computer Science.

Edwards, S.A. (2009) *Retrocomputing on an FPGA*. Columbia University, Department of Computer Science.

Exxum, J. (2015) *Open Tooling for FPGAs*. Available at: https://curtis.io/others-work/open-tooling-for-fpgas/ (Accessed 12 May 2018)

FPGAmstrad. (2018) Available at: http://www.cpcwiki.eu/index.php/FPGAmstrad (Accessed 12 May 2018)

Fenton, C. (2015) *Homebrew CRAY-1A*. Available at: http://www.chrisfenton.com/homebrew-cray-1a/ (Accessed 12 May 2018)

Fickers, A. and van den Oever, A. (2013) Experimental Media Archaeology. A Plea for New directions. In van den Oever, A. (ed.). *Techné/Technology. Researching Cinema and Media Technologies. Their Development, Use, and Impact*. Amsterdam, Amsterdam University Press.

Higuchi, T., Iwata, M., Kajitani, I., et al. (1996) Evolvable Hardware with Genetic Learning. In *Proceedings of ISCAS '96*.

ICARUS 2018. (2018) ICARUS on the Xerox Alto. Video Ethnography. Mountain View, CA, Computer History Museum. Available at: http://www.computerhistory.org/collections/catalog/102738686 (Accessed 12 May 2018)

Iles, J. (2017) S80186: 16-bit 80186 compatible IP core. Available at: https://www.jamieiles.com/80186/ (Accessed 12 May 2018)

Intel 4004 45th Anniversary Project. (2016) Available at: http://www.4004.com (Accessed 12 May 2018)

Ippolito, J. and Rinehart, R. (2014) *Re-collection. Art, New Media, and Social Memory*. Cambridge, MA, MIT Press.

Kittler, F.A. (2013a) Es gibt keine Software. In Gumbrecht, H.U. (Ed.). *Die Wahrheit der Technischen Welt*. Essays zur Genealogie der Gegenwart. Frankfurt am Main, Suhrkamp.

Kittler, F.A. (2013b) Protected Mode. In: Gumbrecht, H.U. (Ed.). *Die Wahrheit der Technischen Welt*. Essays zur Genealogie der Gegenwart. Frankfurt am Main, Suhrkamp.

Kolmogorov, A.N. (1965) Three Approaches to the Quantitative Definition of Information. *Problemy Peredachi Informatsii* 1(1), 3–11.

Krämer, S. (1988) *Symbolische Maschinen. Die Idee der Formalisierung in geschichtlichem Abriß*. Darmstadt, Wissenschaftliche Buchgesellschaft.

KR580VM80A. (2015) KR580VM80A Reverse Engineering. Available at: https://zeptobars.com/en/read/KR580VM80A-intel-i8080-verilog-reverse-engineering (Accessed 12 May 2018)

Mikro-80. (2018) Mikro-80 – a Modern Replica. Available at: http://www.electronicsfun.net/archives/932 (Accessed 12 May 2018)

OpenCores. (2018) Available at: https://opencores.org (Accessed 12 May 2018)

Papilio FPGA platform. (2018) Available at: http://papilio.cc (Accessed 12 May 2018)

Project IceStorm. Available at: http://www.clifford.at/icestorm (Accessed 12 May 2018)

Rinehart, R. (2000) The Straw that Broke the Museum's Back? Collecting and Preserving Digital Media Art Works for the Next Century. Switch 14. Available at: https://web.archive.org/web/20120723084714/http://switch.sjsu.edu/nextswitch/switch_engine/front/front.php?artc=233 (Accessed 12 May 2018)

Rothenberg, J. (1998) Avoiding Technological Quicksand. Finding a Viable Technical Foundation for Digital Preservation. A Report to the Council on Library and Information Resources. Available at: https://www.clir.org/PUBS/reports/rothenberg/contents/ (Accessed 12 May 2018)

Serexhe, B. (Ed.) (2013). *Konservierung digitaler Kunst. Theorie und Praxis*. Vienna, Ambra V.

Shannon, C.E. (1938) A Symbolic Analysis of Relay and Switching Circuits. *Transactions of the American Institute of Electrical Engineers* 57 (12), 713–723.

Strother, D. (2010) FPGA NES. Available at: https://danstrother.com/fpga-nes/ (Accessed 12 May 2018)

Turing, A.M. (1936) On Computable Numbers, with an Application to the Entscheidungsproblem. *Proceedings of the London Mathematical Society* 2 (1), 230–265.

ZX-UNO. (2018) Available at: http://zxuno.speccy.org/maquina_e.shtml (Accessed 12 May 2018)

INDEX

abandonware 116
academia *see* scholarship
Acmade Compeditor *see* Pic-Syncs
actor network theory 22–23
ADAPT research project: documentary practice as a research method 43–56; hands on history approach 13, 15–24, 209; reenactment 36–40
agency, mind and body 22
Agnew, Vanessa 29
Alberti, Samuel 211
amusement arcades 157; contemporary revival 155–157; experience offered by 153–155; historical forces 147–148; moral panic 145–146; perceptions and regulation of 145–147; play as work 148–149; relationship to video games 150–153; research study 149–157
analogue media: forms and formats 116–117; obsolescence 6; optical media 119–121; playback function 111–113; psychic life of dead media 124
anthotype process 94–106
Anthropocene 92–93, 101–102
Apple Macintosh 184–185
Archaeological Media Labs 178; *see also* Media Archaeology Labs
archaeology *see* media archaeology
Arnheim, Rudolph 61–63
artificial intelligence (AI) 2
audiocassettes, for Walkmans 139–141

authenticity: media history 69–71; museum preservation and display 223–224; reenactment 68–69

Back In Time For Dinner 28
Baudrillard, Jean 210
Benjamin, Walter 224–225
Betamax 112, 115–116
black box technologies 11–12, 187–188
Blackpool 147, 150, 151–153
Blockbuster stores 33–35
Boon, Tim 208–209
British Entertainment History Project 49
Bush TV22: brief history 207–208; *Experience TV* gallery 213–215, 218; handling collection 218–219; *Information Age* gallery 216–218, 220; introduction of 206–207; *Making the Modern World* gallery 211–213; in the Science Museum Group 205; *Secret Life of the Home* gallery 215–218; switching on 219–220

cameramen 19–20
Canon Cat case study 182–185
Capitalocene 92–93
cassette tape players 191
Cassirer, Ernst 67
Castells, Manuel 149
casting, ADAPT research project 48–52
CDs 119
cinema 124

236 Index

citizen curation 162, 167–169
citizen science 193
clickbait, reenactment 29–36
communication: distortive effect of
technical media 62; increasing mobility
130–133; relationship with
technology 2
critical conservation practice 222
Cronenberg, David 110–111
curation: Bush TV22 205; critical
conservation practice 222; museum
preservation and display 222–225,
227–231; museums 204–205; Pebble
Mill project 162, 167–169

dark ecology 92–93
Davis, F. 190
Dead Media Streaming Service 5, 111–113,
118–119, 121–124
de-habituation 64–66, 70
desensitization 64–66
digital media: contemporary context
91–92; file formats 121; obsolescence 6
digital videos: clickbait and
procrastitainment 29–36; reenactment
26; streaming software 113–116;
see also YouTube
distortion: distortive effect of technical
media 61–63; media history 69–71;
technology-instigated distortions
63–66
Doane, M. A. 84
documentary practice as a research method
43–56
documentation, hands on history 12–13
Downs, C. 149–151
du Gay, P. 143
dualism 23–24
Dudley, Sandra 210
DVDs 119

editing, ADAPT research project 54–55
Edwards, Stephan A. 228
Electric Dreams 28
electronic waste 6
Elsaesser, T. 190
embedded images 79
environmental context, dark ecology
92–93
Ernst, Wolfgang 4, 187–188, 209
ethnography 14
Experience TV gallery 213–215, 218
experimental media archaeology 12, 60–61,
66–69, 231

Facebook, Pebble Mill project 162, 163,
170
failure, the art of 70–71
Fenton, Chris 229–230
Fickers, A. 160, 161, 162, 189, 209
field programmable gate arrays (FPGAs)
227–231
file formats 121
filmers 19–20
filming for research 13–15, 52–54
Firewire 115
formalization 226–227
format theory 118–119
Foucault, M. 63, 189
Further Back In Time For Dinner 28

games *see* video games
Gardner, Drew 32
Gauvin, Jean-Francois 209–210
Geertz, C. 14
Germono, Gustavo 85
Goggin, G. 130, 131
Google: artificial intelligence 2; YouTube
advertising 31
Graphical User Interface (GUI) 183–184
Gunning, Tom 58, 59

habituation 64–66; *see also* de-habituation
hands on history 2–7; ADAPT research
project 43–44, 209; importance of
11–24; media archaeology labs 177–186,
188; Pebble Mill project 160–171; in
research 11–13, 23–24, 66–69
Haraway, Donna 24
hardware, and preservation 225–228
hedonism 147–148
Heidegger, M. 23, 24
hermeneutics of astonishment 190, 198,
201
Herschel, John, Sir 94–95, 102
historical images 76; Miller, Lee 76–77;
rephotography 77–86
historical reenactment *see* reenactment
Hitchcock, Alfred 120
humanity: call for action 93–94; dark
ecology 92–93; relationship with
technology 1–2
hybrid agents 18–21

images *see* historical images;
photography
Information Age gallery 216–218, 220
interactive overlays 80–81
interactive splits 80

Index **237**

intimacy of media experience 133–141, 142
Ireland, Andrew 36

Jones, Ryan 33–34

Kids React 29–30, 31–33, 35
Kittler, Friedrich 61–63, 121, 226
Klett, Mark 78
Kneebone, Roger 3–4, 36
Kolmogorov, Andrei 226
Krämer, Sibylle 226–227

labs: arts and humanities 175–177; Canon Cat case study 182–185; media archaeology 177–186; a variantology of hands on practices 185–186
language 62, 224–225
Laserdisc 119, 123
Latour, B. 18, 20
learning, hands on history 3–4
leisure, and work 148–149
linear narratives 58–59
Lion Eyes 54

Macintosh 184–185
Maclot, Armand 98
maintenance 70–71
Making the Modern World gallery 211–213
Malafouris, Lambros 20–23
material engagement theory 20–21
media archaeology 4–5, 66–69
Media Archaeology Labs 177–186, 188–191; museum exhibitions vs. the laboratory 191–193; participatory research study 193–201
media cycles 64–65
media history: authenticity, distortion, and the art of failure 69–71; distortive effect of technical media 61–63; hands on history in research 66–69; newness 58–60; re-sensitization of researchers 66; sensorial dimensions 60–61; technology-instigated distortions 63–66
MijnKOOL 103–106
Miles, M. 84–85
Miller, Daniel 15
Miller, Lee 76–77, 78–79, 81–82, 83
mixtapes 139–141
mobile devices: adoption of the Walkman 142; Walkman's portability as the predecessor of mobile phones 130–133
moral panic, amusement arcades 145–146

Morton, Timothy 92–93, 101–102, 103
museums: Bush TV22 210–220; exhibition vs. the laboratory 191–193; materiality 208–211; media and communication 187–189; participatory research study 193–201; preservation and display of media 222–225, 227–231; purpose of 204–205; retrocomputing 228–230; translation 224–227; *see also* Media Archaeology Labs
Muybridge, Eadweard 78
myCABBAGE 103–106

'new media' 59–60, 69
newness 58–60, 63–65, 69
nostalgia, Media Archaeology Labs 190, 197–198
novelty 58–60, 63–65

obsolescence 6; abandonware 116; Dead Media Streaming Service 5, 111–113, 118–119, 121–124; 'new media' 59–60; playback function 111–113; psychic life of dead media 124; *see also* museums
Openshaw, Jonathan 91–92
optical media 119–121
otherness of technologies 190

participatory research 193–201, 199, 210
Pebble Mill project 49, 160–171
personalization of media experience 133–141
Peters, Benjamin 59, 64–65
Peters, John Durham 2
photography 76; anthotype process 94–106; contemporary digital context 91–92; Miller, Lee 76–77; rephotography 77–86
Pic-Syncs 5, 15–16
play, and work 148–149
playback function 111–113
portability, Walkman as the predecessor of mobile phones 130–133
post-digital 91
preservation *see* curation
printed circuit boards (PCBs) 153
privatization of media experience 133–141
procrastitainment 29–36

radio 137, 139
radio car, Pebble Mill project 163
Raskin, Jef 183–185
realist fallacy 65–66

238 Index

recruitment, ADAPT research project 45–47, 48–52
reenactment 7, 26–27, 40–41; ADAPT research project 50; bringing the living back to life 36–40; clickbait and procrastitainment 29–36; experimental media archaeology 66–69; the recent past on television 27–29
repair 70–71
Rephotographic Survey Project (RSP) 78
rephotography 77–78; act of making a rephotograph 78–79; conclusions 85–86; encounters and disappearances 84–85; of Miller's work 81–82, 83; participation and exchange 82–84; types of 79–81
research *see* scholarship
re-sensitization 60–61, 66, 68–69, 70
retrocomputing 228–230
Rinehart, Richard 223

scholarship: documentary practice as a research method 43–56; hands on history approach 11–13, 23–24, 66–69; newness 58–60; reenactment 36–40; re-sensitization of academics 66
Science Museum Group 205, 208–209, 210–220
Secret Life of the Home gallery 215–218
Sensitization Desensitization Cycles (SDCs) 64–66
Shklovsky, Viktor 64
side-by-side images 79
Siegert, Bernhard 120
Slovenia, use of the Walkman 128–130, 139, 142
smooth motion 114
social media, Pebble Mill project 162, 163, 170
software, and preservation 226–228
software, streaming 113–116
Solnit, Rebecca 78
Sony Walkmans *see* Walkmans
split images 79–80
Sterne, Jonathan 118
Steyerl, Hito 114
Strauven, W. 190–191
streaming software 113–116
Stuckmann, Chris 34–35
Sustainist Design 93–94

tacit experiences 210
tactile learning 3–4

Talbot, Henry Fox 94–95
technical media, distortive effect 61–63
technological affordances: hands on history 2–3, 11–12, 24; Media Archaeology Labs 4, 185, 190; social process 5
technological bricoleur 121
technology, relationship with humanity 1–2
teleological narratives 58–59
television: documentary practice as a research method 43–56; reenactment of the recent past 27–29, 36–40; *see also* Bush TV22
That's So Last Century 28, 30
The 1900 House 27–29
Transit project 98–103
translation, and preservation 224–227
Trotman, Dawn 16
Tufano, Brian 19–20, 23

van den Oever, A. 161, 162, 189, 209
Van Doren, Emile 98
VCRs 191
Verdonck, Benjamin 102–103
VHS 111, 112, 116, 119–120, 123, 191, 198
video games: moral panic 145–146; perceptions of 145–146, 147; play as work 148–149; relationship to amusement arcades 150–153
Videodrome 110–111
videos *see* digital videos; YouTube

Walkmans: adoption of 142; historical context 126–130; Media Archaeology Labs 191; portability 130–133; privatization and personalization of media experience 133–141
waste *see* electronic waste
White, Oliver 16
Wilson, Abigail 36
work, and leisure 148–149

Young, J. 146, 147–148
YouTube: clickbait and procrastitainment 29–36; professionalization and advertising 31; reenactment 26
Yugoslavia, use of the Walkman 129–130, 139

Zielinski, Siegfried 4